# DISPERSING THE GHETTO

# Dispersing the
# GHETTO

*The Relocation of Jewish
Immigrants across America*

## Jack Glazier

**Cornell University Press**

Ithaca and London

First published 1998 by Cornell University Press.

Printed in the United States of America

Cornell University Press strives to use environmentally responsible suppliers and materials to the fullest extent possible in the publishing of its books. Such materials include vegetable-based, low-VOC inks and acid-free papers that are recycled, totally chlorine-free, or partly composed of nonwood fibers.

Library of Congress Cataloging-in-Publication Data

Glazier, Jack.
Dispersing the ghetto : the relocation of Jewish immigrants across
America / by Jack Glazier.
p.  cm.
Includes bibliographical references and index.
ISBN 0-8014-3522-6 (cloth : alk. paper)
1. Jews, East European—United States—History.  2. Jews—Europe,
Eastern—Migrations.  3. Industrial Removal Office (U.S.).  4. Jews-
-United States—Charities.  5. United States—Emigration and
immigration.  I. Title.
E184.353.G53  1998
973'.04924—dc21                                               98-4178
                                                                CIP

To my maternal grandparents,

Morris and Deborah Rosen,

and their children,

Rea, Alice, Sarah, Betty, Isidore, and Libby

In Memory

*New Americans when the century was young,*

*they made their way with grit, humor,*

*and boundless hope.*

# Contents

# Acknowledgments

I wish to thank the National Endowment for the Humanities and the Wenner Gren Foundation for Anthropological Research for supporting the initial phase of my study of the Industrial Removal Office (IRO). Thanks are also due to the Research and Development Committee of Oberlin College for a summer grant to continue the project and for a research leave enabling me to complete the investigation and to write a substantial part of this book.

The papers of the IRO are held by the American Jewish Historical Society of Waltham, Massachusetts, and I am grateful to that institution for its generous assistance and welcome. I especially appreciate the help and encouragement of the Society's late librarian, Dr. Nathan Kaganoff, who felt that a book on the IRO was long overdue. I am also grateful for help I received at the Jewish Division of the New York Public Library, YIVO, the American Jewish Archives, and the Hebrew Union College library. Special thanks are due the excellent staff of the Oberlin College library for their cheerful forbearance in the face of my many requests for assistance.

My ideas were sharpened in discussions or correspondence with a number of people, several of whom read parts of the manuscript. They include Woody Watson, Martin Ottenheimer, Betty Messenger, John Messenger, Deborah Pergament, Walter Zenner, Richard Alba, and the late George Pozzetta. At Oberlin, I benefited from the critical suggestions of Jeff Blodgett, Nate Greenberg, Milt Yinger, and especially Heidi Thomann Tewarson, who read several chapters of the manuscript and educated me about German Jewish life in the modern age. In ways that have no measure, her companionship has sustained me over the course of this project.

## ACKNOWLEDGMENTS

I am also indebted to two Cornell University Press readers for their incisive and critical reading of the manuscript. Finally, I thank Peter Agree of the Press for his early interest in my research and his help and advice in bringing this book to publication.

Oberlin, Ohio                                                        Jack Glazier

# Introduction

Preparation of this book began in 1992 amid the celebrations and commemorations marking the quincentenary of Columbus's voyage. Those events unfolded as several versions of how to be an American were put forth. Films, magazine and newspaper articles, books, scholarly conferences and exhibitions, and even a reenacted voyage of replicas of Columbus's ships all marked our collective recognition of the epochal event. Unlike the four-hundredth anniversary centered on the Columbian Exposition of 1893 in Chicago, the commemoration of the early 1990s was suffused with controversy and ambivalence about the meaning of the European arrival, especially for native peoples of the Americas and Americans of African descent. The quincentenary was different because America is different, attentive as it was not in 1893 to the multiplicity of voices emanating from once-excluded segments of the American population.

In the 1890s, a strong belief in inevitable progress and the national future buoyed many sectors of American society. The West had been conquered, and the superintendent of the census declared in 1890 that the frontier no longer existed. In the waning days of that year, the nineteenth-century Indian wars ended when the army unleashed a final devastating blow against a Lakota encampment on Wounded Knee Creek in South Dakota.[1] The contours of the emerging world colossus were taking shape as the country turned its full attention to the continuing transformation of an agrarian nation into an urbanized, industrial power. Despite appalling social dislocations, these profound changes pointed toward an even more expansive American horizon. The sanguine, energetic mood of

1

the country indicated that there was indeed much to celebrate four hundred years after Columbus.[2]

It was not an unalloyed optimism. The manifold problems of a swiftly moving nation sounded a note much less tuneful than the generally celebratory tones of the Columbian Exposition. Problems of rapid industrial and urban growth, the disaffection of a growing labor movement, and economic depression arriving in 1893 were commonly linked to the proliferating numbers of new immigrants. The 1890s bore witness to an uneasy recognition that the social character of the country was undergoing sharp, portentous alterations, perhaps putting at risk the progress that some were beginning to view with less certainty. Not far from the lakeside pavilions of the Columbian Exposition, another part of Chicago exemplified all of the social and physical problems of teeming urban life, including vice, disease, crowding, slums, sweat shops, and child labor.[3]

Many people in the 1890s drew a sharp qualitative distinction not only between Europeans and all others but also between different types of Europeans. They separated the preferred earlier, or "old," immigration of northern and western Europeans from the "new" immigration of eastern and southern Europeans, specifically Jews, Slavs, and Italians. Along with Indians, African Americans, and Asians, these new arrivals from the Old World constituted in political and cultural terms a marginal, nearly muted segment of American life, more often spoken for or about than speakers themselves on the public stage.

Among skeptics and immigration critics, the movement of people from eastern and southern Europe that had begun on a large scale the decade before and would continue until World War I posed a threat to the character of the United States and its institutions. Adding to the growth of cities, one of the hallmarks of the 1890s, the immigrants were closely identified with the social problems and moral derangements of urban life. The extraordinary advancement of cities, particularly those with burgeoning manufacturing and industrial capacities, was a momentous development. It came about not only through the internal migration of rural Americans to urban centers but also through the arrival of the European newcomers. In 1890, 42 percent of New York's population was foreign-born; the comparable figure for Chicago was 41 percent.[4] In 1900, the figures were 37 percent for New York, where 42 percent of the population of Manhattan and the Bronx was foreign-born, and 35 percent for Chicago.[5] Ten years later, the figures were 40 percent for New York as a whole, 47 percent for Manhattan, and 36 percent for Chicago. Factoring in native city residents with one or both parents foreign-born, the numbers for New York, Manhattan, and Chicago were 79 percent, 83 percent, and 78 percent, respectively.[6] Indeed, the life of cities from the 1890s until World War I cannot be understood apart from immigration and the whole panoply of problems and concerns associated with the arrival each year of many thousands from eastern and southern Europe.

Even before the era of immigration and rapid urbanization, the American cultural imagination attributed moral laxity and weakening primary social bonds to city ways. The crowded immigrant quarters of any American metropolis, particularly on the East Coast, served only to confirm and sharpen older ideas about the moral and social corruption inherent in urban existence.[7] The immigrant, more than any other agent in the final years of the nineteenth century, fixed the attention of skeptics and critics on the fateful turn that the United States seemed to be taking.

Immigration became something of a lightning rod for many of the distressing and anxious feelings of those change-filled years. Whether it was the growth of corrupt machine politics, labor radicalism, crime and juvenile delinquency, drunkenness, prostitution, pauperism, vagrancy, or any one of the many other social ills associated with city life, the new immigrants provided an obvious target for nativists and others trying to place blame for the disturbing changes coursing through the country. Resistance to immigration found intellectual and ideological support in multiple sources, including the pseudoscientific racism of Madison Grant and W. Z. Ripley and the status racism of Henry Adams, Henry James, and other northeastern patricians. Although not cast in racialist or eugenic terms, the anti-immigrant bias of unions derived from a fear of displacement of American workers by cheap labor from abroad. The xenophobic populism of political figures and commentators from the Midwest and South also added its angry measure to the weight of opinion against immigration.[8]

Various segments of the American business establishment at certain times also condemned immigration policy, despite labor leaders' claims that business was eager to undercut American workers by exploiting cheap, alien labor. When many unions were identifying the immigrants as a dangerous threat to American workers, the publications of various business enterprises and industries expressed equal vehemence at what they saw as the adverse economic and social consequences of immigration.[9] In hard economic times, business interests pondered the advisability of increasing the number of jobless in the country. As for the social consequences of immigration, American business grew suspicious of foreign workers, seeing them as a large portion of the rank and file of union membership and as prominent in union leadership. More troubling still was the perception that radicalism drew considerable strength from foreign influence. Exploitable surplus labor, although economically attractive to capital, could, however, pose unacceptable dangers to social stability.[10] Only in periods of economic upturn, as in the wake of the election of 1896, did business moderate its view of immigration, finding a new confidence in its ability to control the immigrant workers needed for the resurgent economic expansion.[11]

H. G. Wells distilled the social and political wariness of the time as he began his reflections on America by contemplating the questions he had to answer before gaining admission to the country: "Are you a polygamist?" and "Are you an anarchist?" Once admitted, he criticized immigrant New York in terms that any nativist would have regarded approvingly. Although prescient about future scientific developments and highly critical of prejudice and unreason regarding African Americans, Wells fully adopted the outlook of an immigration restrictionist. Of the new immigrants, he warned that the "dark shadow of disastrous possibility remains."[12]

Not always strident or threatening in the manner of populist or labor resistance to immigration, nativist conviction could also assume an almost genteel quality when voiced by no less a literary stylist than Henry James. Writing at about the same time as Wells, James found cause for lament after returning for a time to America following his long sojourn abroad. Writing in *The American Scene* a series of sketches about various cities in his newly rediscovered homeland, James deplored what he saw in lower Manhattan, where his patrician antisemitism came into full play. He observed, "There is no swarming like that of Israel when once Israel has got a start, and the scene here bristled, at every step, with the signs and sounds, immitigable, unmistakable, of a Jewry that had burst all bounds." The sheer crush of people, the intensity of life, and "the gathered past of Israel pushing through" convinced James of the "Hebrew conquest of New York." Taking changes in language as perhaps emblematic of the dramatic alterations in the New York scene, James allowed, disingenuously, that the future accent in America "may be destined to become the most beautiful on the globe and the very music of humanity." He then continued, more characteristically, "Whatever we shall know it for, certainly we shall not know it for English in any sense for which there is an existing literary mea-

4

sure."[13] Although cultivated and mannerly in style, James's derisive portrait of the Lower East Side was quite in keeping with seamier anti-immigrant sentiments.

Nonetheless, immigrant Jewish life had its defenders among outsiders. Notable among positive representations is Hapgood's *The Spirit of the Ghetto*, which certainly was influenced by the author's friend and fellow journalist, Abraham Cahan.[14] A progressive midwesterner by upbringing, Hapgood was a Harvard graduate and shared with James a patrician origin. In place of James's "swarming" Jewry, Hapgood found individuals—scholars, poets, actors, journalists, and other writers—whom he portrayed in rounded, human terms. As if to counter the commonplace depiction of Jews and the meaner realities of the street, the tenement, and the sweatshop, Hapgood ignored economic life and the harsher features of the East Side.

One could thus find cause for hope or despair about the American future. The ideal of progress and the promise of an even more expansive new century confronted the turbulent realities of the day. Established American Jews shared the concerns of their fellow citizens. Against the widely perceived threat posed by immigration, American Jews began to see their own success as tenuous and their impending prospects less assured. Although very conscious of the historical limitations and dangers faced by their eastern European coreligionists, American Jews feared what a new wave of Jewish immigrants might portend for their own security and social standing. Accordingly, they set about to protect themselves with highly organized campaigns to hasten the social and economic adjustment of the immigrants.

### German Jews in Europe and America

German American Jews constituted the majority of the American Jewish population at the dawn of the immigration era. They derived from an earlier, much smaller nineteenth-century population movement coinciding with the so-called old immigration and had sometimes managed to achieve stunning success. Arriving mainly in the 1840s and 1850s, the German Jewish immigrants flourished as merchants and businessmen. They held to the views of Reform Judaism and looked to a promising future as citizens of the new country founded on the same

Enlightenment principles that had nurtured Reformism. Reform Jews emphasized only the universal features of the Jewish faith that they considered to be rational and fully in keeping with modern life. Their vision of Judaism narrowly circumscribed the areas of religious practice. In spurning the old commitments to the dietary laws, ethnic and linguistic symbols, and the national longings of an exiled people, they shared little with their eastern European coreligionists. Moreover, the German Jewish immigrants of mid-century experienced the Old World in markedly different ways from the eastern European Jews, or *Ostjuden,* as they were sometimes derisively labeled.

Since the eighteenth century, German Jews had not suffered the systematic and forced exclusion that ghetto existence had imposed on eastern European Jews. Often living on amicable terms with their Christian neighbors, German Jews had a considerably weaker conception of themselves as socially distinct. After all, they rejected the markers and practices that had rigidly bounded Jewish life for centuries, thus bringing them closer in practice to their non-Jewish neighbors. The lifting of legal prohibitions— the Emancipation—against their participation in the civil and political affairs of the non-Jewish world further ensured that the German Jews were making a historic break with the Jewish past.

In Europe, the encounter between German and eastern European Jews had produced its own mix of feelings of obligation, sympathy, and accusatory blame. Encouraged by medieval rabbis, Jews were committed to tenets of faith and tradition that reinforced their bonds both to the local community and to Jews in other places. In the German states before the Emancipation in the latter part of the eighteenth century, a sense of collective and mutual responsibility underlay self-governing Jewish communities through political institutions sanctioned by non-Jewish state authority.[15] Although Jews valued mutual responsibility on the basis of religion and tradition, Jewish leaders were also held responsible for other Jews in overtly political terms, requiring the leaders to police the Jewish community. Jewish institutions thus exercised a range of political functions, including controlling the size of a town's resident Jewish population. The maximum number was fixed by the state, but it was left to the Jewish authority to act as gatekeepers, quite literally, issuing passes to enter the city or expelling illegal entrants.[16] Jewish paupers represented a special concern because they were excluded from the hierarchy of categories defining residential privileges in German cities. In New York in the mid-1870s, Jewish immigrants identified as paupers represented the first worrisome concern of the German Jews in America, as if in reprise of their forbears' European encounter with the eastern Jews.

A notable individual meeting resistance when he initially took up residence in Berlin was Solomon Maimon, a Polish Jewish philosopher eager to continue his secular studies in the West. Gaining the protection of a Jewish family against continued inquiries from the Jewish gatekeepers about his presence in Berlin, Maimon was able to meet the philosopher Moses Mendelssohn as well as other enlightened German Jews. Years before, Mendelssohn himself is believed to have faced the same severe questioning on first coming to Berlin and was permitted to enter only because he wanted to study with the chief rabbi.[17] Eventually, Maimon sought from Mendelssohn and his friends suggestions for a project worthy of his education and linguistic skills.

The various proposals and their rationales are indicative of the superior attitude of the German Jews toward their eastern coreligionists. Maimon's patrons generally agreed that he would undertake a translation into Hebrew of some learned works that would "enlighten the Polish Jews still living in darkness." With Mendelssohn's support, one of the German Jews recommended that Maimon translate from the French a work on the history of the Jews. This translation would then help his eastern compatriots properly locate the source of Jewish persecution and oppression in the way of life of the Jews themselves. They would learn, moreover, that "the fall of the Jewish state, as well as all the subsequent persecution and oppression which the Jews had suffered, had arisen from their own ignorance and opposition to all rational planning."[18]

German Jewish sentiment toward the ghetto dwellers of the East thus had deep roots in the European experience. Once in America, German Jews continued to identify culturally with their fellow citizens of Christian faith, from whom they believed themselves to differ only slightly. Likewise, they defined Judaism as culture, religion, and community in narrow terms. Conflict and contention in considerable measure marked their relationship to eastern European Jews, once the immigration of the latter was fully under way. A patronizing style and regular expressions of *noblesse oblige* toward the newcomers on the part of the established community exacerbated the differences and the resentments between the two groups. Concerned about both their own interests and the dangers to them posed by unenlightened but innocent victims of antisemitism, established American

Jews of German origin were in general highly ambivalent toward the new-comers in the 1880s and early 1890s.

American Jewish newspapers as well as the pronouncements of prominent German American Jews pointedly illustrate equivocation and paternalism toward the immigrants. While consistently condemning the antisemitic edicts in Russia and the czarist policies steadily restricting Jewish economic life, the newspapers of the 1880s and 1890s presented an unflattering portrait of the immigrants in articles, editorials, and letters. For example, Augustus Levey, secretary of the short-lived Hebrew Emigrant Aid Society (HEAS), the earliest formal Jewish organization to aid the immigrants, made a number of telling observations. Capturing the essence of the problem of the relationship of German Jews to the immigrants, Levey noted that the HEAS activists "have a reciprocal duty to perform; first, as members of the American community, and next to the refugees under our charge." That the German Jews were caught up in the sometimes conflicting demands of responsibility to the immigrants and their view of the requirements of American citizenship led him to differentiate between those who "will become citizens of whom we may be proud" and those with "neither a future in this nor in any other country." Of the latter, Levey said,

> The mode of life of these people in Russia has stamped upon them the ineffaceable marks of permanent pauperism, only disgrace and a lowering of the opinion in which American Israelites are held by this community can result from the continued residence among us of such an addition to the Jewish population. Every crime against property or the person committed by one of these wretches will throw obloquy over our race throughout the land.[19]

An American Jewish commentary of 1881 even suggested tackling the problem abroad before it reached these shores:

> It is very philanthropic to desire the Jews of Russia to leave that Empire, now that riots have broken out in the Ukraine, but to suggest that three million of them settle in America, evidences more enthusiasm than common sense. A better way. . . would be to send American Jewish missionaries to Russia to civilize them there, rather than give them an opportunity to russianize [sic] us in the event of such a colossal emigration.[20]

The same missionary theme was repeated ten years later when an editorial optimistically predicted that five men "with the energy of a Livingstone" could achieve great results in elevating Russian Jewry.[21]

Cyrus Sulzberger, a prominent leader in New York Jewish affairs, also identified objectionable qualities among some Jews while deploring discrimination "against whole classes," calling it "un-American and bigoted." He was writing in response to a statement in *The American Hebrew* that Jews should be able to find welcome at summer resorts. He argued that the editorial statement ignored differences among Jews, many of whom, for good reason, would find no hospitality because they were ill-mannered and loud. Sulzberger concluded, "Beyond question there is a prejudice against us in Christian hearts. But let us not feed it. Let us not arm hatred with good reason. Let us rather make our social conduct invulnerable even as we strive to make our morals."[22] These remarks capture the source of much American Jewish anxiety. To the considerable extent that the German American Jews feared "guilt by association," they made strenuous efforts to disarm prejudice by exhorting the immigrants toward respectable conduct as they defined it. Not complacent in their success or even their citizenship, German American Jews adopted stratagems for dealing with the immigrants that were fully consistent with Sulzberger's admonition. They hoped to deflect from themselves political and popular opinion critical of immigration and the immigrant and to set a standard of conduct for the immigrants that would effectively neutralize nativist sentiment.

The self-proclaimed duty among established Jews of guiding and enlightening their eastern coreligionists joined assumptions, also characteristic of the European past, about Jewish vulnerabilities. The eastern Jews bore considerable responsibility, as Maimon's patrons had suggested, for the historical debilities that had befallen them. In the United States, it was also widely believed that people who were the objects of discrimination had some control over the acts committed against them. Whereas Russian pogroms were irrational manifestations of hatred against Jews, prejudicial thinking and discriminatory practice in the new country had some logical basis. Jews could thus positively influence American attitudes. This conception sprang from optimism and reason, even when the imprint of race and ethnic bias was deepening in the 1890s. If Jews suffered because of some flaw in themselves, they could effectively diminish discrimination by reforming their objectionable conduct, guided by the wise counsel of their patrons. At stake was nothing less than the Jewish future in the United States.

The relationship between German American Jews and the newcomers was depicted particularly well by Abraham Cahan, the remarkable immigrant man of letters who founded *The Jewish Daily Forward* in 1897 and served for many years as its editor. In his autobiography, Cahan describes his first encounter with an American Jew shortly after arriving in New York. Fresh from his native Vilna, Cahan disembarked at Philadelphia in early June 1882 and, with other immigrants, was transported to New York's Castle Garden, the immigrant reception center at the foot of Manhattan. His meeting at the HEAS office just opposite Castle Garden encapsulated the mix of feelings between immigrants and patrons:

> I departed with a strong impression that he was a heartless bourgeois. And he probably suspected that I was a wild Russian. That is what they called us immigrants at that time, sometimes even to our faces.
>
> The inability to understand each other affected the relationship between the Russian-Jewish immigrants and the American Yahudim or German Jews. . . . Later I realized that there were Yahudim who fervently wished to help us stand on our own two feet in the new homeland.
>
> The reports of the pogroms had stirred them deeply and accounted for their participation in the immigrant society. But agreement between us was practically impossible. It wasn't only the differences in our daily language and manner of speaking that got in the way. That wouldn't have been so bad. It was deeper differences in inherited concepts and customs that separated us. With the best intentions in the world and with gentle hearts they unknowingly insulted us.[23]

Cahan's fiction also illuminates the immigrant experience, including the multilayered relationships of newcomers and German American Jews. His acclaimed novel, *The Rise of David Levinsky,* tells the story of a young man's growing estrangement from religion, the conflicts engendered by his immigration to the United States, and his ensuing success in cloak manufacturing. Although a fictional creation, Levinsky's story resonates with the truth of thousands of immigrant lives, sundered from Europe and recreated in American along new and often troubling lines. In the concluding paragraph of the book, Cahan's Levinsky says simply, "My past and my present do not comport well."[24] Levinsky's prosperity and the accompanying disjunction between past and present—his assimilation—portrayed the dramatic upward mobility of many Jews in America. However, despite ceaseless repetition of this process among the immigrants, American Jewish anxieties about the cultural adjustment of the newcomers, at least regarding the immigrant generation, remained substantial at the turn of the twentieth century.

Before the Jewish immigration from eastern Europe, beginning in the eighteenth century, the *Haskalah,* or Jewish Enlightenment, had introduced secular learning to the communities of the Old World. Orthodox practice and Jewish law were no longer the sole arbiters of how one should live. Still, many German American Jews regarded the immigrants collectively as habitués of practices unsuitable to life in America.

Other immigrant proclivities also invited derision. Typically businesspeople and political moderates, German American Jews worried about the growth of socialist and radical activity among the immigrants; immigrant Jews who called attention to themselves not only as Jews but also as socialists invited particularly scornful criticism. For example, socialists identifying themselves as Jews in a Labor Day parade in 1890 were condemned in the English language Jewish press. *The Jewish Messenger* complained that no other marchers carried banners revealing their religion and that "years of hard work on the part of citizens of the Jewish faith to level all distinctions between Jew and Gentile save those connected with religious doctrines are rendered as naught by the acts of thoughtless and misguided people less than five years in-the country."[25]

Established Jews were relatively successful in blending into the wider society without betraying their Jewishness because they had long before rejected those emblems continuing to mark the eastern Jews as aliens and greenhorns. The reaction of German American Jews to the cultural manner of the newcomers was intense. Apprehensive about what their relationship to the immigrants might augur for their own social standing, they were also restive about their material capacity to fulfill their sense of moral obligation to the immigrants. All of this combined to produce considerable equivocation and consternation.

Because American Jews of German origin had achieved, in their own view, an optimal adjustment to American life, they believed that the immigrants had much to learn from their example. Their Judaism, albeit vastly different from that of the newcomers, comfortably accorded with public sensibilities and the demands and opportunities of American life. To the extent that the immigrants failed to meet or, worse, rejected this standard, frictions between the established Jewish community and Jewish immigrants inevitably followed.

Differences between the two groups of Jews also found psychological expression. Self-defined as modern and rational, the German Jews of Europe and the United States still recognized a kinship, however disturbing, with the Jews of eastern Europe. The latter by force of numbers threatened to overwhelm the carefully cultivated image the German Jews displayed. The aversion to the ghetto and its many associations on the part of American Jews of German origin had assumed a particular kind of intensity characteristic of converts or of people who see disturbing images of themselves in the faces of those whom they would reform. As immigration accelerated, German American Jews continued the process of self-definition, tacitly comparing themselves with the newcomers. Such determinations did not always constitute an active, conscious program to construct an American Jewish identity but were at the least implicit in every effort, institutional and personal, to assist, encourage, or criticize the Jewish immigrants. The new Jewish immigration had thus provoked American Jews to undertake a collective cultural and political self-assessment. It was reminiscent of the efforts of their German Jewish forbears in Europe to forge a modern identity in the wake of the Jewish Emancipation, which, in their view, rendered retrograde and anachronistic the culture of their provincial, ghettoized coreligionists.[26]

### Old Promise, New Peril

To established American Jews, the danger of immigration was especially great because it threatened the messianic promise of their adopted land. The lead article in *The Menorah,* the official organ of the B'nai B'rith, of October 1892 referred to America as "the redeemer . . . born on the 12th day of October, 1492" and as "marching on . . . until the redemption of the human race is achieved."[27] Another reflection of 1892 on the meaning of the Columbian voyage pointed out that the four-hundredth anniversary of Columbus's landfall, 12 October 1892, coincided with the Hebrew date marking the seventh day of the festival of Sukkot. That holiday represents both harvest thanksgiving and the commemoration of Jewish wandering in the desert prior to entering the Promised Land. The 1892 convergence of the Gregorian and Hebrew dates occurred for the first time in four hundred years, for the previous coincidence of 12 October and the seventh day of Sukkot was in 1492, even falling on the same week day as the 1892 date.[28]

The symbolism could not have escaped readers who shared the Reform Jewish leadership's view of America as the promised land of the Jews, the New World Israel. Columbus was a latter-day Moses. His voyage of discovery set the stage for a wholly new covenant, not with God but with Washington and Jefferson. Perceived threats to this millennial dream would accordingly spur established German American Jews to the most determined, defensive counteraction, especially when the menace came from other Jews, however foreign and unlike themselves the newcomers appeared. As much as some might have wished, established Jews could not dissociate themselves from the immigrants.

Tumultuous social forces set in motion by the wave of immigrants thus provoked anxious feelings in American society and even unsettled American Jewish faith in the New World. Such were the portents of American social and political life that German American Jews feared an erosion of the foundations of their own religious freedom and economic opportunity. While recognizing the necessity of assisting eastern European Jews appearing in increasing numbers on the East Coast in the early 1880s, many established Jews were for the next ten years nervous critics of immigration. Their own standing in America was at issue.

### Fear and Responsibility: American Jewish Ambivalence

In a plea for "more stringent emigration laws" in view of the "utterly helpless emigrants to these shores," *The Jewish Messenger* voiced an opinion widely shared among German American Jews.[29] In the early 1880s, no apprehension among the Jews of New York was greater than the looming specter of a permanent class of immigrant Jewish paupers cast ashore in the city. Their fear manifested itself in telling and dramatic ways. Even the Jewish charities of New York were not above draconian measures against desperate and helpless people vulnerable to dependency.[30] The response to pauperism on the part of the United Hebrew Charities (UHC) consisted of "forwarding" immigrants back to Europe if, for any reason, they were unable to support themselves. In 1887, for example, the UHC reported that 414 Jewish arrivals were provided with steamship tickets back to Europe. These individuals made small contributions of their own or received some assistance from friends toward the cost of their passage. They returned, according to the UHC, because they could not make a satisfactory living. Another 1,082, "unfitted [sic] to cope with the necessities of employment," had been in the United States for less than a year when they were sent back to Europe on cattle boats. The 1,496 repatriated from New York constituted about five percent of the 30,866 Jewish immigrants reaching Castle Garden in 1887.[31] Given the publicity and the embarrassment, those returned to Europe were more apparent than their numbers might otherwise indicate. They were a visible disgrace, risking the reputation of New York's established Jews.

At the same time, German American Jews were impassioned in their consistent condemnation of the conditions in eastern Europe that had set the Jewish immigration in motion. Many of these people were not far removed from Europe themselves, although they had neither lived in ghettos nor suffered the legal and political debilities of the eastern Jews. American Jewish awareness of European antisemitism and the economic privations driving the newcomers to American shores set against their own dread of mass immigration gave them an ambivalent outlook on the problem of Jewish suffering. The American Jewish press reflected this conflict in the 1880s and 1890s, sometimes supporting open immigration and other times expressing alarm.[32] Likewise, the UHC conveyed the same ambivalence, nowhere more clearly than in the following juxtaposed paragraphs from its 1887 annual report:

> The thoughtless immigration of people unable to work, with the impossibility of granting them sufficient help presented to us the danger to the community at large of a further increase of such elements.
>
> We cannot concur with measures proposed by the public press to restrain immigration—if such measures would prevent even one of our oppressed co-religionists from seeking the hospitality of this country.
>
> Next to caring for our own poor, we fully recognize the propriety of the duties imposed upon us, through our better social position in this country, to aid the persecuted and oppressed of our old home.
>
> But in careful consideration of such duty, we must deliberate how to reconcile our means and our inclination.[33]

The UHC pointed out that its primary responsibility was "to distribute relief among the needy Hebrews of the *City of New York*."[34] It did not see organized efforts on behalf of arriving immigrants as a major part of its charge. Before 1881, Jewish immigrants in need of assistance received it ei-

14

ther from the Commissioners of Emigration or other national societies charged with looking after immigrants. Some Jewish immigrants were sent to the UHC, where they received aid.[35] In 1874, the UHC supported the distribution of immigrants in its first annual report: "When the prospect of improvement in this city was hopeless, the Board have [sic] assisted deserving families to homes West or South, or on their return to Europe."[36]

## *The Industrial Removal Office: Origin and Outlook*

In February 1901, the Industrial Removal Office (IRO) was founded as part of the nascent Jewish Agricultural and Industrial Aid Society (JAIAS). The latter was founded in 1900 and was devoted both to assisting would-be Jewish farmers and to encouraging Jewish immigrant settlement beyond New York. Underwritten by the Jewish Colonization Association (ICA), headquartered in Paris, the IRO for just over two decades promoted the distribution of Jewish immigrants from the eastern seaboard to the interior of the country. Although the organization had branch offices in Boston and Philadelphia, New York commanded virtually all of its attention.

The immediate cause of the IRO's formation was a sudden and relatively large influx of Rumanian Jews to the United States in 1900, following antisemitic decrees by the Rumanian government. The Rumanian Committee was hastily formed in New York to distribute the refugees to other towns and cities where they might more easily find employment. The committee enlisted the cooperation of the lodges of the B'nai B'rith. Located throughout the United States, the lodges received the Rumanian Jewish newcomers and found them work in local businesses, commercial establishments, and industries. The Rumanian Committee quickly evolved into the IRO, embracing the same goals of Jewish immigrant distribution but doing so more systematically and on a much larger scale. The IRO directed its attention to unemployed Jewish immigrants regardless of their origin. Although most of its clients were Russian Jews and others of eastern European origin, the IRO also assisted Sephardic Jews, whose emigration from the Balkans to the United States coincided with the middle years of IRO activity.

The IRO was organized, led, and staffed primarily by German American Jews and generally assumed the paternalistic stance characteristic of other German Jewish philanthropies. Although the IRO actively supported an open immigration policy against the growing force of restrictionism, it defined the immigration of eastern European Jews as a major problem confronting both the Jews of New York, where most of the immigrants disembarked, and American Jews generally. The IRO regarded immigration as a great national asset but only if the massive human capital were not degraded by dependency and unemployment, which the organization hoped to arrest by helping to match the skills and abilities of the newcomers with the labor needs of various American locales. The nub of the problem was absorption, both economic and cultural. How could many thousands of Jewish immigrants arriving each year find self-sustaining employment in New York's labor market, where unemployment and underemployment were chronic predicaments? If people remained in New York on the economic margins, how could they avoid falling victim to the vices flourishing in the squalor of the crowded immigrant districts? If they continued to live on the East Side, where the language and culture of the *shtetlekh,* or small towns of the Pale of Settlement flourished, how could they adopt the values and styles of living that were the end point of the widely embraced process of Americanization? With assistance and guidance, immigrant clients of the IRO might assimilate themselves into American society and thus substantially mitigate the apprehension of their patrons.

The IRO thus fostered Jewish immigrant distribution throughout the United States. Assisting only unemployed Jewish immigrants, the IRO for two decades expedited the resettlement of some 80,000 people to more than 1,000 towns and cities. Enlisting the cooperation of Jews in interior communities, the IRO depended on them to secure employment for the immigrants and to ease their settlement into the community. The Jewish immigrants would embark on a new life of self-respect, built on decent if not lucrative employment that would benefit both themselves and the country. At the same time, moving away from the dense immigrant enclave of the city would hasten their adoption of mainstream values, language, and culture. Achieving these ends, the immigrants would find "their own salvation," as David Bressler, the long-time general manager of the IRO, frequently remarked. The ideology of distribution depended on a social, economic, and moral rationale. It was summed up by Morris Waldman, the assistant manager of the IRO in its early years: "No saner or more reasonable method of aiding the unemployed could be conceived than 'removal.' It is not merely palliative; it is preventive, and strictly so, because it attacks the root of evil."[37]

Discussions of immigrant adjustment at the turn of the twentieth century were often phrased in terms of "Americanization," although the older image of the melting pot amalgamation of many old country patterns into a new, American synthesis was weakening under the force of nativism.[38] The new immigration had spawned widespread disquiet about the capacity of the nation to absorb newcomers under the old terms, for questions were raised about their adaptability. Doubts about the possibilities of Americanization—or assimilation—met sharp criticism from Jewish as well as other European ethnic organizations. Taking inspiration from an ideology of nativism and scientific racism, the most virulent skeptics claimed that immigrants outside of the old stock of northern and western Europe were incapable of fitting themselves into American life.

The following editorial remarks, under the heading, "The New Know-nothingism," in a 1910 number of *The American Hebrew,* typify the Jewish institutional reaction to such sentiments:

> But the opponents of free immigration rest their case mostly upon . . . the fear that Americanism will be overrun and swamped by the lower culture of the new arrivals. This . . . indicates a despicable want of confidence in the capacity of American institutions to mould the character of the immigrant and his descendants. Nothing is more remarkable in the history of mankind than the Americanization of the second generation of immigrants, which is to be observed in all directions, whether the parents were English or Slavs, Italians or Jews.[39]

Sharing this view, the IRO predicated Americanization on the immigrant embrace of civic, democratic values and the duties and privileges of citizenship, which would not be possible unless they first obtained decent employment. The IRO perspective was consistent with the fledgling modern view of culture. It assumed that immigrants from any land were amenable to assimilation because culture was plastic and mutable.

These views stood in opposition to scientific racism, which was pervasive and influential in the discourse on race and ethnicity early in the century. It merged culture and biology into a retrograde model emphasizing the fixity and genetic determination of behavior. Supporting xenophobic tirades against immigration, scientific racism viewed the newcomers as so unlike their British, German, and Scandinavian predecessors that the differences were interpreted in racial terms. It was as though the disagreeable social characteristics linked to them were as natural and unchanging as their physical features. Accordingly, nativist alarms about race mixing and masses of unassimilable and polluting aliens cast some of the darkest shadows over the immigrants and the prospects of continued immigration.

Although the IRO view of Americanization did not sanction a wholesale abandonment of traditional culture, it implied that Old World custom should adapt itself to the mores of the new country. That such adjustment was believed possible, even inevitable, put the IRO and allied organizations at odds with all immigration restrictionists. Opposing scientific racism and immigration restriction then reaching their apex, the IRO viewed its work as especially urgent. It would relieve the suffering and despair of unemployed and poverty-stricken immigrants by enabling them to construct lives of self-respect and independence beyond the stultifying confines of the eastern ghetto. At the same time, the IRO joined the movement against immigration restriction by making it possible for immigrants to contribute actively and productively to the economic development of the country.

To immigration supporters, desirable change in culture—in other words, the adjustment of immigrants to American society—could best proceed under conditions approximating mainstream life. The dispersion of concentrated immigrant settlements would bring the newcomers into contact with non-Jews, thus providing an important key to the acculturation process. Many German American Jews hoped that under their benevolent tutelage the immigrants would learn to conduct themselves acceptably by rising above old, benighted practices that would otherwise inhibit their adaptation. On the assumption that much prejudice against immigration and the immigrant had a rational basis, the IRO also asserted that dispersion would diminish restrictionist clamor.

The encouragement of immigrant accommodation to America also defined the institutional response of other prominent Jewish organizations and philanthropies toward the newcomers. It underlay every plan for Jewish immigrant distribution antedating the founding of the IRO. Seventeen years after warning of the dangers of "arming hatred with good reason," Cyrus Sulzberger became the first chairman of the IRO and helped set a course that he and others hoped would indeed disarm hatred. Otherwise, the immigrants themselves, their patrons, and the continuing prospects for immigration would be jeopardized.

## From Ambivalence to Activism in the New Century

The IRO joined a discourse on immigrants and immigration begun more than two decades before its founding. It put into sharp relief the uneasy relationship between established American Jews and the newcomers while actively supporting liberal national immigration policies. The old ambivalence of German American Jews toward the new Jewish immigrants had given substantial ground before the increasing persecution of eastern European Jews in antisemitic edicts and pogroms, particularly in Rumania and Russia. Moreover, the sheer volume of Russian Jewish immigration and the emergence of articulate immigrant spokesmen critical of patronage and paternalism compelled the serious notice of German American Jews. Although the paternalism and equivocation of the 1880s and 1890s had been moderated dramatically by the early twentieth century, the American Jewish leadership remained confident that it had a keener understanding of the problems of immigration than did the newcomers themselves. This confidence was abundantly clear in the work of the IRO. Still, from the outset, the IRO operatives never doubted that German American Jews and their immigrant coreligionists had come to share a common interest and a common fate.

Beginning work at 104 Rivington Street before moving in 1905 to 174 Second Avenue for the remainder of its existence, the IRO-gathered reports on local labor markets and their capacity to absorb both skilled and unskilled immigrants. Such an orderly gathering of information was a requisite feature of the scientific and rational procedures the IRO valued, representing in its view a marked improvement over earlier unsystematic attempts at distribution. The IRO defined the problem of overcrowding as a national concern, not simply an inconvenience for New York's Jewish population and its charities. Jewish communities in the interior were asked to share the burden of assimilating the newcomers.

Accordingly, the IRO assisted immigrants to do more than simply leave New York. It directed them to particular destinations, determined by the capacity of the receiving community and its labor market to absorb them. Applicants were investigated by the IRO in a highly selective procedure to determine their suitability for resettlement. Thus, distribution represented neither an end in itself nor a wholesale scheme to relocate under any circumstance New York's unemployed immigrant Jews. Rather, it would make possible the self-support thousands could not achieve in New York,

19

which was a single crucial step pointing the way toward a new, responsible life in the United States.

Moreover, the IRO represented "the inauguration of a movement which should and must be greatly extended . . .[for] the experience of past years has proven that, almost every family removed becomes a center around which, immediately, and with ever-increasing force, others congregate.[40] The IRO believed that distribution would create a chain migration. Resettled individuals or families would become links to which kin and friends in Europe or on the East Coast could subsequently attach themselves. Two individuals sent to Detroit in 1904, for example, were reported to have drawn sixty additional people to the city.[41] Sometimes characterized as the "magnet effect," it was described by Sulzberger in 1904:

> The total number of removals from New York made by the Society in its three years of work now aggregate 13,000. In the face of the tremendous number of arrivals this would seem useless but for the thought that those established elsewhere will serve to attract their relatives and friends to the same places, and thus ultimately secure the diversion of a considerable number from New York.[42]

In a similar vein, Waldman explained that the diversion of immigrants from New York would be accomplished "by establishing in each person removed a center of attraction for other individuals from this city and Europe."[43]

By the end of 1917, when IRO work ground to a virtual halt, the organization had resettled 78,995 individuals, including 2,459 and 2,576 people from its Philadelphia and Boston offices, respectively.[44] In line with Sulzberger's early observation, this number represented only a small proportion of the steadily increasing Jewish immigrant population of New York and, in itself, fell far short of the demographic shift the IRO sought. Still, Bressler asserted in 1914 that "it would be a conservative estimate . . . to say that at least one quarter of a million persons have been directly influenced to leave the metropolis by the educational and practical work of the Industrial Removal Office."[45] It is unclear on what basis Bressler made this claim. Nonetheless, given the general pattern of Jewish immigration whereby new settlers attracted Old Country kin and friends, there is no doubt that the IRO reinforced the process of chain migration and utilized it to disperse the ghetto.[46]

Both the IRO and preceding American Jewish programs for distributing the immigrants sprang in part from self-protective motives. Given the nagging worry that even the most exemplary American Jewish citizen would be judged as no better than the worst of the immigrants, American Jews took measures that they thought would preserve their own standing. They responded cautiously and defensively to a worrisome climate of opinion that they thought might put them at risk owing to their perceived connection to the eastern European Jews.[47] They trembled at the possibility of a "Jewish question" entering American politics.[48]

Reducing the IRO and American Jewish efforts on behalf of the newcomers to mere self-interest, however, flattens the contours of an extremely complex historical terrain wherein matters of value, world view, and religious teaching have no bearing on human motives. If self-interest alone prompted American Jewish action toward the immigrants, one would be hard-pressed to explain the sustained actions of established Jews to lobby strenuously against every move after 1890 to restrict immigration.[49] American Jews went to great lengths to ensure that immigration would continue, even when the mass movement of eastern European Jews was straining the resources of their charities and fledgling communal institutions. The steady arrival and settlement of immigrants in New York also continued to generate the very problems against which the IRO set itself. Moreover, the mass immigration and its supporters were drawing the malignant attention of the scientific racists and nativists, who were unconcerned about distinctions among the Jews themselves. American ports of entry remained open as long as they did owing in some measure to the efforts of Simon Wolf, Louis Marshall, Jacob Schiff, and like-minded American Jews of German background. The quota legislation of 1924 shutting down the European immigration culminated decades of restrictionist activity, but the victory occurred in spite of the determined opposition of Jewish immigration advocates and organizations, including the IRO.

### Persistent Paternalism

The IRO represented a unique experiment among the many ethnic organizations aiding the European immigrants. Although concerns about urban crowding, immigrant unemployment, and distribution were not unique to Jews, only the IRO among immigrant ethnic aid organizations defined its *raison d'être* as immigrant dispersion. It also functioned as a kind of labor clearinghouse serving the broader purposes of immigrant accomodation and the self-protection of American Jews. At the same time, the IRO believed that the continuation of an open immigration policy depended on undercutting the arguments of the restrictionists, a task that could best be accomplished by demonstrating practically the utility and adaptability of immigrant labor.

The IRO was caught up in the major questions of the day, including the fate of national immigration policy, the relationship between immigration and labor markets, the cultural accomodation of immigrants to American society, and the tension between assimilation and cultural persistence. The latter, particularly, was encapsulated in the relationship between the earlier German Jewish immigrants and their children on the one hand, and the eastern European Jews on the other. German Jewish philanthropies and social service organizations assisting the immigrants were an extension of that relationship. The sheer number of newcomers posed enormous challenges to such organizations and to those who had already found their niche. The German American Jews were exemplars of adaptation to the United States, but their radical narrowing of the spheres of religious and ethnic life could not easily serve as a model for the new Jewish immigrants, at least in the short term. Tensions were inevitable. The immigrants brought a very different version of Judaism to the United States, where it began to take root and flourish. Not homogeneous, the culture of the new Jewish immigration encompassed religious orthodoxy, secular learning, Zionism, and various versions of socialist or anarchist thinking. Despite the differences among these several cultural movements within the Jewish immigrant settlement, all contrasted with the German Jewish world view, including its forceful critique of the East Side. The IRO unavoidably provided a platform on which some of these contested ideologies were expressed.

After reviewing various periods of Jewish life in America, a newspaper story of the mid-1880s simply remarked, "The Russian period has begun in earnest."[50] The threshold of the new century also witnessed the substantial economic success of numbers of Russian Jews, some of whom were managing to send their children to college. Many more immigrants, however, joined by the uninterrupted stream of new arrivals from Russia, continued to wage an arduous economic and social struggle to create better lives, usually against enormous odds.

The IRO intended to reduce the odds, not by any guarantee of success but by trying to provide the immigrants with a probable chance of finding an economic niche outside of the urban ghetto. Once achieved, what the IRO considered the highly desirable process of adjustment, or "Americanization," would run its welcome course. That it might mean the eclipse of some eastern European cultural patterns was of no special concern, except, of course, to the immigrants themselves. Once resettled in the interior, they had to determine how much and to what extent they would accommodate Old Country habits to American life. Beyond self-support and good citizenship, the IRO remained flexible about the terms of accommodation.

Any study of the origins, workings, and ultimately the significance of the IRO must confront its unsettling name. The JAIAS promoted Jewish farming as well as light industry in the vicinity of Jewish agricultural communities to make farming settlements more viable. Industrial enterprises located in New York were encouraged to set up shop in rural areas—to remove themselves from the city to the countryside—thus originating the concept of "industrial removal." The IRO, after gaining partial autonomy from the JAIAS and then eventual administrative independence in 1907, devoted none of its attention to industrial removal. However, the name persisted.

Retrospectively, the well-intentioned and humane goals of the IRO seem inconsistent with the idea of industrial removal applied to people. The phrase is jarring. Moreover, in some of the correspondence between the main office and its various cooperating communities, IRO officials wrote or wired about "shipments" and "consignments," referring to immigrants in transit or ready to depart from New York. One cannot help but wince at the startling irony of such terms, especially among Jews, in light of the euphemisms of four decades later, when "shipments" and "consignments" thinly shrouded unspeakable evil.

Neither the reification nor the social distance connoted in these designations is a mere accident of language. Rather, they convey the mix of feelings that German American Jews held toward the newcomers, whom they were helping at arms length. "Removal" in its most benign usage at the time referred to what we would now term a household move or transfer. That it was applied to people rather than goods signals both their objectification and the undesirability of their presence in crowded immigrant New York. "Removal" further suggests a determination by its originators that the immigrants were more to be acted on than to act on their own—a paternalistic notion regularly borne out in the pronouncements of the IRO leadership.

Yet no coercion marked the work of the IRO. Immigrants had to apply if they wanted IRO assistance, and the numbers of applicants consistently exceeded by a wide margin those whom the organization could help. Assistance was rendered in the genuine belief that it would materially and psychologically ameliorate the lives of dispirited and desperate people. Still, "industrial removal" conveys a particular attitude, coldly objective and superior, toward the formidable economic and social problems of Jewish life on the East Side. The reified designation also indicates the increasing scale of the Jewish immigrant settlement of New York and the enormous task the IRO had set for itself. Although immigrant distribution was nothing new, the scope and urgency of the problem in 1901 far exceeded what had gone before, and nothing less than a "scientific" and "rational" approach to the problem would do. The managers and board of the IRO confronted the extraordinary challenge of reducing the steadily increasing Jewish immigrant population of unemployed. As the problem became objectified, the partial, often ad hoc measures of the past yielded to a more organized, large-scale effort proceeding along orderly, efficient, and impersonal lines. Given the scope of its self-defined mandate, the IRO in rhetoric and action sometimes subordinated the distinctive human quality of individual cases to the broad aggregate of unemployed thousands, requiring "removal," "shipment," and "consignment."

Following this introduction, Chapter 1 places the IRO in the broader context of other American Jewish efforts at self-protection through immigrant distribution, beginning in the 1870s. Distribution was also encouraged as essential to the widely valued "normalization" process—the outward movement of Jews from their narrow economic niche in Europe into farming and an array of skilled and unskilled occupations. Chapter 1 also considers the growing support of immigration by German American Jews and their continuing opposition to charges that their institutions were inducing immigration in violation of the law.

Chapter 2 examines the IRO in relationship to the rancorous debate on immigration. Unreservedly supportive of liberal immigration policies, the IRO expressed its views in various reports and in the public statements of its staff, especially David Bressler. Arguing for the positive benefits of continued immigration, the IRO also used its various platforms to rebut the racial and economic arguments of prominent immigration restrictionists.

Chapter 3 moves beyond the official pronouncements of the IRO to consider the internal Jewish debate on issues motivating the organization. This intramural discussion included immigrant intellectuals, the IRO and its immigrant clients, and the Yiddish as well as the Anglo-Jewish press. Among these issues were distribution and assimilation, philanthropy and charity, the patronage of German American Jews, and the place of the East Side and ethnic enclaves in the American Jewish future. The immigrants, in their letters to the newspapers and to the IRO, expressed vigorous and diverse opinions. However poor and powerless, they were never simply passive, mute objects of American Jewish philanthropy. Rather, they actively provided their own representations, both approving and oppositional toward dominant views of immigrant life and labor in the United States.

Chapter 4 discusses the operation of the IRO in several communities of the Midwest, including particularly Indianapolis and Terre Haute. IRO activity at the local level provides a counterpoint to its hopeful statements of purpose expounding the idea of a single, unified American Jewish community willing to shoulder the heavy burden and inconvenience of relieving the plight of the immigrants. The IRO assiduously cultivated the spirit of self-sacrifice throughout the country, but it frequently encountered local resistance. The daily reality of IRO work in many towns and cities sometimes produced conflicts between local concerns and the organization's sweeping goals. Cooperating Jewish communities frequently placed their self-conceived best interest ahead of the IRO program, for the newcomers sometimes proved costly, troublesome, and embarrassing. The dialogue between the main office and cooperating communities shows a continuing tension between the IRO's conception of an American Jewish commonweal and the limits of local altruism.

Chapter 5 concludes with a consideration of contemporary immigration issues in comparison with those of the earlier era. Nearly one hundred years after the founding of the IRO, the face of the United States is again changing through large-scale immigration. Unlike the earlier era, assimilation in the 1990s is not the nearly universal value it was in 1901. Changes in American society have made possible more overt expressions of cultural difference than was the case when the IRO was active. A controversial and divisive issue at the dawn of the twentieth century, immigration is contentious once more at its close.

Finally, an appendix consisting of eleven tables summarizes and interprets demographic and economic data on Jewish immigrants, particularly those assisted by the IRO.

# — 1 —

# Jewish Immigrant Distribution

The first stirrings among German American Jews regarding immigrant distribution occurred in the 1870s, when the United Hebrew Charities (UHC) of New York devised plans for resettling eastern European Jews in interior communities. Organized in 1874 through the union of five charitable and relief associations, the UHC in its first year formed an Emigration Committee for "assisting families and individuals to more promising fields of residence than our city." Between October 1874 and April 1875, the UHC contributed to the transportation of ninety-two adults and children, only forty of whom settled in other parts of the United States. The remaining fifty-two returned to Europe with UHC assistance.[1] Although the first UHC annual report does not detail the reasons that people returned to Europe, later explanations disclosed that such returnees were predominantly individuals incapable of self-support. They included the old and infirm as well as younger men who were unable to secure employment. Their return to Europe reduced UHC charity obligations and was no cause for regret.

The UHC made some effort to match immigrants' skills with the needs of potential receiving communities or to ensure that immigrants sent from New York would at least have friends or relatives in the designated community to look after them. Like the IRO to follow, the UHC wanted to take into account both the needs of particular families and individuals on the one hand, and interior communities on the other. Both organizations eschewed any intention simply to dump immigrants elsewhere, particularly if they were paupers. The Emigration Committee disapproved of "the pernicious system of sending paupers from city to city" and argued instead "that no persons be sent elsewhere in this country unless they can give satisfactory proof that they better their condition by the change intended.[2] Still, whatever the concerns of the UHC with immigrant welfare, its program of dispersion sprang in large measure from fears that its financial resources would collapse under the weight of an increasing immigrant population. The UHC greatly preferred to commit its funds to the resident needy of New York.

Between its founding and 1911, when the UHC abandoned its own distribution program, the organization had assisted resettlement to the interior of just over 24,300 immigrant Jews. In most years, only a few hundred immigrants were aided. The peak years of resettlement were 1890 to 1896, when the UHC helped slightly more than 16,000 immigrants.[3] Although the organization managed to relocate a very small number of immigrants in proportion to the total Jewish immigration, it provided some precedent for the IRO.

The distribution activities and immigration concerns of the UHC in the 1870s were only a prelude to larger-scale efforts provoked by the notorious May Laws of 1882 following the assassination of Czar Alexander II the previous year. These enactments succeeded in worsening the already onerous conditions of Jewish life in Russia by further limiting where Jews could live, and especially how they might earn a living. Various vocations in agriculture and industry were simply closed to Jews, and professional careers were similarly restricted. The growing threat of pogroms and impoverishment initiated the mass movement of Jews to American shores. In four decades, immigration began to shift the center of Jewish life from Europe to the United States, producing stunning effects on American society. The sudden appearance of large numbers of eastern European Jews in the United States confounded their American coreligionists with a major economic, social, and moral crisis.

In the fall of 1881, following antisemitic outbreaks in Kiev and other cities, thousands of refugees quickly fled to Brody, Galicia, which was then part of the Austro-Hungarian Empire. Threatened with repatriation by the government, 1,500 of the hapless refugees made their way to the United States with the assistance of the Alliance Israelite Universelle. Support committees were quickly formed and included the Russian Jewish Committee in America (composed of the Emigration Committee of the UHC and a committee of the Union of American Jewish Congregations), the Mansion House Committee in London, and similar organizations in Berlin,

Vienna, and other continental cities.[4] The European organizations joined the Alliance Israelite in trying to relieve the plight of the Brody refugees by assisting them in settling in other countries, particularly the United States. The Russian Jewish Committee, however, proved ill-equipped to deal with the refugees. The UHC reported in 1882 that "receiving, caring for, and distributing our unfortunate brethren fleeing from persecution . . . became too vast and difficult for the temporary committee, and . . . the Hebrew Emigrants' Aid Society [HEAS] was formed and is now doing noble work."[5]

The HEAS reported that the sudden, large immigration of Brody refugees unrestrained by the European committees was placing enormous burdens on its resources. While trying to find occupations for the new arrivals, the HEAS faced the disembarkation of 4,000 people in June and July of 1882 for whom it could not care without "incurring great cost." Small hotels were rented for 250 people, and another 250 were housed on Wards Island. That number soon doubled, and the crowding became so severe that the Health Department objected. One thousand people were cared for at Castle Garden until the oppressive summer heat required that the refugees there move to hotels.[6]

Founded in 1881 with financial support from the Baron de Hirsch and disbanded in 1883 after some slackening in the rate of Jewish immigration, the short-lived HEAS succeeded the Russian Jewish committee. The concern of the HEAS for the welfare of the immigrants was secondary to coping with the problems and threats that large-scale immigration posed for American Jews. Distribution and colonization emerged as prominent strategies for diffusing the sudden influx of refugees and thereby protecting the Jewish position in the United States.[7] Complaining that refugees were dispatched to the United States without regard to whether they could become independent, the HEAS despaired of finding them occupations. Many lacked professions, and others were old and frail.[8] The European committees did not want to direct the refugees to their own countries, and the HEAS adamantly opposed what appeared to be a wholesale export to the United States of immigrants likely to become public charges. The HEAS felt its control over Jewish immigration was thereby undermined. Similarly, its criticism focused particularly on the actions of the Mansion House Committee, authorized by the other committees to direct immigrants to various American destinations.[9] The HEAS complained that the Mansion House Committee's dispatch of Jewish immigrants to different parts of the United States was haphazard and ill-considered.[10]

For example, some refugees were sent directly to towns and cities, "which was a great embarrassment to the Society."[11] The New York Jewish leadership preferred that the immigrants first pass through New York. They wanted to exercise some control over the disposition of immigrants, many of whom were being returned to New York by the receiving communities, although they had come through other ports.[12] The Mansion House Committee believed that labor markets in England were so glutted that, were it not for the American outlet for Jewish emigration, pressures would have been overwhelming, especially in view of the restricted range of vocations pursued by Jews.[13] In the second year of its three-year life, the HEAS was overwhelmed by the number of immigrants arriving in New York:

> At State Street, this week, the scenes were the same as heretofore. Owing to lack of funds, the society has found it a matter of impossibility to take charge of the emigrants, and . . . the emigration Commissioners will have to look after all the emigrants arriving henceforth. The Emigrant Aid Society will assist cases of destitution and illness, but able-bodied immigrants will have to shift for themselves.[14]

Soon after, the European committees remitted funds for the HEAS to continue its work, and the Mansion House Committee ceased directing immigrant refugees to the United States.[15]

The HEAS utilized previously established local resettlement committees to aid the refugees fleeing the antisemitic outbreaks in Russia. In 1882, immigrant assistance organizations coalesced in twenty-two American cities and in Toronto and Montreal.[16] The HEAS faced complaints from its American committees about immigrants who were unable to find work. Demands were made that the HEAS send no additional immigrants. Alluding to the agricultural settlement of Jews, which had received considerable emphasis on both sides of the Atlantic, one representative critic remarked that his city, Buffalo, seemed to be the endpoint of "farmers" manufactured for the purpose. He continued, "We are now overcrowded with people without work, and worse than all, unable to work. I hope you will . . . under no circumstance allot any more to this city, till you hear from us, nor send any, who may even have been ticketed . . . at Liverpool, as we shall be forced to at once return them to New York."[17] Criticism of this sort was not unusual at the start of the first distribution efforts.

Beginning in the 1880s, German American Jews thus confronted the nettlesome and fateful problem of how to cope with the movement of eastern European Jews to American shores. On the one hand, they felt sympathy and obligation by the bonds of common faith, however differently it might be observed and interpreted. On the other hand, they were apprehensive about what this new association and the enormous responsibilities it brought might augur for their own position and future in American society. Thus *The Jewish Messenger,* in urging the UHC to establish an emigration bureau to assist immigrants on arrival, argued that it would "constitute one link in the chain of protection for exiled Hebrews and of self-defence [sic] for American Israelites."[18]

Fear of disease and the consequences of widespread poverty also provoked concern. The following UHC comment in 1889 on the hygienic and social dangers of urban congestion is illustrative:

> Overcrowding is the greatest burden from which the Jewish communities in the Tenth and Thirteenth Wards are suffering. The condition of the Jewish quarter—as it is now generally and, unfortunately, with peculiar propriety denominated—has too often been the subject of extravagant word-painting in the daily press, but any passer-by cannot be blind to the fact that the good name of New York Judaism is endangered unless remedial measures are promptly devised to correct the evil . . . of this unlawful and farspreading [sic] feature of our tenement-house system.[19]

American Jews were also fully aware that popular opinion and the mainstream press took skeptical note of the immigrants. *The New York Times,* for example, observed that immigrants remaining in the city would "appreciably swell the ranks of our beggars, ragpickers, organ grinders, low criminals, and other objectionable classes."[20]

Reflecting American Jewish self-interest, the UHC and the HEAS supported control over the numbers and quality of the immigration. The UHC reiterated these concerns throughout the 1880s. American Jews of a liberal religious outlook saw themselves as models of citizenship and took a dim view of beliefs and practices that might set Jews apart from their neighbors. Self-support was also a vital step toward exemplary citizenship and, as immigration increased, productive labor by the newcomers received commensurate emphasis. In 1888, the UHC remarked that when the 20,000 or 30,000 Rumanian and Russian Jews arrived, "dejected, apprehensive, half-clad, miserable," in flight from persecution, little concern was expressed about the economic consequences. The UHC Report continued,

> But times have changed. It is no longer a matter of a few thousand immigrants, whom American freedom welcomes with open hand. It has become a social, financial and business question, this annual increase of our population, indiscriminately contributed by European nations, and the time has come when, in the best interest of American Judaism, we should solemnly warn our brethren in Europe not to encourage the emigration of people who cannot earn their livelihood, and who cannot be deemed welcome accessions. We have burdens enough. . . . Our newspapers have had daily records of misdemeanors, marital misery and petty quarrels, that may largely be attributed to the same source.[21]

The American Jewish leadership was especially apprehensive about the possibility of very needy Jewish immigrants concentrating in urban areas, particularly East Coast points of disembarkation—New York, Boston, and Philadelphia. Such dense urban reserves of Old World practice would only call into doubt the assimilation process. The ethnic community represented an obstacle to Jewish progress in the United States, a retrograde way of life that inhibited or forestalled altogether immigrant adjustment to the new country. Critiques of the East Side struck a very sensitive chord among German American Jews, who determined that dispersion of the newcomers offered the best possibility of achieving assimilation into the economic and social life of the country.

Concerns about immigration continued into the 1890s, when urban concentrations of immigrants grew even more acutely dangerous. Accordingly, the Lower East Side—the largest and most visible Jewish immigrant concentration—was regarded in increasingly desperate terms. After a brief discussion of the problem of adaptability, *The American Israelite*, a strong voice of the American Reform outlook, noted,

> Ignorance and depravity born of oppression is at the bottom of it all and it is therefore no wonder that a well-defined demand is arising for discrimination in immigration. The American does not want a little Bohemia, Hungary, Italy, Ireland, Germany or Russia in every one of his large cities, and to him who has ears to hear and eyes to see, it must be evident that this question will sooner or later become a burning issue.[22]

Claiming that Jews do not assimilate as easily as non-Jews, the article reminded its readers of their paternalistic responsibilities: "It behooves the Jew . . . who has already made evident his right to enjoy the privilege of this free county [sic], to see that the Russian Jew, whom Slavonic ignorance and oppression has [sic] degraded, is educated and lifted up to the level of the intelligent citizen."[23]

Well before the founding of the IRO, immigrant distribution was regarded as the solution to the problem of adjustment and assimilation. Yet Jewish institutional support for dispersion in the 1880s and 1890s or, indeed, for any program addressing perceived Jewish problems of national scope, was little more than rudimentary. The IRO emerged when Jewish community institutions and philanthropic activity had succeeded in coalescing to the point that coordination and implementation of projects beyond the local level became feasible. The IRO formalized the nonagricultural efforts at immigrant dispersion in a manner that would improve on the various piecemeal efforts and local committees of the previous two decades through a process that was "thoroughly rational and scientific."[24]

## Jewish Farming, Normalization, and Outward Mobility

Immigrant dispersion in the 1880s and 1890s also included several concerted efforts to set up Jewish newcomers as farmers, particularly in agricultural colonies. The HEAS sent out six families to settle in Rosenhayn, New Jersey, where off-farm factory work, as in other south Jersey farming experiments, was essential for survival. The best known and largest of the agricultural schemes among the New Jersey Jewish settlements were in Woodbine and Vineland, although it was clear by the 1890s that colonies were not practicable.[25] Modest achievements notwithstanding, farming ventures repeatedly collapsed throughout the country. The reasons for failure in particular cases varied, but a general pattern emerged, including inattention to the quality of the land acquired, insufficient capitalization, lack of agricultural experience, diminishing spirit after the initial enthusiasm, and poor access to rural markets. Idealism and energetic commitment could not overcome the harsh realities of nineteenth-century American agriculture.

In addition to removing Jewish refugees and immigrants from congested American cities, settlement on farms also sprang from much older, if less expedient, motives. German Jews in Europe and America were stung by stereotypes depicting Jews as suited only to commercial activity, trading, or other endeavors not requiring arduous physical labor. They hoped to expand Gentile perceptions of Jewish capabilities by encouraging immigrant Jews to break with the past and become producers. The entry of Jews into agriculture would represent a major step on the road to "normalization," or the movement of Jews from their economic confinement into the same range of occupations available to their Christian neighbors.

Jewish organizations, such as the IRO and the UHC, fully embraced the idea of normalization to diminish the differences, except those of faith, between Jews and non-Jews. Normalization would dissolve the barriers between typical Jewish vocations and the skilled and unskilled occupations open to others. Popular opinion, including pernicious nativism and antisemitism, regarded Jews as unfit by reason of biology or history for any productive enterprise, especially farming. Instead, they were destined to continue to play a parasitic role on the social body as speculators or middlemen, such as sellers, hawkers, and peddlers. The IRO, for example, had to combat narrow public attitudes about the capacity of Jewish labor to work at tasks not customarily performed by Jews. Such opinions, if they persisted, could only hinder immigrant efforts to exploit the gamut of occupational opportunities in the United States.

Many observers identified the historical limitations preventing European Jewry from achieving normalization. David Philipson, for example, an American-born Reform rabbi, articulated the sensitivity of many Jews, particularly among the leadership and intelligentsia:

> Time and again the reproach has been uttered against the Jews that they are only consumers and not producers. Time and again we have been told that among farmers, handicraftsmen, artizans [sic], the Jew is a rarity; all his ambition lies in the lines of trade and commerce. . . . Mendelssohn . . . in answer to that same reproach, pithily said: "Our hands are bound, and we are blamed for not using them."[26]

Philipson then went on to explain the social and historical origins of limitations placed on Jews, who, in ancient times, had participated in the productive trades. In the United States, he argued, the European conditions of exclusion did not prevail and therefore the mission of the Jew in America was "to remove all past false traditions regarding the Jew; to in every way

34

make himself one with his neighbors; to stand off from them only in his religion."[27]

In the liberal view, Jews should aspire to their neighbors' expectations of what constitutes a normal style of living. Their unimpeachable conduct would also help to dispel anti-Jewish feelings. The dominant image of the eastern European Jew as middle man loomed as a dark shadow over efforts to encourage full Jewish participation in modern social and economic life, including farming. It was believed that, above all other work, farming would contribute most to the refiguration of customary understandings and images of the Jew, formed over centuries by severe European constraints on Jewish economic life. By becoming producers, especially on the land, Jews would achieve the kind of social normality promised by the Emancipation and pursued so resolutely by Reform Jews.

German American Jews shared a number of attitudes with some of the thinkers in the young Zionist movement regarding normalization. This shared perspective was ironic on two counts. First, the leaders of the JAIAS were ardently anti-Zionist, ideologically opposed to Jewish nationalist aspirations. The social and political means to Jewish liberation, they believed, had to be found in the countries where Jews had settled, assuming that legal and customary restrictions did not *ipso facto* preclude Jewish integration into community life. Accordingly, the United States represented the best hope of world Jewry. Second, the philanthropists among the German Jews of the United States and Europe were not landed gentry. They were urban financiers, actively promoting Jewish agriculture from the comfort of New York, Philadelphia, Paris, and Berlin, where they had made fortunes in commerce and finance.

On the Zionist side, figures such as Aaron Gordon, who, in middle age, had begun a new life in 1904 on the land in Palestine, argued that the Diaspora had deformed Jewish communities by inhibiting farming and the natural dignity of agricultural labor. As a Zionist theorist, Gordon believed that farming and manual labor in Palestine would revitalize the Jewish people by ending the centuries-old alienation between Jews and nature. In forging a national culture, Gordon claimed, Jews must value manual labor, not merely as a means of survival or as an instrumental activity in itself, but as a fundamental element in the reconstitution of the nation and the individual Jew. Normality depended on it, for "a normal people is like a living organism which performs its various functions naturally, and labor is one of its basic and organic functions." Jewish nationhood also required that Jews perform "all the work, from the least strenuous, cleanest, and most sophisticated, to the dirtiest and most difficult."[28] In this way, they would break free from the unnatural limitations of commerce and trade to which life in Europe had consigned them.

Agricultural movements had sprung up among eastern European Jews quite independent of the encouragement of their coreligionists in Germany and the United States. The *Am Olam* (Eternal People) movement emerged in eastern Europe in the 1870s. Influenced by socialism and the secular thinking of the *Haskalah*, or Jewish Enlightenment, the idealistic young people of *Am Olam* envisioned, consonant with Gordon's romantic view, a kind of self-confident, muscular Judaism, dignifying manual labor and agriculture as these would be freely practiced in the New World. Fired by passion and idealism, some arrived in the United States only to face disappointment at the failure of their agricultural colonies.[29]

Although the political goals of Zionism would certainly be rendered nugatory without occupational shifts in the Jewish communities Gordon envisioned, the most fundamental transformations had to occur in the very outlook and self-conception of the Jews themselves. Shlomo Avineri has aptly summed up Gordon's attitude: "Zionism . . . was not merely or even primarily a political revolution but a socioeconomic and psychological revolution as well, without which the political revolution would remain hollow and meaningless."[30] A remarkable consequence of the normalization of labor in the Zionist plan for Palestine was that many European Jews would propel themselves downward in the conventional economic hierarchy.

Likewise, the German Jewish ideal of economic life in the Diaspora envisioned the participation of Jews in agriculture and in occupations that had historically excluded them. If not as downwardly mobile as the Zionist strategy, the plan of the Jewish leadership in the United States at the turn of the twentieth century was no less ambitious in trying to transform Jewish social and economic experience. Stereotypes about Jewish middlemen would yield before the burgeoning numbers of Jews breaking out of their historic confines to enter all economic spaces. It is thus with some satisfaction that the IRO summarized the distribution of occupations of their clients in the years between 1902 and 1914:

The most interesting feature . . . is a comparison of the number of beneficiaries engaged in the needle industry (which is commonly believed to be the most prevalent trade in which our people engage) and the number of our beneficiaries in miscellaneous unskilled occupations (in which our people are supposed to engage infrequently); such a comparison will show that there were less people engaged in the needle industries than in unskilled occupations, thus indicating a most healthy condition in the industrial life of our people.[31]

The variability of Jewish labor was appreciated for its historic importance. Immigrants might now effectively enter the mainstream of economic life. They would not simply be Jews working in familiar European pursuits but rather Americans in the making, indistinguishable occupationally from their neighbors. The ghetto would be a bad memory, an image grown faint from the bright light of a normalized life in the United States, where Jewish labor would not be narrowly channeled.

The UHC also expressed satisfaction as early as the mid-1890s when it collected evidence of the diversity of trades and occupations that Jews were entering. In a 1926 retrospective on fifty years of UHC activity, the organization noted the "bitter complaints" of the 1880s and early 1890s that Jewish labor was suited only for peddling and tailoring. But by 1895, the UHC annual report registered more than 150 different kinds of jobs filled by immigrant Jews.[32] That a lack of skills among many Jews was actually acclaimed is a telling index of the debilitating yoke that for centuries had controlled Jewish social and economic participation in eastern Europe. Even if Jews might be working in lowly occupations offering less monetary reward than peddling or other middleman endeavors, they were breaking free from European economic restrictions.

In view of their unique historical position, it is not surprising that Jews alone, among the many immigrant groups in the United States, found cause for celebration because the ranks of the unskilled included so many of their own. However radically opposed their political outlooks, Zionists and German American Jews alike hailed the outward economic mobility of uprooted European Jews. Jewish farming schemes and an abundance of unskilled Jewish labor in the United States thus fit a programmatic change. Jews would cease to inhabit the ghetto, both as a locale and as a state of mind.

The challenge of Jewish farming notwithstanding, some immigrants remained determined to shatter the hardened mold of European Jewish life that had excluded the agricultural option. A few managed to achieve a limited, hard-won success through individual farming rather than colonization. In a charming memoir of growing up in rural North Dakota, Sophie Trupin, the daughter of Jewish immigrants who wrested a difficult living from the Plains, recalls her father's motives in seeking an agricultural life. After Trupin's father arrived in Chicago in 1904, his younger brother, an earlier immigrant making his living as a peddler, tried in vain to persuade the newcomer of the fortunes that awaited them in the city:

> He painted a glowing picture of the goals they could reach working together, but my father was unimpressed. He had not come to this country to be a merchant. He had left his family and his homeland for nobler purposes. Too long had Jews been identified with trading and dealing. Somehow, my father felt it necessary to change that image. To win the respect of the Christian world, Jews must work with their hands—not in shops and factories, but on the land, producing food.[33]

And so the young man joined a very small number of other immigrant Jews willing to endure the arduous life of homesteading.[34]

Despite the process of outward mobility, stereotypic images about Jewish labor persisted well into the twentieth century. John R. Commons, the economist and consultant to the Industrial Commission on Immigration of 1901 and the Commission on Industrial Relations organized in 1912, exemplified the older views of Jewish occupations and economic proclivities: "The Jewish immigrant, particularly, is unfitted for the life of a pioneer. Remarkably individualistic in character, his field of enterprise is society, and not the land."[35] Likewise, Prescott Hall, founder of the Immigration Restriction League, dismissed with shopworn disdain agricultural schemes for Jews because "long residence in the ghettoes [sic] of Europe has unfitted most of the Jews to be independent farmers." Hall also criticized the nonagricultural distribution efforts of the IRO as too meager when measured against the annual Jewish immigration.[36] Jewish organizations had no choice but to persist in their efforts to ameliorate the poverty of the newcomers and to facilitate their adjustment to the United States. In this way, they hoped to counter prejudicial thinking while expanding the possibilities for Jewish economic life.

### Baron de Hirsch Philanthropy and "Assisted Immigration"

Aid for Jewish immigrants received an enormous boost in 1890 when the Jewish financier Baron Maurice de Hirsch established the fund bearing his name. It was prompted most immediately by an increase in Jewish immigration from Russia following an upturn in antisemitic actions. The fund totaled 2.4 million dollars and was to provide for the amelioration of the plight of Jewish immigrants fleeing from persecution. Through its appointed board of American Jews active in philanthropic work, it supported numerous projects, including agricultural instruction, loans to Jewish immigrants engaging in agriculture, assistance to newly arrived immigrants to travel from the port city to a place where they could secure work, and mechanical and technical training, as well as the formation of schools for this instruction. The fund subsidized instruction in the English language and in the duties of citizenship.[37] Its various programs thus promoted immigrant accommodation to the new country. Seeing a defensive and redemptive value in the fund, *The American Israelite* welcomed its establishment. The newcomers would be

> wisely cared for and the citizens of our country will be protected against an increase of the proletarian population in the cities, manufacturing or mining districts; also against an increase of beggars and what is next to it, peddlers and small hucksters; against the increase of Nihilism, Socialism, Communism and such other extravagances to which people just escaping the bonds of slavery are most prone. . . . The redemption of those persecuted, downtrodden and degenerated Hebrews is in agriculture, which in one or two generations will restore the race to its pristine character.[38]

The fund also enhanced UHC distribution efforts, particularly in reuniting immigrants with previously settled kin or friends and in aiding the move of immigrants to more congenial labor markets where their self-support was more probable. Throughout the 1890s, distribution continued to be a primary concern of the UHC "in connection with the burning question of the increased immigration from Russia and its absorption into the industrial market of the country in order to prevent a further increase of the Jewish proletariat in this city and the dangers connected with it."[39] In addition, the UHC used its subvention for industrial training, the purchase of tools for craftsmen, and essential fees for trade union membership. Almsgiving or any temporary relief of the sick or infirm was explicitly precluded as out of keeping with the goals of the Baron de Hirsch Fund.[40]

The best-known American projects of the fund were Jewish settlements in New Jersey, particularly in Woodbine, which incorporated farming, agricultural training, and light industry.[41] Of all of its well-intended agricultural efforts, only Woodbine, in the view of the fund's chair and IRO board member Eugene Benjamin, achieved any degree of success.[42] Because agriculture represented just one of several projects, it was decided that all farming activities could more effectively proceed through a separate organization underwritten by the fund. Toward this end, the JAIAS was founded in early 1900.[43]

The largess of the fund was interpreted by some critics as encouraging and assisting the least desirable immigrants. This view underscored the charges of immigration detractors that the United States had become a dumping ground for Europe's outcasts. These immigrants would likely become the permanent class of paupers so feared by the UHC.

The record number of Jewish immigrants arriving in the year before 30 September 1890 suggested to the UHC that some immigrants believed financial support awaited them. Stories were circulating in Europe that money from the fund would be distributed to the new arrivals regardless of their economic circumstances. The improvident and others unprepared to struggle for their living were thus induced to emigrate by false rumors. The UHC feared they might then resist any effort to find employment.[44]

Such reports, of course, did nothing to discourage the close scrutiny under which American immigration policy fell in the early 1890s. Simon Wolf, chairman of the Union of American Hebrew Congregations, denied that the Jewish immigration was induced or assisted.[45] The issue was growing particularly charged because a flourishing nativism was joined by restive labor alert to the importation of poor immigrants who were willing to work for the lowest wage.

Wolf offered assurances directly to the secretary of the treasury, Charles Foster, whose department then administered immigration. He informed Foster that "no organization exists in the United States that in any way directly or indirectly aids, assists, or encourages introduction into this country of [that] class of people . . . on the contrary, their arrival is deplored." While he urged that Russian Jewish refugees continue to be granted a safe haven in the United States, he also petitioned the government to work for the amelioration of those conditions in Russia that were prompting the Jewish immigration, "which by removing the cause, will prevent the baleful effect that arouses natural apprehensions." Moreover, Wolf pledged to Secretary Foster that he and his colleagues would inform Jewish organizations in Europe that assisted emigration violated American law. Then Wolf asserted that the Russian Jewish immigrants did not fall within the excluded classes.[46]

Although concern about assisted immigration of the poorest people had been voiced throughout the 1880s, the immediate impetus for Wolf's communiqué in defense of the Russian Jewish immigrants and of Jewish immigration itself was the passage of the Immigration Act of 1891. That act refocused attention on restricting immigration to self-supporting new-comers responsible for their own livelihoods at the outset of their disem-barkation. The critical, restrictive phrase of that act, as quoted by Wolf, excluded "any person whose ticket or passage is paid for with the money of another or who is assisted by others to come, unless it is affirmatively and satisfactorily shown on special inquiry that such person does not belong to one of the foregoing classes."[47]

Wolf conceded that although many of the new arrivals were desperately poor and may not have paid for their own steamship tickets, they were nei-ther paupers nor likely to become so. They should therefore have been classified under the exceptions clause as not belonging to the prohibited category of indigent or assisted immigrants. Rather, they were immedi-ately taken in hand by their coreligionists, who helped them gain a liveli-hood and an understanding of the duties of citizenship. He stated, "Hands of help and welcome are outstretched to elevate them to the exalted posi-tion of American citizenship, without demanding any contribution from national or local taxes." Furthermore, Wolf defended the Russian Jewish immigration to the secretary by pointing out that over the previous ten years of Russian Jewish flight the refugees had succeeded in assimilating themselves into American life without ever becoming public burdens. He was sanguine about the ability of American Jewish institutions to continue to bear whatever financial and practical burdens Jewish immigration, even if increased, might create.[48]

Appended to Wolf's letter to Secretary Foster were the plans of the B'nai B'rith, the Jewish Alliance of America, and the Baron de Hirsch Fund for aiding the immigrants to become good, self-supporting citizens.[49] Reflect-ing continuing American Jewish concerns, a central feature of these pro-grams aimed to disperse the immigrants across areas of the country where employment was available.[50] Above all, American Jewry would guarantee that the Jewish immigrants would not require public resources for their support. Shortly before Wolf's pledge to the secretary, the UHC had re-ported that of 1,300 people in the almshouse of New York there was only one Jew, whereas the statistical proportion of Jewish immigrants would have been 200.[51] The UHC, in line with the organizations cooperating in the

Wolf deposition, was in effect arguing that any needs of the Russian Jewish immigrants would be attended to privately by American Jewish institutions.

Considering the mixed sentiments of American Jewish organizations and the English language Jewish press toward immigration throughout the 1880s, Wolf's arguments to Secretary Foster are especially noteworthy. Instead of hesitation, Wolf expressed unabashed support for the immigrants and immigration, consonant with American law. That the tone and content of his communication did not betray any of the ambivalence of the UHC and HEAS reports over the previous decade derives in part from two factors. First, the munificence of the Baron de Hirsch Fund incorporated in New York State at about the time of Wolf's remarks reduced the financial pressure on Jewish organizations devoted to immigrant aid. Second, the record of good citizenship already established by the Russian Jewish immigrants of only a few years before indicated the probable success of future immigrants following their course. The hand of immigration supporters was thereby strengthened.

Secretary Foster's response to Wolf acknowledged the desperation of many Russian Jews in seeking safe haven in the United States and praised "American Hebrews," both for aiding the immigrants to become self-supporting and for actively working to distribute them widely across the country to areas where their labor was needed. Still, the secretary's letter cast a shadow, for he regarded the support of dependent persons as "a tax upon the resources of the country, even though paid from private funds." Likewise, in the secretary's view, danger also lay in the disruption of industrial conditions by the labor competition many impoverished people would create. It was vital, in his view, for American Jews to act patriotically by discouraging European emigration, thus reducing both dependency and the possibility of undue competition for jobs. Foster found the plans for dispersion "most gratifying" and linked, in a *quid pro quo* fashion, the success of immigrant distribution to "the possibility of the Government meeting your views in other respects."[52]

In other words, a liberal interpretation of the exclusionary provisions of the 1891 Immigration Act would turn on the capacity of Jewish organizations to do their part in inhibiting labor problems by ensuring an expeditious and wide distribution of the newcomers. The commitment to distribution by the B'nai B'rith, the Jewish Alliance, and the Baron de Hirsch Fund was especially important in view of Secretary Foster's remarks and the growing labor opposition to immigration in the 1890s, of which the 1891 Immigration Act was symptomatic. Should American Jewry not successfully contend with the increasing urban congestion of Jewish immigrants, then Jewish immigration itself would be imperiled. The Wolf–Foster exchange reinforced the already prominent American Jewish institutional commitment to immigrant dispersion. It also linked the distribution of Jewish newcomers to continued immigration, thus establishing the terms of a major strategy later taken up by the IRO to counter the restrictionists.

Despite the denials of Jewish communal organizations, allegations about assisted immigration persisted. They seemed to keep pace with the rising tide of arrivals. Testifying before the Industrial Commission ten years after his exchange with Secretary Foster, Wolf again declared, "There is no fund available in this country, either out of the funds of the Order of B'nai B'rith or out of the Baron de Hirsch Trust Fund, for paying the transportation hither of any of these refugees or unfortunate immigrants."[53]

Immigration critics vented their charges against the Baron de Hirsch Fund before the same commission. A representative of the American Federation of Labor, for example, complained that the "Hirsh [sic] Immigration Society expects to bring all the pauper Jews to America."[54] Yet the only influence of the fund on immigration lay in the acceptable support of the reunion of immigrant residents in the United States with their families—a point also made before the Industrial Commission.[55] Still, five years later in reporting on the programs of the Baron de Hirsch Fund, Benjamin felt impelled to confront the old charge once again, pointing out that the directors of the fund "assist the immigrant, but we do not assist immigration." He asserted that the fund was not in conflict with national policy and that even the most deserving prospective immigrant would get no aid until arriving in the United States through his or her own means.[56]

Other agents charged with inducing immigration also were identified. Commons asserted that "had it been left to the initiative of the emigrants the flow of immigration to America could scarcely ever have reached one-half its actual dimensions . . . [and] it is scarcely an exaggeration to say that even more important than the initiative of immigrants have been the efforts of . . . ship-owners to bring and attract them."[57] Likewise, the restrictionist economist Henry Fairchild asserted that the new immigration was not a natural movement. Rather it was prompted by various interested parties, including transportation companies. Consequently, immigrants arrive "with misconceptions and delusions, and without any natural fitness for American life; and as a result many of them suffer bitter hardships and add nothing to the life of this country."[58]

Claims about assisted immigration willfully ignored some fundamental features of the process. Like earlier or old immigrants, Italians, Jews, and Slavs left Europe for a combination of reasons closely linked to their economic and sometimes religious standing in Europe. Concomitant perceptions of more promising opportunities in the United States were also instrumental. These factors, different in their details, were not qualitatively distinct from those propelling the earlier groups of Germans, Irish, and Scandinavians. The entire matter of assisted or induced immigration was a canard boosting restrictionist opinion. However much steamship companies advertised in Europe, such appeals could not induce immigration without more fundamental motives already established on firmer grounds.[59]

Questions about European Jewish organizations assisting immigration arose once more before the Immigration Commission, but it concluded that these organizations "do not assist emigrants to the extent of affording them transportation to the United States." Paying particular attention to the ICA, the commission ascertained that it helped the would-be immigrants obtain free passports and aimed to protect them from predatory agents and others eager to defraud them. During the European investigations of the commission, one member interviewed workers in a Bucharest sweatshop. Virtually everyone wanted to emigrate to the United States but could not for financial reasons. When the commissioner suggested that the ICA could offer help, he was told that financial assistance was not available from the organization. The Alliance Israelite Universelle also assured the commission that it too refrained from providing any material assistance to Jews embarking for the United States.[60]

Opposition to the new immigration sprang in part from a profound discontent at the decline of farming in favor of industry. The conception of the old immigration as constituted mostly of hardy northern Europeans bent on domesticating the American wilderness and wresting a living from the land dove-tailed with the values of nativist populism. The new immigrants, in contrast, populated the teeming, heterogeneous, and polyglot cities of industrial America. They worked in factories and mills yet often returned to Europe. Although Jews were not prominent in heavy industry, they definitely were city dwellers. None of the newcomers seemed given to the more natural, rural labors typified by the robust and self-reliant German and Scandinavian farmers of the upper Midwest, whose lives were more in keeping with the rural and communitarian ideology embraced by many immigration opponents. Although the restrictionists steadily gained ground and ultimately won a series of legislative successes closing four decades of immigration, many among them were fighting a losing battle against the changing economic character of the country.

## Jewish Agricultural and
### Industrial Aid Society and Industrial Removal

In 1900, the Baron de Hirsh Fund supported the formation of the JA-IAS, the parent organization of the IRO. In 1922, the JAIAS became known as the Jewish Agricultural Society (JAS). Succeeding the Baron de Hirsch Fund, the JAIAS intensified the efforts of the previous decade to resettle immigrants on farms or in outlying industrial areas.[61] The JAIAS emerged in a climate of doubt, when stereotypic ideas about Jewish disinclinations toward farming were supported by the poor record of Jewish agriculture during the 1880s and 1890s.

The JAIAS acknowledged the severe obstacles facing Jewish farming and colonizing programs. In 1902, William Kahn, the JAIAS manager, estimated that there were 1,000 Jewish farmers in the United States. Accordingly, the JAIAS concluded that relatively few people of the East Side would gravitate to farming and that, instead, it had to attend to a vastly greater number who were willing to change locales without necessarily shifting occupations.[62]

In 1915, Benjamin offered a particularly critical but thoroughly realistic assessment of Jewish farming schemes dating from the early 1880s. Although many were encouraged by the Baron de Hirsch Fund, none was successful, excepting the Woodbine colony. Failed colonies brought hardship to the would-be farmers who invested all of their money in the enterprise. Even Woodbine's success was costly, for it was achieved "by expenditure of a sum of money altogether out of proportion to the number of individuals permanently removed." In Benjamin's view, if the money had been directed to immigrant distribution, it might well have succeeded in relocating ten times the number of Woodbine, estimated at 2,500 people. He had high praise for the IRO, believing its program of distribution to be "eminently practical and thoroughly successful." Regretting that its founding had not occurred ten years earlier, Benjamin claimed, "Many of the evils of overcrowding in our large seaport cities would have been avoided, or at least greatly diminished, and more important still, we would have materially helped and benefited practically every man, woman and child removed by us."[63]

The JAIAS continued to assist Jewish farming in spite of its dismal record. Instead of supporting agricultural colonization, the newly named JAS opted in the early 1920s for assistance to individuals. The JAS provided its clients with loans on a strict business basis, regarding farming as an individual enterprise rather than as a collectivist, ideological experiment.[64]

In also turning to nonagricultural immigrant distribution schemes, the JAIAS embarked on an imaginative plan to induce urban contractors and manufacturers to relocate their businesses and industries to more sparsely populated areas. Immigrant labor, it was hoped, would follow. This strategy represented true "industrial removal," referring specifically to the physical transfer of light industry and manufacturing outside of New York. A short time later, the Industrial Removal Office (IRO) drew its name from this plan, although it concentrated on the "removal" of people rather than industrial enterprises.

The JAIAS sometimes provided a manufacturer assistance in moving his factory or in constructing additional buildings. Towns were also persuaded to offer attractive rental terms to concerns interested in relocating. For their own part, the immigrants might find inducements to move if a factory where they were already employed was changing locale. In addition, the immigrants could find cheaper rents in areas beyond New York, and the JAIAS would advance money to aid them in getting reestablished in a new home, where the possibility of owning land was also much greater than in the city.[65] However, like the agricultural schemes, industrial removal fell far short of expectations as the JAIAS managers faced consistent, expensive, and sometimes spectacular failure.[66] The JAIAS rather quickly after its founding recognized the impracticality of removing entire industries to rural or suburban areas or in sending groups of immigrants to a single industrial concern. It continued to assist Jewish migration from New York but concentrated its resources on the distribution of individuals and their families.[67]

### Other Distribution Plans: The United Hebrew Charities and the Hebrew Sheltering and Immigrant Aid Society

Without encouraging industrial removal, the UHC also experimented with industrial colonies by assisting immigrant resettlement in areas around

New York where industry and manufacturing were already established. In its 1887 report, the UHC Committee on Employment noted its cooperation with manufacturers in several locations in New York, New Jersey, and Connecticut who offered to provide housing for immigrant workers and their families. The UHC also arranged training in machine sewing and cigar making. This attempt to create industrial colonies collapsed quickly and dramatically when only 19 of 365 workmen remained on the job. The other 346, after only a brief period of work, returned to New York "to lead in the Jewish quarter a life of poverty and distress." The UHC attributed the failure to the "physical incapacity" of the Jewish immigrants and a lack of "diligence and perseverance."[68] Subsequent efforts along these lines yielded only modest success, including the employment of immigrants by garment manufacturers in areas not far removed from New York.[69] The numbers of workers resettled were not significant in proportion to the scope of the problem that Jewish philanthropies had defined. The 1926 UHC retrospective on its distribution activities frankly acknowledged a record of ineffectiveness.[70]

Concurrent distribution efforts were under way by the Hebrew Sheltering and Immigrant Aid Society (HIAS). Like the UHC, HIAS counted distribution among its many activities on behalf of arriving immigrants. HIAS, too, achieved only negligible results in relieving immigrant congestion in New York. In 1912, for example, HIAS aided the resettlement of 844 persons, and in 1913, 1,979 persons.[71] For the same two years, the IRO managed to resettle 6,025 and 6,469 persons, respectively.[72] HIAS's marginal achievement in immigrant resettlement has been attributed to the psychology of the Jewish newcomer, unwilling to relinquish the cultural security of New York or the bonds of kinship and friendship binding them to other settlers in the city.[73]

## The Rumanian Committee and the Industrial Removal Office

The formation of the IRO in 1901 represented the culmination of numerous efforts since the 1880s to confront unemployment, urban crowding, and ghetto-like conditions. Both earlier and contemporaneous programs of distribution by the UHC, the HEAS, the Jewish Alliance, the B'nai B'rith, HIAS, and the various agricultural colonies of the Baron de Hirsch Fund were of limited effectiveness. None undertook resettlement as its exclusive task or accomplished a significant shift of the Jewish immigrant population away from New York. The old problem of congestion had simply worsened by the time the IRO was founded.

Between May and July of 1900, persistent Rumanian antisemitism had intensified, prompting the flight of approximately 20,000 Jews out of the country. In 1900, more than 6,000 Rumanian Jews arrived in the United States. From 1901 to 1904, 28,000 more immigrants arrived. In the five years before 1900, fewer than 4,000 Jews had emigrated to the United States from Rumania.[74] The Dreyfus Affair in France had also fueled antisemitic feeling in Rumania. Rumanian Jews lost previous civil guarantees in a continuing abrogation of their rights. Citizenship for Jews became virtually impossible. Jewish children were barred from public schools, and Jewish institutions were harassed and threatened by official financial exactions. Just as the desperate Jewish exodus of twenty years before had led to the sudden formation of the Russian Committee, the arrival of many Rumanian Jewish refugees in New York necessitated the formation of an emergency committee, which was overseen by the JAIAS.

The new committee was headed by Leo Levi, president of the B'nai B'rith. The Rumanian Committee employed David Bressler, a twenty-two-year-old attorney; as a child, he had emigrated with his parents from Germany to the United States. Bressler and his staff determined which immigrants were best suited for life in the interior and arranged the terms of their resettlement with local committees.

The crisis atmosphere occasioned by the sudden arrival of refugees inevitably resulted in errors of judgment, especially regarding the suitability of particular immigrants for the communities to which they were sent. The latter found their resources strained by the precipitous influx of new immigrants ill-equipped to care for themselves. Difficulties in placing the Rumanians were compounded by some immigrants' claims that they had job skills they in fact did not possess. The Rumanian Committee worked hastily under unusual pressure and was sharply criticized by various receiving communities. According to the JAIAS, "A little forbearance and consideration on the part of our coreligionists, throughout the country, would have been welcome; but apparently every mistake made by the superintendent was harshly criticized, and led to the cancellation of further orders."[75] It was an inauspicious start.

The Rumanian Committee rapidly evolved into the IRO when it was determined that success in the resettlement of Rumanian Jews and other

Jewish immigrants necessitated a single, well-coordinated program of distribution. The IRO was formally created in February 1901 at a meeting of the directors of the nascent JAIAS, headed by Sulzberger. Its formation came in the wake of the sharply increasing number of immigrant Jews in the United States and the ineffectiveness of other distribution programs. In the 1880s, 193,000 Jewish immigrants had arrived, whereas the figure doubled during the next decade. At the end of the first decade of the twentieth century, the number had grown to approximately 976,000.[76] An adequate program of Jewish immigrant distribution would require a more intensive, large-scale, and systematic effort than any previously undertaken.

## American Jewish Support for Immigration and Distribution

Levi's remarks to the B'nai B'rith in 1901 conveyed a sense of desperation in view of the plight of the refugees from Rumania, the modest achievements of all previous distribution efforts, and the steady increase in the immigrant Jewish population of New York. Moreover, as immigrant numbers rose, the idea of distribution as a defensive strategy for the American Jewish community grew even more salient. Levi explained to his brethen that the overriding concern of the order was to "limit, retard and regulate the immigration to the United States" and "to widely distribute those who came, so as to prevent the augmentation of existing Ghettos or the formation of new ones." With some hyperbole, even in view of the severity of the social conditions prevailing on the Lower East Side, Levi described the objectives of the Rumanian Committee and its successor as the prevention of "our indigent coreligionists from becoming or remaining Ghetto dwellers [because] every family raised in that home of horrors faces the grave peril of shame for its daughters and crime for its sons."[77] Portraying the moral dimension of distribution became a leitmotif of the IRO's many efforts to enlist the cooperation of American Jews.

Of course, condemnation of ghetto conditions extended well beyond the Jewish critics of congestion. In 1901, the Industrial Commission also noted that for both Italians and "Hebrews," "tenement-house life tends to their physical and moral deterioration."[78] In addition, the prevailing critique of the ghetto dove-tailed with alarms about the metropolis as a locus of political corruption, often dependent on the support of unsophisticated newcomers. The B'nai B'rith Committee on Removal Work described municipal affairs in American cities as "weak spots in our Republic" and noted lowering standards of citizenship. The committee then asked, "What will posterity think of us if these unfortunate refugees are permitted to be transplanted in solid phalanxes, without preparation or experience, to the most debasing environments of city life, where vice and ignorance concentrate their allied forces upon the weaknesses of humanity?"[79] Levi's statement said nothing about plans or strategies for the limitation or regulation of immigration, beyond identifying it as one of the two "controlling features" of B'nai B'rith policy.[80]

Immigration regulation had been an issue of overriding importance to American Jews since the very beginning of the eastern European exodus. These concerns were also voiced, although with diminished vigor, at the time of the IRO's founding. Levi's remarks endorsing immigration regulation appear in a communiqué that goes on to say: "They [American Jews] must be taught that they by their conduct will decide whether the doors of this country shall remain open to their persecuted brethren in Roumania [sic] and elsewhere, or be closed against them entirely."[81] His statement about immigration regulation consists of a single sentence, and the remainder of his commentary addresses immigrant distribution. Although the Jewish leadership had become less ambivalent regarding immigration, scrupulous obedience to the law, including the prohibition of assisted immigration, was essential. Levi's statement must thus be seen in this light. It would have been very unwise for people highly attuned to political opinion to convey the impression that Jews in the United States favored an immigration policy devoid of any control.[82]

American Jewry was, of course, well aware of the grievous conditions under which eastern European Jews were struggling. The particularly draconian measures in Rumania were only the latest in a series of outrages driving Jewish immigration over the previous twenty years. These conditions were widely known in official circles and reported in the press. Congressmen might well have expected Jewish support for unlimited immigration at such times. Jewish spokesmen, while favoring very liberal policies, never endorsed indiscriminate immigration.

Wolf's testimony to the Industrial Commission shortly before the founding of the IRO must also be seen in this context. Alluding to the HEAS, Wolf noted that only in 1882 did Jews in the United States undertake "to care for, to distribute, and to assimilate" the immigrants. However, fearing the effects of such a large number of immigrants on their coreligionists, the Jewish leadership sent representatives abroad to persuade European Jewish leaders to divert immigration away from the United States or to prevent the dumping of large numbers of people. Wolf also informed the commission that notices were placed in the European Jewish press warning "against indiscriminate emigration to America." Yet Wolf's deposition reflected a broadening spectrum of Jewish opinion supporting liberal immigration with few stated restrictions. Although he subscribed to the laws preventing the landing of criminals, paupers, and others, Wolf questioned the concerns motivating such restrictions:

> [W]e do know one fact, and it can not be too strongly emphasized, and that is that the vast majority of the immigrants of all nationalities who have in the last 50 or 60 years come to this country, and who are now the bone and sinew of American citizenship, came in practically the same condition of financial poverty as that in which the majority of the immigrants come now, a poverty which is often made the pretext for projects of exclusion.[83]

As long as conditions in Russia remained oppressive, he contended without qualification, the United States must offer asylum.[84]

Levi's case for distribution before the Second Conference of Jewish Charities in 1902 contained no mention of immigration restriction or regulation. Regulation was losing its cogency for many Jews in the increasingly restrictionist and nativist climate of the early twentieth century and in the wake of the Rumanian Jewish flight. Moreover, Levi was convinced that the immigration of eastern European Jews to the United States was virtually unstoppable, so intense were the forces motivating it.[85] While eschewing any design to encourage immigration, Levi and others not only pressed the cause of Jewish dispersion within the United States but also opposed any effort to staunch the tide of people fleeing Europe on their own account.[86]

The immigration from eastern Europe represented for Levi an epochal event, every bit as momentous as other massive Jewish population movements, including the Spanish Expulsion. Whereas Jewish communities regularly condemned the travail of Jews at other times and in other places, the same people expressed only "loathing and disgust" at the poverty and suffering close to home.[87] One of Levi's primary objectives was to expose the danger of such attitudes to stir interest in the new exodus. Then it might be possible to secure the active cooperation of American Jews on whom the success of distribution would turn. In a 1903 address, Levi considered the sharply critical attitudes of some Jews toward the immigrants and their reluctance to assist them. He said simply that were it "necessary to choose between the welfare of the one million Jews in this country and the millions who must ultimately come here, justice would turn to the greater number."[88]

Distribution was no simple matter. Beyond the problem of gaining the cooperation of sponsoring communities, the IRO had to contend with the fact that many immigrants would not consider leaving New York. As Levi pointed out, the Lower East Side provided cultural security. Everything encountered by the immigrants on the East Side—signs, goods for sale, synagogues, cafes, theaters—was familiar, a part of their European idiom, and they clung to it. An entire way of life in many respects fully continuous with Old World experience served to insulate them from the cultural shocks and dislocations of the New World.

> For them to come to America means for them to come to New York. They have an idea that what lies beyond the limit of New York is a wilderness; that once they get away from the Ghetto they lose the friends they were accustomed to; that if sickness, trouble, or death comes they have no one to turn to. If they are religiously inclined . . . they have no place in which they can worship in harmony outside the Ghetto. And so they cling there tenaciously, even to the brink of starvation rather than go out into a wilderness or to give up that which is so precious to them.[89]

Arguing that the "limit has been reached," Levi described conditions on the East Side, exemplified by a young girl of thirteen selling newspapers on Canal Street at eleven o'clock at night in order to contribute a few pennies to the support of her family. Reflecting on the "inevitable fate" awaiting that child, Levi exhorted his audience to know "that the care of that child's purity is no more my business because I live in the upper portion of Manhattan Island than it is the care of a Jew who lives in Oregon."[90]

The next year, in an address delivered before the Jewish Chautauqua, Bressler pressed the same point, saying of the immigrants, "[T]hese people do not come to New York; they come to America."[91] With some seventy percent of the Jewish immigrants remaining in New York, down somewhat from even higher percentages staying in the city in the 1880s and 1890s, Bressler and his colleagues faced a formidable challenge. They had to convince the immigrants of the need to disperse while persuading Jews of the interior to help the process.

In defining the problems of the Lower East Side as a challenge to the entire Jewish community of the United States, Levi also spoke in familiar, patronizing tones, although rather more benignly than earlier utterances by German American Jewish leaders or the English language Jewish press:

> It is not to be left to those people to choose where they shall live. They are unable to form a fair judgment. They are no more qualified to form a fair judgment as to where they shall locate when they land as foreigners from Europe than your children or my children to determine what is best for them. They must be guided, led until they are strong enough educationally to move for themselves. They must be educated to a better understanding of the conditions that prevail in the interior of this country, of opportunities offered everywhere for men able to work.[92]

Kahn, at the same conference, also phrased the job at hand in paternalistic terms. The immigrants had a "moral right" to be "uplifted" by those who had enjoyed the privilege of American life, and he asserted that

> . . . they come from a stock that cannot be suppressed by temporary disadvantages, and that to remove these temporary disadvantages and to help these people to cast off their long beards, their soiled clothes, and outlandish habits, and even their moral faults and weaknesses caused by long years of oppression and suffering, is a work which will result in producing self-supporting, industrious and progressive citizens, who will be a benefit to the communities in which they settle, and will reflect credit on the philanthropic gentlemen who have assisted them, in the eyes of both Jews and Gentiles.[93]

Although condescending, Kahn, Levi, and others also emphasized the success that some eastern European Jews were beginning to enjoy. Levi, borrowing Wolf's "bone and sinew" metaphor of the previous year, argued that eastern European Jews not only had become a large, productive part of American society, but also had exposed the unfounded anxieties of a few years before:

> They have been coming here for 20 odd years. Their coming has been looked upon with fear and trembling, but they have come nevertheless. Those who

predicted untold disasters 20 years ago because of the influx of the Russian Jews have been refuted by the developments of the last two decades, because the refugees of 20 years ago are the artisans and manufacturers and the merchants and the bone and sinew of the Jewish part of this country today.[94]

Levi publicized the removal work at the 1902 Charities Conference while virtually commanding the assistance of the Jewish community workers in attendance. In setting forth the broad responsibilities of American Jews, he and others sought a further development of philanthropic programs that would broadly encompass an emergent American Jewish community. By the turn of the twentieth century, a process that would render obsolete the purely localized, independent, and self-interested Jewish settlements and welfare organizations was unfolding. By 1903, the IRO had established agencies in eight cities, coordinated by the main office in New York. Bressler believed that the formation of these agencies sprang directly from the presentations at the 1902 conference on behalf of the IRO.[95]

For the IRO, the solution to the moral and economic problem of the immigrant thus lay in active and receptive interior communities facilitating the social and economic absorption of the immigrants. Nothing could prove more disastrous to the entire design than a haphazard, poorly conceived unloading of immigrants into American cities and towns. Doing so would undermine all efforts to secure the sustained cooperation that an orderly, coordinated plan of resettlement necessitated. The methodical reception and integration of immigrants in communities across the United States required that the IRO convince its cooperators that their efforts were essential yet ran no risk of unusual cost or sacrifice.

### Industrial Removal Office and Jewish Colonization Association Conflicts over Immigration and Distribution

The IRO consistently gauged the political climate to avoid strategies that might further burden the cause of liberal immigration. It thus contended with European Jewish organizations promoting immigration to the United States. An ill-conceived immigration to the interior, abetted by European agencies, could only play into the hands of the immigration restrictionists eager to use assisted immigration as leverage in seeking tighter statutes. A preliminary plan set forth in 1903 by the ICA to encourage the emigration of Jews directly from Europe to the interior encountered the strongest objections from the IRO: "No movement that has for its aim or its result the stimulation of immigration to the U.S. can have encouragement from us. The enormous natural growth of immigration is all that can possibly be cared for . . . . To receive these and to overcome the growing objection to increased immigration on the part of lawmakers and publicists will exhaust our every effort."[96] Fearing "disastrous results" and "chaos" should the ICA direct immigration from Europe to the American interior, the IRO referred to its own singular mission with some justification: "Only New York City has an organization capable of dealing with the question and of giving to the new arrival such assistance and advice as he requires."[97] The ICA proposal "would be fatal to our work and could only result in injury to the cause we all have at heart."[98] Three years later, the Rumanian branch of the ICA promoted subsidized immigration through an advertisement that, in the critical view of Morris Loeb of the JAIAS, was in "direct contravention of the present immigration law." The ICA effort was dangerous and without reason, for "political and economic conditions . . . should make any artificial stimulus superfluous."[99]

The IRO's adamant response in early 1904 to the initial ICA proposal was undoubtedly conditioned by its illegality as well as by prior problems of distribution. The HEAS had encountered difficulty two decades before, and the IRO program itself began inauspiciously. In the former instance, the poorly organized resettlement efforts of the early 1880s met local resistance. Likewise, various complainants reproached the IRO early on at the precipitous arrival of jobless newcomers, who were said to strain economic resources and threaten the social standing of Jewish communities utterly unprepared to receive them. The activities of the Rumanian Committee had also resulted in a number of problems attributable to a fledgling organization quickly responding to an emergency. Some communities were resistant to collaborating with the successor organization, the IRO, and it soon became apparent that the IRO would face the continuing imperative of prodding its network of agencies and committees to cooperate.[100]

Even under the best of organizational circumstances, when IRO agencies existed in cities with large Jewish populations, problems developed. Thus, the IRO informed the ICA that despite the expenditure of a large sum of money—$4,000—to resettle about 400 people in Milwaukee, the agency there requested that the IRO discontinue sending immigrants owing to its inability to assist those already sent. A similar problem also developed in Cincinnati, another early agency city.[101] Accordingly, the ICA plan, without provision for gauging the capacity of interior communities to absorb immigrants in various occupational categories, was strongly resisted. As such, the plan would discourage interior communities from continuing their vital cooperation with the IRO, thus undermining the very foundation of immigrant distribution based on rational principles.

Relatedly, the IRO exercised control over ICA efforts to assist would-be immigrants in joining their relatives already in the American interior. In the early years, the reunification of families focused on Rumanian Jews in the United States who were seeking to bring their relatives from the Old Country. Such reunions were to be predicated on the ability of those already settled to lend assistance to their kin.

A member of the local IRO committee would ascertain this information, specifically whether the person could contribute toward the transportation of his relatives and share his living quarters with them. On the recommendation of the local IRO, the main office proposed to the ICA that it arrange the transportation. Rabbi Feuerlicht of the Indianapolis IRO committee, for example, commended a Mr. Kuppermann as "an industrious young man" seeking to bring his mother and two siblings from Bucharest yet without sufficient funds to provide for their transportation without some assistance.[102] In response, the IRO informed the sponsoring immigrant, through Rabbi Feuerlicht, about the necessary steps to follow for securing help. The IRO could not affect immigration independently undertaken. However, to protect interior communities from newcomers who might be dependent on charity, it advised the ICA about abetting family reunification.

When IRO control over ICA-sponsored family reunification was abrogated, the IRO vigorously complained. For example, in early 1903, the ICA directed Abraham Herskowitz to an interior city without receiving prior approval from the IRO. The latter knew nothing of the circumstances of Herskowitz's relatives in the United States, for no IRO correspondent had investigated the family, particularly regarding its ability and willingness to assist him. Instead, the ICA proceeded on the recommendation of a rabbi. The IRO's response to this episode is especially revealing of its stratified conception of American Jewish communities and the locus of influence within them:

In the present instance you accepted the recommendation of Rev. S. Lifsitz, of whom we have never heard, and who in all likelihood is an obscure Rabbi of a very obscure little synagogue. The fact that this recommendation was written in Yiddish appears to us to have been ample proof of his lack of standing in the community. However, that may be, whether he was a prominent Rabbi or an obscure Rabbi, this family should not have been forwarded without the express approval of our office.[103]

This intramural candor regarding status and authority within Jewish communities indicates in unusually clear terms the German Jewish character of the IRO, both in its upper echelons and in various local agencies and committees. Although eastern European immigrants often held local positions, their participation did not diminish the elitist distinctions implicit in the IRO. "Standing in the community" unambiguously referred to respect and recognition mutually granted among German American Jews.

### Converging Interests and the Moral Crusade

By 1901, Jewish leaders were coming to recognize a shared future with the immigrants. At the Jewish charities conference in 1904, Levi gave one of the clearest, most forthright statements about the new identity of interests:

No amount of labor, or sacrifice, must be too great, for in their welfare in their happiness lies our welfare and our happiness. He who for a moment believes that his or her future as an American citizen is assured by virtue of his wealth or his social condition, and ignores this great responsibility, will be woefully and sadly awakened by finding the Jewish question injected into the turmoil of American politics . . . . something that we must under no circumstances permit, for its admission would be not only fatal to those who are unfortunate, but equally disastrous to those whose lives have been cast in more pleasant places.[104]

Of course, settled Jews and immigrants continued to differ from each other in many respects. Between them lay a great divide of culture, class, religious practice, and even politics.

Poverty and alien culture had rendered the immigrants vulnerable from the outset of the immigration era, and an equivocal attitude on the part of German American Jews toward the burgeoning immigrant population did little to improve their plight. Only a few years before Levi's admonitions, many Jews in the United States had made enormous efforts to distance themselves from their eastern European coreligionists and would have been loathe to cast their lot with them. Levi's pronouncement was thus especially significant, for a very prominent leader unequivocally asserted that established German American Jewish citizens and Russian Jewish immigrants shared a common destiny. He pleaded for a new consciousness because the Jews of the United States could no longer regard their wealth and status as guarantors of security and privilege. They, too, would be buffeted by the immigration issue.

Doubtless many established Jews individually continued to harbor the same old feelings of aversion toward the eastern Europeans, but the organizational response to the immigrants had certainly shifted course. This change came in part from perceived threats that Levi left unspecified, except by his reference to a much feared "Jewish question" in American politics. The source of apprehension lay in the growing specter of nativism. Not only did the Jewish leadership feel a distinctive moral obligation to assist their coreligionists, but they also believed that antisemitism, parading under a banner of nativism, made no distinction between Jews of German or Russian origin. The prospect of a "Jewish question" intruding itself into American political discourse emboldened the most perceptive and politically adroit of Jewish leaders to work assiduously to negate the dreadful possibility.

The IRO described a multifaceted crisis. Although the mass immigration of Jews and their congestion on New York's Lower East Side certainly had profound social and economic implications, much of the ideology and rationale of the IRO was also moral. Sulzberger described immigrant distribution as a "vast religious and social movement."[105] The rhetoric intoned "salvation" and the arrest of the moral as well as the social deterioration pervading the East Side. Immigrants were to be uplifted—economically, socially, and morally—thereby ending the malaise and frustration of daily struggle in the city. In 1912, the IRO described its clients: "Thwarted by the lack of opportunities in the metropolis and harassed by problems of unemployment, they seek an outlet for their energies, and a refuge which shall mean their eventual rehabilitation and the realizing of their potentialities for efficiency, for normal living and for advancement."[106] Lack of action on the immigrant problem or a failure of distribution could only hasten moral and social decline.

This apprehension stimulated a kind of apocalyptic forecast of the sort associated with social movements. The menace would only grow more threatening if the Jews of the United States did not act collectively and decisively to reverse the trend. They were called on to join the task of moral recovery, uplifting immigrants ground down by poverty, despair, and the corrosive effects of tenement life. The discourse of peril also aimed to mobilize German American Jews in defense of their own interests, now defined as inseparable from those of the immigrants.

Immigrant distribution was also the constructive alternative to restriction. It promised benefits not only for the immigrants and their sponsors, but also for the United States: "Removal is not merely a benevolent effort, but a sociological movement of value, not only to the beneficiary but to the country at large, because it is circulating labor to those parts of the country where it is most needed."[107] The liberating effects of economic self-sufficiency on the immigrants would in turn contribute to the standing and respect of Jews throughout the United States. At the same time, economic independence would help transform the immigrants, degraded and humiliated by the antisemitism and oppression of the Old World, into model, self-respecting citizens. An American Jewish failure of will to address these issues would imperil their own position while compounding the multiple problems of immigrant life in the big city ghetto. As for continued immigration, the collapse of rational dispersion could only encourage even more determined efforts to curtail it.

### Distribution through Galveston

Inspired by the accomplishments of the IRO and sharing its commitment to immigrant distribution, financier Jacob Schiff formulated an ancillary distribution plan. He reasoned that the goal of Jewish immigrant distribution could be facilitated if disembarkation from Europe did not occur on the East Coast. Accordingly, the Galveston Movement, founded in 1907 and operated until 1914, encouraged the immigrants to book passage from Europe to the Galveston, Texas port.[108] Then, the Jewish Immigrants' Information Bureau, also referred to as the Galveston Bureau, would direct the newcomers to towns and cities west of the Mississippi River. Along the same lines established by the IRO, the Galveston Bureau organized agencies throughout the American West in cooperation with B'nai B'rith Lodges to facilitate immigrant distribution. The bureau existed under the auspices of a committee headquartered in New York and chaired by Schiff. Morris Waldman, assistant manager of the IRO, served as the first manager of the Galveston Bureau. Bressler became the "honorary secretary."[109]

Bressler summed up the relationship of the IRO to the Galveston Bureau, beginning with the service of Waldman and extending to that of two successive managers: "His [Waldman's] administration, founded in the experience and policy of the Industrial Removal Office, gave a direction to the Bureau which, for all practical purposes, was maintained in the succeeding seven years. He worked hand in hand with the general manager of the Industrial Removal Office . . . as did his successors at Galveston."[110] Bressler characterized the Galveston work as "essentially an experiment in human dynamics, a shifting of environments to release the industrial and spiritual potencies of oppressed men and women."[111]

In Europe, the Jewish Territorial Organization (ITO) headed by Israel Zangwill lent support to the Galveston Bureau.[112] The ICA, the mainstay of the IRO, remained uninvolved, despite various efforts to enlist its help. In Rumania and Russia, the ITO advertised the benefits of booking passage to Galveston rather than to the eastern ports. The ITO offered no financial assistance to immigrants so that it would remain within the purview of American legal restrictions.

The experiment in Galveston lasted only seven years and achieved meager results. Ten thousand immigrants disembarked at the Texas port and fanned out across the West, where they attracted an unknown number of friends and relatives to their new locales. Bressler praised the results: "The Bureau succumbed to obstacles which could not be overcome. But it is in no sense a failure; 10,000 people will have arrived at Galveston by the closing date. The way is pointed; the route is open. The thousands have been rehabilitated; their physical and moral welfare has been conserved. The human contribution cannot be overestimated."[113]

Schiff, a few months before the bureau's termination, assessed some of the major problems that led the governing committee to dissolve it. Immigrants booking passage to Galveston had a single choice—the North German Lloyd ships departing from Bremen. With no alternative, the immigrant was "more or less at the mercy of this single steamship company."[114] The passage to Galveston required twenty-three days—a considerable sacrifice for immigrants, most of whom were ticketed in steerage. Many lodged justified complaints about the voyage, which exceeded by more than two weeks the journey to New York. These inconveniences strongly militated against recruitment efforts in Europe. At the beginning of the Galveston plan, Bressler and Schiff were, of course, well aware of the greater number of days that the passage required. They hoped to persuade the transportation lines to improve the voyage with faster service, but were unsuccessful.[115]

The probability of deportation represented the greatest limitation on the ability of the Galveston Bureau to attract a much higher volume of Jewish immigration. The rate of deportations at Galveston was 5 percent, compared with an average of 1.2 percent at other American ports.[116] This greater likelihood of deportation certainly discouraged many immigrants, who might otherwise have been willing to endure the hardships of the longer voyage.[117] Given these liabilities and the cultural appeal of New York, the Galveston Movement could attract only a negligible proportion of the European Jewish immigration.

## Conclusion

The IRO, the Galveston Movement, and earlier Jewish immigrant distribution plans sprang from the mixed motives of anxious German American Jews. They were morally bound by a sense of responsibility toward their eastern European coreligionists while profoundly concerned about their own fate in the midst of the controversies over immigration. Closely attuned to American political and social currents, the organizers and operatives of Jewish distribution embraced the ideal of rapid immigrant accommodation to American life. Dignified self-supporting labor in the American interior would point the way to that accommodation, untainted by the retrograde practices flourishing in the big city ghettos. The supporters of distribution, by helping to solve the social, economic, and moral problem of Jewish immigration, would themselves remain untainted. Thus liberated from the last vestiges of European oppression, the immigrants could then become exemplary citizens contributing productively to their adopted country. Their own salvation, in the IRO design, would also be the salvation of their patrons.

# — 2 —

## Confronting Immigration Restriction

In 1903, early in his tenure as general manager of the IRO, David Bressler asserted that the passage of increasingly stringent immigration laws was provoked in part by "congestion and its resultant economic and social evils." Consequently, any measures to reduce congestion would also weaken the position of immigration restrictionists, for "[without] so-called Ghettos and Jewish East Sides, there would be no logical reason to oppose or restrict the immigration of Jews into this country."[1] In the same vein, *The American Jewish Yearbook* of 1906 stated simply: "The work of distribution of the immigrants is still the greatest problem that besets American Jewry.... It is generally recognized, that if a feasible plan were worked out, by which the congestion of the Jewish quarters in the large cities would be reduced, there need be no fear of restriction of immigration."[2] Indeed, for the American Jewish leadership at the turn of the twentieth century, immigrant distribution dominated discussions of how best to cope with the continuing tide of arrivals in the eastern ports. With little equivocation or dissent, American Jews were committed to a continuation of liberal immigration so that their eastern European coreligionists might find safe haven in the United States. Dispersion represented for them not only the key to the economic and social adjustment of the newcomer but also the pivot on which immigration policy would turn. The stakes could not have been higher. If the United States were to remain a refuge for the oppressed, immigration activists would have to demonstrate that the recent immigrants were conforming to the highest standards of Americanization, achievable, in their view, only if urban immigrant concentrations were diffused into other areas of the country.

Confident and optimistic about the capacity of the IRO to bring about positive changes in Jewish immigrant life, Bressler in 1903 overestimated the force of "logical reason" in diminishing the clamor for immigration restriction. Of course, Bressler's confidence in the power of reason to allay national anxieties was not unique. The spokesmen for other American Jewish organizations shared this sentiment. It was incumbent on Jews to diminish the ghetto problem on which the critics of immigration had focused. The pressures for restricting immigration would then naturally abate as the major prop supporting restrictionism gave way. Jews, from this perspective, thus bore some responsibility for the criticisms leveled against them, and the IRO determined to confront the criticism head on and defuse it. American Jews had to chart an activist course, solving their own immigration quandary—the high ethnic density of the city and its attendant problems—by showing critics that an orderly thinning out of immigrant settlements was possible. Failure would certainly bring restrictionist legislation. It was all very logical, but much restrictionist assertion was impervious to rational argument.

The restive power of anti-immigrant feeling, especially pernicious when cloaked in the mantle of science or learned authority, outweighed reasoned discourse in shaping much popular and official thinking. Although sanguine about the mission of the IRO, Bressler and his colleagues were realists, fully understanding the increasing opposition to immigration and, in some quarters, distribution itself. Thus, in its annual report for 1911, the IRO lamented the attacks on the latter:

> It is generally conceded that so far as the problem of immigration is a problem at all, it is in the matter of distribution. This is practically admitted by the immigration restrictionists who do all in their power to discredit the value of the work done in this direction, and the Commissioner General of Immigration in his last annual report opposes distribution on the ground, among others, that every immigrant sent into the interior makes room for others.[3]

Because restrictionists believed that the wrong kinds of immigrants were arriving, programs of distribution could treat only symptoms, not the underlying malady.

The IRO had little choice but to continue its program, showing how organized resettlement could immediately begin to effect the Americanization of the immigrants. The practical value of a rational dispersion would thus be demonstrated. Strong opposition notwithstanding, the IRO remained confident that its modest but steady successes could influence national policy directly. Although valuing practical work over arguments in the fight against restriction, Bressler and his colleagues were not content simply to publicize the record of successfully resettled immigrants. While hoping that such demonstrable achievements would blunt restrictionist criticism, they also actively combated restrictionist arguments with reasoned rebuttal. They repeatedly stressed the value of immigration and the economically beneficial consequences of reducing the density of immigrant enclaves.

The publication of reports of three government commissions critical of immigration—the Industrial Commission on Immigration (1901), the Immigration Commission (1911), and the Commission on Industrial Relations (1916)—reflected the growing strength of restrictionist sentiment. Still, congressional action to curtail immigration was ineffective in the immediate wake of each report. The outbreak of World War I, however, had practically the same result. This unexpected *de facto* victory for the opponents of immigration led economist and staunch restrictionist Henry P. Fairchild to gloat, "The war did to immigration what all the restrictionist agitation in the world could not have accomplished—it stopped it altogether."[4]

The IRO pressed for an immigration policy unspoiled by ethnic bias or artificial barriers, but such efforts met severe opposition from several sectors of American society. Bressler's faith in the capacity of a rational plan of distribution to neutralize the pressures for restriction proved illusory. It underestimated the influence of spurious race-based claims about the dire consequences of continued immigration and the credibility of questionable economic and social arguments.

The immigration question remained prominent in IRO annual reports and the speeches and articles of its leadership. As a contributor and editor of *Jewish Charities*, Bressler also used this venue to examine immigration issues and impugn restrictionist claims. In addition, the IRO's monthly bulletin, published from mid-1914 to mid-1917, confronted restriction at a particularly critical juncture in the history of the organization. Although IRO activity diminished sharply with the onset of World War I, the organization believed that large-scale immigration would eventually resume.[5] In 1916, Bressler predicted that the end of the war would bring a great stimulus to the movement for distribution of Jewish immigrants and that "the fullest powers and experience of the Removal Office will then be needed to take hold of the situation."[6] Consequently, it was essential to maintain the cooperating network and the machinery of resettlement. Toward that end, the IRO published its monthly bulletin.

Notwithstanding the steady annual influx of thousands of Jewish immigrants adding to the pressures on IRO resources, the organization never relented in its stand for liberal immigration. The IRO added its voice to those of other groups contesting restriction, such as the National Liberal Immigration League and the American Jewish Committee. These organizations also pressed the value of distribution in their respective presentations before the U.S. Immigration Commission.[7]

Allies in the struggle against restriction at times disagreed over appropriate courses of action. Although only implied, the management of Gentile opinion was a general concern, yet one that might lead to tactical disagreements. Louis Marshall, one of the founders of the American Jewish Committee, emphasized judicious, quiet strategies of back-stage lobbying and the exercise of discreet influence on members of Congress rather than visible protests that would bring problematic publicity. Marshall found the tactics of the National Liberal Immigration League particularly unwise in its conspicuous protest meetings and leaflets.[8] The IRO also preferred politic strategies and shared Marshall's fear of immoderate gambits that might bring unintended, destructive consequences. With the movement for restriction gaining ground, ill-considered ploys by immigration advocates would only strengthen the hand of the opposition.

A case in point was the HIAS plan to establish closer ties to various European immigration societies and to station a HIAS representative in Europe. In addition, the HIAS Board of Directors wanted to include European members on the organization's advisory board to bolster the relationship between HIAS and other Jewish immigrant societies abroad. None of these plans was carried out after encountering opposition from the Baron de Hirsch Fund Committee, which furnished HIAS with annual support.[9] Bressler, writing as the editor of *Jewish Charities*, also strongly disagreed with the plan. He believed that it would be interpreted "in certain quarters" as encouraging immigration and therefore wanted to avoid any move that even hinted at "ulterior motives."[10]

A formidable, if groundless, argument in the restrictionist arsenal, assisted immigration had provoked responses from immigration advocates since 1890, as noted in Chapter 1. Bressler's caution was understandable. Any plan, however innocent, that smacked of cooperation with foreign immigration organizations could prove disastrous. It would certainly vitalize charges heard over the previous two decades that the southern and eastern European immigration was not the natural, spontaneous movement of people that supposedly defined the old immigration of a generation before.

Likewise, the IRO criticized academic opinion about immigration, emanating not only from committed restrictionists but also from immigration supporters. A particular instance centered on Horace Kallen, whose two-part *Nation* article, "Democracy Versus the Melting Pot: A Study of American Nationality" unwittingly provided grist for the restrictionist mill, in the view of the IRO. Approvingly, the IRO noted Kallen's argument that Jewish immigrants sedulously prepare for American citizenship and make great strides in effacing the differences between themselves and their social environment. Then Kallen asserted, "Once the wolf is driven from the door and the Jewish immigrant takes his place in our society a free man and an American, he tends to become all the more a Jew."[11] Kallen's voice was in the minority calling for the preservation of immigrant traditions that would form a pluralist America quite out of keeping with the prevailing assimilationist vision.[12] The IRO lamented that Kallen's article had already elicited a letter to *Nation* from a restrictionist jeeringly proclaiming that the "cat has been let out of the bag." The organization did not take issue with Kallen's claim that Jews were culturally self-conscious; rather, his point was overstated, thus encouraging restrictionist arguments that Jewish immigrants resisted assimilation because of their heightened sense of cultural self-awareness. Admonishing "those who desire to befriend the immigrant against being too academic," the IRO restated its familiar argument that the Jewish immigrant assimilates sufficiently "to become a worthy American citizen."[13]

In the main, the IRO had to contend with racial and economic arguments against immigration. Whereas the economic arguments fastened on questions about the effects of immigration on employment, wage scales, and the standard of living, racial critiques played on a deep-seated nativist fear of outsiders as different beyond all hope of absorption into the American nation. Together, they comprised a formidable bulwark against a continuation of immigration on the scale it had reached. Restrictionist arguments presented, on the one hand, a welter of fallacious racial interpretations of social conditions and, on the other, social and economic data deployed as damning evidence against continued liberal immigration.

## The Literacy Test

Although some resumption of immigration occurred at the end of the war, restrictionist views remained prominent and began to achieve their legislative aims in 1917. That year, Congress passed a literacy test over President Wilson's second veto. The literacy test was, however, believed "to afford only a frail barrier" against the tide of desperate immigrants. Therefore a quota act in 1921 aimed to stifle a feared postwar immigration of people displaced by the conflagration. Annual immigration was limited to three percent of a given nationality resident in the United States in 1910. The Immigration Act of 1924 provided further restrictions, tightening annual quotas to 2 percent of a nationality resident in the country in 1890.[14]

Endorsed by the Immigration Commission, the recommendation for a literacy test was rejected, although not strenuously, by Congressman William S. Bennett, the lone signatory to the very brief "views of the minority." The commission found "The reading and writing test as the most feasible single method of restricting undesirable immigration."[15] Bressler and his former IRO colleague Abraham Solomon called the literacy test "the great subterfuge" and charged its advocates with using the test as "a disguised expression of their dislike for 'foreigners.'"[16] With praise for President Wilson following his veto of the bill sanctioning a literacy test, the IRO prophetically observed, "Of course it would be a sheer waste of time to argue this Literacy Test on its merits. It does not require any subtle penetration to understand that the Test is a disguise. Its advocates care little about Literacy or Illiteracy. What they desire is an entering wedge for later and more drastic legislation ending up in a carnival of exclusion."[17] For the advocates of liberal immigration, the literacy test represented the cruelest and most arbitrary of restrictionist efforts, an irrational drive to exclude immigrants who were on all other grounds desirable.

Characteristically, the IRO explained illiteracy as a product of social conditions—obstacles to elementary education faced by Jews in Russia and Rumania or poor educational institutions in Italy. Efforts to deny admission to sober immigrants determined to make their own way were built on the "fallacies of restrictionists and the sophisms of the special interests."[18] The United States would be poorer from the restrictionists' victory. Ostensibly, they aimed to apply a literacy test universally to all immigrant groups; then, the standard of literacy, and thus desirability, would raise the general level of immigration. However, in actuality, the test indirectly aimed to exclude large numbers of southern and eastern Europeans on racial or ethnic grounds. The IRO praised Senator Reed of Missouri, who supported Wilson's veto of the literacy test. Reed asked, "Are the children of immigrants the equals of our native population in education, intelligence and patriotism? If the foregoing question can be answered in the affirmative, then restrictive legislation is not only unnecessary but a serious mistake." Reed argued that the literacy of immigrant children was higher than the general American average and that states with the lowest percentage of immigrants had the lowest literacy rates.[19]

For the IRO, all attempts to establish a literacy test were built on mistaken premises. If successful, such efforts would prove counterproductive in curtailing a process ultimately beneficial to the country. Illiteracy bore no relation to crime, to which it was often linked; in fact, most criminals were literate. Nor did a literacy test provide a valid measure of individual value and therefore would not exclude undesirable newcomers. People did not choose to be illiterate, but instead could not read owing either to an absence of opportunity to learn the written language of their native countries or to systematic persecution based on race or creed. Illiteracy lay beyond anyone's control, and exclusion on this basis was undemocratic and un-American.[20] A literacy test would undermine the national good, for the freedom of American life liberated the energies and resources of immigrants to their benefit and that of the country. American self-interest thus required liberal immigration policies.

The irrationality of the literacy test was also apparent in the high rates of literacy among the children of immigrants as well as by their record of achievement in public schools. With opportunities available, immigrants would respond, both for their own interests and for the commonweal.[21] In its hardest-hitting attack on the literacy provision of the Burnett Bill just after its passage in the House of Representatives, the IRO labeled it "vicious" and "a combination of race prejudice and class legislation of the rankest kind." Invoking American ideals to oppose restriction, the IRO criticism continued:

> The literacy clause is aimed at certain races without . . . having the courage to name them specifically. Such race discrimination is as mediaeval as Russia's oppression of the Jews and Turkey's persecution of the Armenians. If this literacy test finally becomes enacted into law, we must recede a century in civilization. It may not be that "all men are created equal," the solid heart of this

nation knows that there are no bad races, that there are only bad individuals. . . . The "high-falutin" talk of restrictionists, which unctuously speaks of superior races, overcrowding, and other equally shoddy phraseology should have absolutely no significance for us.[22]

The rising tide of restriction finally proved too powerful, even for the presidential veto, successfully wielded by three chief executives—Cleveland in 1897, Taft in 1913, and Wilson in 1915. In 1917, an immigration bill providing for a literacy test—"the obnoxious fetish of the Honorable Mr. Burnett"—successfully passed the Congress.[23] Lobbying by the American Jewish Committee succeeded in excluding from the test immigrants fleeing religious persecution. Vetoed again by President Wilson, the Burnett Immigration Bill became law following a congressional override. For twenty years, recommendations for a literacy test occasioned intense discussion that was in some ways emblematic of the entire debate about immigration policy.

The 1917 defeat for immigration advocates proved very disheartening. It represented a victory for New England patricians wedded to caste-like values at odds with the democratic ideals of the country; southern politicians suspicious of foreign laborers and their possible impact on the South; and "the oligarchy of labor [trying] to limit the labor supply in the United States."[24] Labor's support of the literacy test was, of course, ironic, for many recent immigrants had swollen the ranks of American unions. Union leaders appealed to the rank and file with alarmist warnings that unskilled and illiterate newcomers would reduce American wages.

### Racial Arguments

The surging nativism of the 1890s condemned the newcomers as a different "stock," inferior to the northern and western European immigrants of a few decades earlier. Using a pastiche of coarse biological observations and social stereotyping, nativist critiques of immigration usually played on crude racial images, augmented by scientific racism and rank xenophobia. The emotionalism of nativist argument gained strength through the imprimatur of science, as major figures in biology, sociology, and anthropology lent strong support to the racialist rationale for the severest constraints on immigration.

The recalcitrant Immigration Restriction League presented its argument against distribution before the Immigration Commission. The league's executive secretary, Prescott Hall, contended that a change of location would do nothing to alter the "character and tendencies of an immigrant." The likely consequence of distribution would be the dispersion of large slums to create many small slums around the country. With its attachment to eugenics, the league believed that only exclusionary measures would prevent the proliferation in the United States of immigrants "coming from races and countries . . . which have not progressed, but have been backward, downtrodden, and relatively useless for centuries." Distribution could hardly mitigate such circumstances, for there was little justification in thinking "that a change of location will result in a change of inborn tendencies."[25]

Consistency in the conception of race among restrictionists is not to be found. The usages of race by the Immigration Commissioners, for example, vary. They range from allegedly innate social characteristics and biological features to a much greater emphasis on linguistic and cultural qualities. The concoction of somatic, cultural, and linguistic attributes in classifying races is indicated in the commission's *Dictionary of Races or Peoples*. The commission depended on "the primary classification of mankind into five grand divisions . . . made upon physical or somatological grounds, while the subdivision of these into a multitude of smaller 'races' or peoples is made largely upon a linguistic basis."[26] The commission believed that this classification had important practical implications. An immigration inspector, wholly unequipped to make a racial determination on physical grounds, might easily classify an individual according to native language.

Prominent authorities, including Edward A. Ross, John R. Commons, and Madison Grant, offered a melange of biological and social explanations for the alleged corruption of American life at the hands of the immigrants. Their race-based suppositions about human behavior attracted the support of diverse figures in the social and biological sciences. They emboldened and sanctioned the efforts of the Immigration Restriction League and helped catalyze opinion against liberal national policies by warning of the heritability and immutability of tendencies among the new immigrants toward pauperism, dependency, disease, and other social and biological pathologies. The doomed future that the new immigration augured for America—the America descended from northern and western

Europe—is indicated by the title of Madison Grant's nativist lament, *The Passing of the Great Race.*

Increasingly, the racial critique charged that eastern and southern Europeans were incapable of assimilation, thus leading to a fundamental questioning of the very possibility of Americanization. That is, despite the values attached to the assimilation process, implying that one could become an American by culture as well as by citizenship, racial arguments denied the capacity of the eastern and southern European immigrants to adjust to the new social conditions that they encountered. Grant, the best known and most influential of the prophets of scientific racism, bitterly characterized the conviction that immigrants could adapt: "With a pathetic and fatuous belief in the efficacy of American institutions and environment to reverse or obliterate immemorial hereditary tendencies, these newcomers were welcomed and given a share in our land and prosperity."[27]

In crude racial arguments, southern and eastern Europeans were regarded as naturally inferior to the old stock of immigrants. Considered culturally unmalleable owing to the fixed, natural limitations of biological race and temperament, the newcomers could not fulfill the expectations of the new country by adopting a way of economic and social life suitable to American circumstances and values. Moreover, eugenic alarms warned of a steady social decline and that, in the words of Ross, "a deterioration of popular intelligence" would ensue.[28] Equally lamentable in Ross's Malthusian, racial critique of immigration was a birthrate among immigrants greatly exceeding that of the "precious stock of pioneer ancestry."[29]

The dire economic consequence of this differential was the inability of pioneer descendants "to compete in a labor market overstocked with subcommon representatives of certain unachieving and undistinguished strains of southern and southwestern Europe."[30] With his fellow midwesterner and academic, economist John R. Commons, Ross also opposed immigration as a threat to American workers likely to be displaced by newcomers willing to work for less or to serve as strikebreakers. They lowered the general level of life in the United States, tainting it socially and politically with their alien and debased manners. The social problems of burgeoning cities were the direct result of the new immigration. Ross also mustered a tangle of negative ethnic stereotypes and antisemitic gibes. Jews were powerful and wealthy out of all proportion to their numbers in the United States, and Jewish financial support and influence within the National Liberal Immigration League and the Baron de Hirsch Fund spearheaded the battle against immigration restriction.[31] Expressing the anxious concerns of many, Ross lent the restrictionist movement the authority and influence of his professional standing.

The IRO did not shrink from confronting Ross's views. Following the publication of his article, "Hebrews of Eastern Europe and America," in *Century Magazine* (September 1914), the IRO called Ross one of "those Don Quixotes of the intellect who have been fighting the windmill of Jewish vices." The shopworn caricature of Jews presented in that article was extended in his 1914 restrictionist volume, *The Old World in the New*. Calling malicious Ross's stereotypic representation of Jews as cunning, powerful, clannish, unproductive, and dirty, the IRO was particularly combative, claiming that "the article is vicious in its tendency and corrupting to the intelligence of that vast number of non-Jews who have no real understanding of Jewish character or ideals and who are ready to accept any caricature which makes them laugh." Instead, by examining the social and economic circumstances of Jewish life, "Insight replaces snap judgment":

> Has the Jew proved an economic asset to the United States? Has he shown a tendency to assimilate rapidly? Has he a civic conscience and has he a moral life? If he has all these then he is sound at the core and an asset to any country. . . . Assuming, for the sake of argument, that the Jew is uncouth, that he loves profit, that he takes to the pack and the professional pursuits rather than to manual labor—do these detract from his moral or mental make-up? What other nation so readily appreciates the best in American institutions? What other immigrant takes so much pride in his American citizenship? What other class of voter is so intelligent and discerning of the political problems of the day? What immigrant more avid of culture? What immigrant more efficient, more sober, more steady? These are the qualities which make for sound citizenship.[32]

Anthropologist Franz Boas, a courageous scientific dissenter from conventional theories of race, argued forcefully against the kinds of views promulgated by Ross. A German Jewish immigrant, Boas was the most important progressive anthropologist of his day in vigorously opposing all efforts to explain social conditions by recourse to biology, race, or some putative inherited temperament. Boas argued the then-radical thesis that mutability characterized all racial types and that the latter bore no necessary relationship to cultural forms. Boas, among American anthropologists, stood prominently at the forefront of the debate about race and culture in relationship to the immigration issue.

Consequently, any indictments against anthropology as a critical source for racialist explanations of culture or similar rationales against immigration require some qualification. Certainly, unschooled dilettantes, such as Grant, writing outside of innovative currents within professional American anthropology, supported their retrograde views with sources heavily freighted with the typological racial formalism of Blumenbach or the racist hierarchies of Gobineau. Finding little interest in race among American anthropologists, Higham observed that "a perfected racism depended on amateur handling of imported ideas."[33] Whereas European classificatory theories of race pervaded amateur opinion in the United States, Higham understated the racialist views of some influential professional American anthropologists.[34] Whatever their provenance, racial explanation was pervasive in popular opinion and professional pronouncements. Against this tide, Boas pointed the way to a wholly new understanding about the sources of human behavior that would ultimately transform his own field and seep into public consciousness.

Radical in their implications and inconsistent with the prevailing politics of restriction, Boas's views had no effect on the national political figures shaping immigration policy. The latter included the members of the Immigration Commission, which ironically, engaged Boas as a consultant. His research on behalf of the commission bolstered his critique of nineteenth-century racial formalism, which was woven into the biases of the commissioners. They found more to admire in the extant racial theories of the day than in the new thinking of modern anthropological science exemplified by Boas.

Following nearly four years of study and hearings, the published findings of the U.S. Immigration Commission appeared in 1911 and comprised forty-one volumes. Not surprisingly, these volumes contain no bibliographic entries for Boas, with the exception of the volume he authored. This omission is especially glaring in Volume 5, *Dictionary of Races or Peoples*. Written by the French-trained anthropologist Daniel Folkmar, it is a muddle of somatic and linguistic characteristics that were used to classify racial types and subtypes. The *Dictionary* aimed to clarify "the true racial status" of the new immigrants.[35] The selected bibliography includes the work of Blumenbach, Ripley, and other racial theorists of that time.

Boas's detailed study on the mutability of physique among immigrants over a single generation comprised the entirety of Volume 38, entitled *Changes in the Bodily Form of Descendants of Immigrants*. His radical conclusions, however, exercised utterly no influence on the commissioners. The substance of Boas's research was at odds with many of their preconceived views. His thesis represented nothing less than a paradigmatic shift within anthropology about conceptions of race. Had the implications of Boas's findings been seriously attended to, the members of the commission would have been hard pressed to sustain the argument for their restrictionist recommendations. Although the final report of the commission recognized Boas's surprising results, its recommendations were submitted as if Boas had assumed no research role on behalf of the commission.

Boas's research in New York on Jewish and Italian immigrants and their children provided scientific and empirical evidence contradicting every effort, including the *Dictionary,* to classify and order races according to static criteria—the methodological core of scientific racism. The primary somatic indices of race, such as head form, had long been regarded as stable hereditary features of groups over many generations, thus providing reliable standards for racial classification. Boas demonstrated statistically that the head form—the cephalic index, or the ratio of head width to length—of the immigrants differed from that of their European-born children and, to an even greater extent, from their American-born children. Moreover, the determining role of environment was further corroborated by the fact that the numerical difference in head form between immigrant parents and their American children varied with the length of time that the mother had resided in United States before the birth of her children.[36] The commission granted that Boas's demonstration of differences in bodily form between immigrants and their children was "a discovery in anthropological science that is fundamental in importance."[37]

Boas also pioneered research on the relationship between race and culture. Throughout his long professional life, he maintained that biological factors and culture varied independent of each other. Old claims to the contrary were insupportable. Boas's *The Mind of Primitive Man*, published in 1911, the same year that the findings of the Immigration Commission appeared, laid out the argument against singular deterministic views of culture, including, especially, biological or racial causation. It was instrumental in relocating the wellsprings of human behavior from race to culture and effectively set the course of modern anthropology. As to the immigration controversy, if biology and culture are independent of each other and variable within and between generations, then allegations about unassimilable eastern and southern Europeans are exposed as only crude prejudice. The commission conceded only that some people believe that "under the influence of the existing educational, social, and political conditions the immigrants gradually change their habits of life and their ways of thinking."[38] The full purport of Boas's conclusions, considered seriously, would force recognition of the plasticity and flexibility of human behavior over the course of a generation. For if somatic features shift so rapidly within a population owing to environmental influence, then the cultural acquisition of new traits—assimilation in effect—could certainly proceed apace.

Regarding the claims on behalf of northern Europeans made by Jeremiah Jenks, a restrictionist economist on the Immigration Commission, the IRO rebutted his views in terms fully in accord with Boas's research: "This notion of race superiority is, perhaps, the most interesting and the most persistent of the fallacies of restrictionist philosophy. The very conception of race superiority should be revolting to the scientific mind, especially in view of the recent anthropological evidence adduced, which shows that there is more vanity than truth in the idea of inherent race superiority."[39] In this light, the apocalyptic warnings of the most diehard restrictionists about unassimilable alien hordes from the other side of Europe would have to give way. The new immigrants were, instead, prospective Americans, whose children and grandchildren would be no less subject to the influence of the American social and political environment than the children of patrician New Englanders. The IRO pressed this point repeatedly, never more strongly than in response to such stalwarts of the Immigration Restriction League as Ross and Hall. The latter asked, "Is it possible that flag exercises in the schools, teaching American History, and the use of patriotic speeches and songs, can change the fundamental attitude of Mediterranean and Asiatic races within one generation?" The IRO replied wryly,

Assuming that this were not possible, may we ask Mr. Hall, what difference does it make? Supposing it does take two generations for the poor immigrant to get Americanism into the marrow of his bones, who suffers? Slow but sure, the process may be a little tedious to impatient restrictionists, but the process is there, works out successfully, and the children of the unfortunate immigrant who could not change his fundamental attitude, are now successfully Americanized, and in time they too may become sufficiently Americanized to advocate restriction.[40]

The entire rationale of IRO activity and the organized Jewish communal support of immigration and the immigrant turned on this particular scientific anthropological truth—the plasticity of human behavior. This view was as radical in the first decades of the new century as it was to become commonplace in social science in later years. The institutions and democratic traditions of the United States would transform immigrants and their children into Americans, making a lie of any assertion that allegedly inherited racial or temperamental characteristics of a particular group would impede the process. To claim otherwise was un-American because it denied the salutary and formative power of American life to break the shackles that for so long had limited the progress of immigrants in their lands of origin. As represented by the IRO, history and social circumstance, not nature, explain human action:

> Those in favor of the restriction of immigration usually mistake effect for cause. It is their belief that the immigration to these shores is responsible for a good deal of the improper functioning of this country's nervous system. Now if one studies the question with an eye to the truth, one perceives that all these evils arise not from the nature of the immigrant, but from the nature of the surroundings in which he lives. . . . Guide the immigrant, open his eyes to the vastness of the country, enable him to start in a locality where he has a normal environment, where his trade obtains, where the market is not so overcrowded, and where life, even though slower is still fuller—you will remove the evil which you imagine inherent in the immigrant.[41]

The irrelevance of Boas's findings to the Immigration Commission and the incongruity of his association with an enterprise that was dominated by restrictionist sentiment are at first glance puzzling. Jenks received all of Boas's communications and exercised considerable influence on the final report and recommendations. His role helps to explain why Boas's scientifically significant findings proved nugatory. Less crass and contemptuous in his observations than either Ross or Hall, Jenks nonetheless ranked among the most effective of the many academic restrictionists. George

Stocking points out that the initiative for Boas's research came not from the commission, but from Boas himself, who took advantage of available research funds by proposing a project germane to the concerns of the commission.[42] Maurice Fishberg, a medical doctor with research interests in physical anthropology, had studied somatic differences between immigrant Jews and their New York–born children and had called Boas's attention to the research funds available from the Immigration Commission. Fishberg had already begun to establish that the American-born children of immigrants tended to be a good deal taller than their parents.[43] Boas continued this research, swimming against the rapid restrictionist current of the commission and much popular opinion.

In 1924, the year that the already reduced European immigration was virtually arrested by congressional action, Boas repeated his by then familiar argument in the popular *American Mercury* that neither heredity nor anatomy could explain the culture history of any group of people. Moreover, he exposed the smug assertion of European superiority over African culture and the Negro. Boas argued that such claims neglected the "cultural primitiveness of the great mass of individuals, which finds expression intellectually in the uncritical acceptance of traditional attitudes and emotionally in the ease with which they succumb to the power of fashionable passions."[44] Boas's words might well have been taken as an ironic commentary on much restrictionist thinking—primitive, uncritical, and slavishly bound to the authority of unexamined popular sentiment.

### Economic and Demographic Arguments

The economics of immigration proved even more contentious than race in the continuing debate, although race and economic factors are not consistently separated in the restrictionist assertions. Reflecting the mix of prejudicial feeling against the current immigration—"very little of it is high class"—and economic concerns, *The New York Times* in 1903 found the economic aspects of immigration "obscure":

If the labor of these hundreds of thousands of relatively unskilled immigrants is needed, and shall continue to be needed until the movement is checked and those already here are absorbed and assimilated, they will be of benefit to the country. If, on the contrary, it is giving us a supply of unskilled labor in excess of our needs, and to find work the latecomers must break down the established rate of wages, strikes and riots are to be expected, and Socialism in its more dangerous aspects will receive a great impulse.[45]

The editorial concluded that only a continuation of national prosperity could promise a positive outcome. Indeed, the periods of industrial depression and downturn brought forth passionate opposition to immigration. The uncertainty about the economic consequences of immigration in the editorial foreshadowed much of the subsequent argument about the impact of the newcomers on wages and the standard of living of the American worker.

Anti-immigration issues came into sharp focus within the Immigration Commission. It is thus important to examine the commission's work more closely, beginning with consideration of the demographic character of the new immigration, and its Jewish component in particular, to provide a context for the IRO's arguments against restriction. Although biased against immigration from the outset, the commission still provided an invaluable store of data regarding wages, housing, immigrant children in schools, conditions in Europe, return migration, and the like on the many ethnic groups making up the new immigration. Commission data and conclusions offer a clear window through which to see the sharply defined contours of Jewish immigration after 1899 and the arguments, however self-contradictory, for immigration restriction. Conclusions palpably at odds with the evidence of the *Reports* themselves once again show the groundless faith in "logical reason" that Bressler believed would keep restriction at bay.

The new immigration stood among the most highly charged domestic issues in the early years of the twentieth century, and "the changed character of the immigration movement to the United States during the past twenty-five years" prompted the commission's formation. The restrictionist movement sought to extend the limitations of then current laws preventing the admission to the United States of criminals, the mentally disturbed, and others deemed undesirable for reasons of health or morality. Even the strongest proponents of liberal immigration supported such limitations, based as they were on the personal deficiencies of individuals. The movement for restriction, however, also pressed for policies that would create exclusionary measures against particular groups, defined by nativity. For the first time in the history of American immigration, people of specific ethnic origins would face severe numerical limits on their admission. The commission set out to document the differences between the old and the new immigration and, in regard to the latter, to gauge "the effect of such immigration upon the institutions, industries, and people of this country." Impaneled through the Immigration Act of 1907 with the broad mandate to "make full inquiry, examination, and investigation . . . into the subject of immigration," the commission was to report to Congress with any recommendations deemed appropriate.[46] The commission presented its reports, with several strategies for restricting immigration, to the 61st Congress.

The restrictionist measures supported by the Immigration Commission sought to control the alleged overabundance of unskilled labor in the United States. One aim was to establish certain criteria to determine which people among the unskilled could be admitted. The commission recommended restrictions on those who entered the United States without any interest in becoming citizens or even permanent residents but came instead to accumulate money before returning home. Usually single men, such individuals were willing to live at a very low standard. Little attention was given to the contribution of these "birds of passage" to the American economy—the goods and services they produced, including the massive building projects that employed them in the construction of bridges, tunnels, and the edifices of urban America. The commission also urged restrictions against people likely to be undesirable citizens or resistant to assimilation owing to what were regarded as unsavory personal habits.

Although many of the commission's anti-immigration arguments were ostensibly driven by economic concerns, its sentiments were certainly conditioned by a diffuse nativist suspicion about peoples of eastern and southern European origin. To implement restrictions, race quotas could be established. In addition, unskilled workers arriving without their wives or families could be excluded, and the head tax could be levied in a way that favored men arriving with wives and families. The commission also suggested an increase in the minimum amount of money an immigrant was required to possess on arriving at an American port.[47] In these criteria for exclusion, one can readily discern the kinds of immigrants who were valued: permanent settlers, not transients; families arriving together; immigrants who would eventually send for their families remaining in Europe, thus establishing a fairly balanced distribution of men and women rather than a sex distribution skewed toward single males; skilled craftsmen;

and immigrants not driven to the United States by economic hardship. Selectively reading the evidence on the old and new immigration, the commission juxtaposed an old immigration of families headed by skilled workers determined to settle permanently in the United States against a new immigration of largely single men, for the most part unskilled and determined to return to their European homes after laboring for American salaries far surpassing what they might earn in Europe.

The commission's mandate was clear. Empirical investigation was to yield data on the new immigrants, which would in turn lead to recommendations deriving from the scientific findings of the commission and its staff. An enormous compendium of data and statistics was gathered, both from previously published government reports and from new research sponsored by the commission. Shortly after they were empaneled, six commissioners even sailed for Europe, where they investigated, over the course of several months, the sources of the new immigration and its causes. The ideological center of gravity among the commissioners was so weighted toward restriction, however, that the panel's final recommendations were virtually a foregone conclusion, bearing in many instances very little relationship to the mass of research findings of the final report. The data frequently suggested conclusions directly at variance with the commission's own restrictionist recommendations, despite the assertion by Jenks and Lauck that the facts brought to light "seem to point clearly to a rather rigid restriction on immigration for the present, until more progress can be made in solving the problems of assimilation and distribution."[48]

This statement derived from a conception of scientific explanation as simply a discovery procedure. Social policy could then follow logically from the patterns laid bare by empirical research. The significance of scientific data is self-evident, clearly outlined within the numbers for any trained eye to discern. This naive empiricism left no room for the possibility of distortion, which worked its way into the commission's procedures and recommendations.

That the commission supported restrictionist measures in its final report to congress came as no surprise at the time, given the widely known anti-immigration stance of the commission chairman, Senator William P. Dillingham of Vermont, and his fellow senatorial and congressional commissioners, including Senator Henry Cabot Lodge of Massachusetts (a member of the Immigration Restriction League) and Congressman John Burnett. The like-minded views of Jenks, head of research for the commission and the most important presidential appointee, became widely known. Six editions of his anti-immigration volume, *The Immigration Problem: A Study of American Immigration Conditions and Needs* (with W. Jett Lauck) were published between 1911 and 1926 and were dedicated to Senator Dillingham. In all, the commission consisted of nine members, including three senators appointed by the president of the Senate, three members from the House of Representatives appointed by the speaker of the House, and three people appointed by President Theodore Roosevelt.[49]

The skewed nature of the commission's recommendations in light of the complex and internally variable quality of the post-1881 immigration was very much a function of the putative opposition between the old and the new immigration. The commission's commitment to that distinction was unwavering, resisting its own closely documented social and economic profile of the newcomers since the early 1880s. Between 1820 and 1883, the old immigration comprised more than 95 percent of the entire European immigration and derived primarily from Britain, Germany, Scandinavia, Holland, Belgium, France, and Switzerland. The commission noted a "rapid change in the ethnical character of the European immigration" after 1883 and that "in recent years more than 70 percent of the movement has originated in southern and eastern Europe."[50] Although the dichotomy reflected a temporal difference in the two migrations as well as aggregate ethnic distinctions, the alleged social variations between old and new were by no means so clear cut. In other words, although the Commission conceded that new immigrants did not always fit the generic characteristics of the post-1881 immigration, its findings were stretched to fit the Procrustean bed of the old/new dichotomy.

Methodologically, procedures were suspect. For example, new and old immigrants were compared along several dimensions but usually without any clear, consistent delineation of how long people from each category had been living in the United States. The European-born generation of new immigrants was thus compared to the second or subsequent generations of old immigrants. The limited assimilation of the former compared with the thoroughgoing Americanization of the latter cast a shadow over the new immigrants.

A case in point concerns boarders and lodgers, who frequently lived in the households of the new immigrants. The propensity of the new immigrants to live in the "boarding-boss system," that is, for lodgers to pay the household head a monthly fee for boarding, cooking, and washing, was said to promote unsanitary, congested conditions, preventing the development of satisfactory family life. This type of living arrangement contrasted sharply with the household patterns of the old immigrants and native born, where a more wholesome family life presumably emerged. Although the commission mustered an impressive array of statistics on the frequency of boarding among various ethnic groups and the size of households where boarding occurred, the absence of a diachronic perspective could only reinforce the commission's negative *a priori* assumptions about the new immigrants. Without accounting for longitudinal patterns of upward mobility and residential and household changes over time among both old and new immigrants, the frequency of boarding among recent immigrants and its allegedly damaging effect on family life further distorted their image.[51]

When the commission did chart the course of assimilation over time across a range of old and new immigrant groups, the positive implications of these trends had no bearing on the final restrictionist recommendations. For example, it was noted that the extent to which "non–English-speaking races" acquired English provided "one of the most important indications of the degree of their assimilation." Drawing on data from a sample of immigrant employees numbering more than 200,000, the commission found, predictably, that English-speaking ability increased, often dramatically, with length of residence in the United States. Likewise, English language competence was extremely high—approaching 90 percent—among immigrants arriving before the age of fourteen years.[52] This evidence was quite at odds with anxieties about unassimilable aliens or new immigrants resistant to Americanization.

With no indication that decline of the old immigration would be reversed nor that the new immigration would attenuate naturally, the commission observed that the large number of new immigrants "has provoked a widespread feeling of apprehension as to its effect on the economic and social welfare of the country." Permanence of settlement focused some of this "apprehension" and was taken as a critical point of contrast between the old and new immigrants. The former came in family groups to stay, casting their lot with the new country. The latter consisted mostly of men who, in many cases, did not intend to settle in the United States, but rather sought only to take advantage of the wages they could earn in American industry before returning to Europe. Regarding the returnees as exploiters of American opportunity without a concomitant personal and social investment in the new land, the commissioners were little concerned with the tangible results of their labor in agriculture, industry, and construction. While conceding that this profile did not describe all of the new immigrants, the commission argued that "the practice is sufficiently common to warrant referring to it as a characteristic of them as a class."[53] Questionable generalizations or composite statements of this sort would thus outweigh consideration of the distinctive social and economic characteristics and achievements of people within each ethnic group in the formulation of recommendations.

The Immigration Act of 1907 established procedures for keeping a formal record of immigrants departing from the United States, and the commission made use of these new records to press its point. The commission cited figures for the period 1908–1910, indicating that the return migration of immigrants from the old category constituted 16 percent of those admitted. The comparable figure for immigrants in the new category was 38 percent.[54] When the fiscal years 1906–1907 to 1907–1908 are compared, the result is particularly telling. Heightened industrial activity in 1906–1907 was accompanied by the largest immigration to the United States before the publication of the Immigration Commission volumes. By October 1907, an industrial depression had begun, followed by a large-scale return migration of aliens to Europe. During these successive years, the Jewish immigration to the United States was 149,182, or 12 percent of the total of 1,237,341 immigrants. The Jewish return to Europe constituted 2 percent of the total 381,044 returnees. The highest percentage of returnees was registered by southern Italians at 39 percent, well beyond the next highest figure of 12.3 percent for Poles. The return rate for Jews differed little from many of the old immigrant groups and was in fact less than the 3.8 percent registered for the German immigrants. For the same two-year period, 91.1 percent of returnees were part of the new category and 8.95 percent were part of the old category, thus leading the commission to see the old immigrants as permanent settlers as opposed to the transient new immigrants drawn to the United States only by labor opportunities. Repatriation figures show that between 1908 and 1910 when eight Jews returned to Europe for every 100 immigrating to the United States, the comparable figure for southern Italians was 56.[55]

This pattern continued until the eve of World War I. Thus between 1908 and 1914, the ratio of immigrants returning to Europe to the total immigration to the United States was 7.1 percent for Jews and 32.2 percent for

non-Jewish immigration.[56] Not only did the commission recognize the
Jews as permanent settlers; its figures on immigration and return for
1907–1908 indicated that the Jewish settlement was characterized by "a
degree of permanency not reached by any other race of people in either
class."[57] Still, the commission voiced apprehension over the new immigration as a whole, however it might vary from group to group. Consequently,
its restrictionist recommendations aimed to limit severely the immigration of all southern and eastern European groups.

Certainly, familial stability and permanent American settlement were
highly germane to the work of the IRO. It supported the reunion of wage
earners, newly settled in the interior, with their wives and children left behind either in New York or in Europe. Indeed, both in popular Jewish consciousness and in the scholarly literature, the determination of Jewish
immigrants to settle permanently in the United States with their families
long ago became an unquestioned truth.[58] The May Laws, customary restrictions against Jewish participation in economic life, and physical attacks combined to drive thousands of Jews annually to the safety of
American shores. The debilities under which the Jews of Russia had to live
were duly noted by the Immigration Commission in its detailed assessment of emigration conditions in Europe. It included a memorandum
from the ICA detailing the residential, occupational, and educational restrictions enforced on Jews by Russian law.[59] Whereas the "birds of passage" phenomenon aptly characterized Italian and other new immigrants,
the character of the Jewish immigration was vastly different. Yet to the restrictionists, it remained a subset of the new immigration by reasons of
timing, origins, and racialist views of eastern and southern Europeans.

The demographic profile of Jewish immigration is clearly discernible in
the annual reports of the Bureau of Immigration after 1899, when the designation "Hebrew" was first utilized for arriving immigrants. Before that
time, Jews disembarking at Castle Garden or, later, Ellis Island, or at the
ports of Philadelphia, Baltimore or Boston were simply identified in federal immigration records by country of origin.[60] Data nonetheless exist for
the period before 1899, when the UHC systematically recorded Jewish
arrivals at the port of New York. Equivalent Jewish organizations in
Philadelphia and Baltimore maintained similar records. The result, when
combined with federal records from the Bureau of Immigration, is a clear
demographic picture of the new Jewish immigration dating from just after
its onset. The figures show the enormous discrepancy between the Jewish

immigration and the composite characteristics of the new immigration, particularly in regard to the ratio of men to women and to large numbers of children. Even in its earliest stages, Jewish immigration stood apart from the new immigration.

From 1886 until 1898, the UHC logged the arrival of 380,278 Jewish immigrants in New York, of whom 147,053 were men, 104,570 were women, and 128,655 were children (under sixteen years of age). Of the adult immigration, men constituted 58 percent and women 42 percent.[61] In 1894, 13,142 adult immigrants landed, of whom 6,738 were women and 6,404 were men—the only year when the UHC recorded an adult female immigration in excess of male immigration.[62] Even more telling of the familial nature of this massive movement of people are the data on immigrant children. During the twelve-year period under consideration, the percentage of the total immigration of adult males, adult females, and children was 38, 27, and 34, respectively.[63] Some returnees to Europe notwithstanding, immigrant Jews were not temporary sojourners but links in a severed chain that would subsequently reconnect itself in the United States. Sometimes, the first link was a young husband who would eventually earn enough money to send for his wife and children. Other immigrants arrived to join already established adult children, siblings, more distant kin, or even friends from the same town. Less commonly, entire families might have the means to travel together. But whatever the sequence of arrival of family members and kin, reunification in the New World defined Jewish immigration, which depended most immediately on the policies of the American government.

If the proponents of restriction acknowledged with favor the more permanent and familial nature of the Jewish immigration compared with other segments of the new immigration, they also could point to one of its least acceptable features. It was overwhelmingly an immigration to the cities, and to New York in particular. The annual reports of the UHC clearly indicate the decidedly urban character of Jewish immigration, with New York representing the most egregious manifestation of a teeming immigrant metropolis. The UHC reports from 1885 until the eve of the new century indicate that 72 percent of the Jewish immigrant arrivals remained in New York; the other 28 percent eventually left the city to rejoin family and friends elsewhere.[64] The IRO thus confronted an enormous problem that the UHC, concerned with multiple projects in addition to distribution, had not materially affected.

Presenting formidable social service problems to Jewish organizations, the congested city was also a highly visible target for the restrictionists with their invidious and statistically questionable comparisons between the old and the new immigration. The squalor and congestion of immigrant New York in the 1840s and 1850s somehow escaped notice because the distorted frame of comparison usually juxtaposed the recently disembarked new immigrants with the successfully adapted and assimilated older immigrants. The propensity to dwell in cities was regarded, moreover, as an undesirable Jewish characteristic.

Against the menace of tenement life and associated urban social ills, the IRO found itself in odd agreement with the immigration restrictionists. Ghettos were profoundly objectionable to both sides. To the IRO, they retarded assimilation. To the restrictionists, ghettos were the embodiments of American decline. Enclaves of foreign custom, in the IRO view, could only insulate their inhabitants from the positive values and laudable cultural influences of American society. They created immense social problems and nurtured a criminal class and also preserved outmoded Old World customs and habits of mind out of step with normal life in the United States. However, whereas the restrictionists wanted to curtail the admission of allegedly unassimilable aliens from the wrong side of Europe, the IRO sought to keep the doors open and to solve the ghetto problem.

The IRO remained convinced that assimilation would go forward if only a proper domestic policy toward immigrants were adopted, both by private organizations and by the government. Despite some periodic disagreements among the most prominent American Jewish organizations, virtually all embraced immigrant distribution as the key to gainful self-reliance, to rapid incorporation of Russian Jews and others into American society, and to a continuing immigration.

To that end, the IRO, the Jewish Immigrants' Information Bureau, the American Jewish Committee, and the National Liberal Immigration League each submitted statements to the Immigration Commission. Distribution, of course, represented the prominent theme in the presentations of both the IRO and the Jewish Immigrants' Information Bureau.[65] It also was strongly endorsed by the National Liberal Immigration League and the American Jewish Committee as part of their opposition to restrictionist measures, including the literacy test and an increased head tax. The former noted that the "problem of immigration is a problem of distribution" and that in the decade to come the most pressing task "will be the relief of the congestion in our large cities by aiding the unemployed to go to small towns and to the farming districts—the more distant parts of the country where their services will be more useful to the nation."[66] Likewise, the American Jewish Committee urged the government to assist organizations, including the IRO, engaged in diminishing the urban congestion of immigrants and in seeing to their economic, educational, and housing needs.[67]

The Immigration Commission emphasized the negative economic consequences of the existing immigration and believed that American interest required further restrictive legislation that would narrow the criteria for admission to the United States.[68]

Following on the heels of the Immigration Commission, the Commission on Industrial Relations was created by Congress in 1912. It conducted most of its investigations in 1914 and submitted a report to the Sixty-Fourth Congress the following year. Its primary purpose was the investigation of the causes of industrial unrest in the United States. The commission was, in many respects, the high-water mark of Progressivism, forthrightly exposing the abuses of special interests at the expense of working people. In line with the restrictionists, it unequivocally blamed immigration for the most intractable industrial problems, from undermining the standard of living to inhibiting the formation of unions. Consequently, the commission recommended the passage of the Burnett–Dillingham Bill with its restrictive literacy provisions.[69] A lengthy section of the final report coauthored by Commons endorses immigration restriction after the following sweeping indictment: "Underlying the entire problem of self-government in this country and placing a limit on the ability to remedy abuses either through politics or labor unions, is the great variety of races, nationalities, and languages."[70] A population that varied by race, ethnicity, and language could only undermine the economic and political health of the nation.

### Economic Rebuttals of Commission Findings and Fallacies of the Old/New Distinction

Whether they alleged a reduction of American wages, a lowering of the standard of living, or increasing pauperism, the immigration critics were unable to sustain a consistent line of supportable economic argument. For example, at the same time that the restrictionist movement complained about the new immigration undercutting the wages of domestic workers, it also claimed that exclusionary measures were essential if immigrant pauperism and dependency were to be reduced. The IRO attacked this view at a time when the Manufacturers' Association in New York declared a lockout in the garment industry. Forty thousand people, mostly immigrants, had taken to the streets in a public demonstration of their rights. Without considering the issues involved in this dispute between capital and labor, the IRO instead wanted to use the occasion to challenge people to consider the positive impact of this immigrant-dominated industry on the American economy in terms of spending capacity, production, and consumption:

> We offer these suggestions especially to our misguided friends, the restrictionists, who are constantly casting into our face the argument that the immigrant entering our country frequently becomes the pauper and dependent, rather than a cooperator and industrial as well as national asset. Here . . . is the answer to your ever exaggerated and fallacious argument. This industry calling for investments in millions having a turn-over annually of more than a billion dollars, is composed mainly of immigrants. The investor is a product of our new immigration, the producer is his fellow immigrant, and the consumer[s] with the spending power of many millions, are largely immigrants. Are these the characteristics of paupers?[71]

This line of argument was not new for the IRO, which in its annual reports of 1906 and 1911 offered estimates both of the earnings of its clientele and the value of the products they produced. In the latter report, for example, the IRO pointed out that by the end of 1911, approximately 30,000 wage earners had been resettled. Based on wage reports to the main office, the IRO estimated that the people it assisted were earning between fifteen and eighteen million dollars a year. The sum was doubtless even greater because many of their children had reached working age since resettlement. Following estimates from the U.S. Census that earnings constituted about one-fifth of the total value of a product, the IRO concluded that its clients were contributing between seventy-five and ninety million dollars per year to the industrial output of the country.[72]

Whereas the restrictionists argued that the economic data lent strong support to policies that would sharply diminish immigration, proponents of the more open policy argued from the same data that the new immigration was an economic boon. Following the publication of the Immigration Commission's findings, Samuel Joseph's 1914 study, *Jewish Immigration to the United States, 1881–1910,* criticized misconceptions about Jewish immigrants that ignored their demographic and economic similarity to earlier European newcomers.[73] Indeed, the IRO held the book in great esteem, optimistically suggesting "that if our restrictionist friends would take the patience to read Dr. Joseph's contribution and give it unbiased consideration, they might radically modify their views on the immigration question."[74]

The selective and ahistorical reading of the data presented by the Immigration Commission pit the IRO against Jenks three years after the commission's findings were published. Jenks undoubtedly was familiar with Joseph's book, but the IRO's hope that Joseph's study would force a rethinking of the restrictionist position was not realized. The restrictionists were not persuaded of the economic value of the Jewish immigration. Following an interview with *The New York Evening Post* in which Jenks argued that the northern European immigrants were more desirable than their southern or eastern European counterparts, the IRO countered his view with a different interpretation of the statistics at issue.

Jenks noted that the immigration from southern and eastern Europe from July 1914 to January 1915 had been negligible, whereas that from northern Europe showed uniformity and steadiness, thus demonstrating the greater desirability of the northern European immigration. Arguing that Jenks unfairly selected his data to make a restrictionist point, the IRO extended the comparison to include the months between July 1913 and January 1914—in other words, a six-month period before the outbreak of World War I, which severely disrupted migration patterns. The northern European immigration in the earlier six-month period totaled 106,533; in the later period, it was 74,398, a decline of more than 30 percent. Pointing out the hazards of ocean transport, the IRO argued that such perilous conditions accounted for the decrease in northern European immigration. At the same time, the government of Italy, owing to its uncertain position in the war, had reduced emigration, exercising a greater control over the issuance of passports. The IRO concluded that the statistical picture of immigration during the periods in question derived from political factors, not from the temperament or psychology of particular categories of immigrants.[75]

In addition, the IRO demonstrated from official statistics that for the years 1911–1914, the rate of immigrant return was approximately the same for northern Europeans as for southern and eastern Europeans. Jenks, in contrast, argued from statistics on particular ethnic groups rather than from figures on all ethnic groups of northern, southern, and eastern Europe. Thus, using more comprehensive data, the IRO claimed that in normal times there appeared no significant difference in repatriation rates between categories of old and new immigrants. During the same period, 39 percent of English immigrants returned to their homeland, whereas the comparable figure for Irish immigrants was 17 percent. Yet no one would assert that English immigrants were less desirable than others or that the English immigration was less stable.

Arguing from statistics proved, in many respects, highly selective and arbitrary. At the least, a more comprehensive view was in order. Even so, the IRO contended that statistics about any class of immigrants provided a poor guide to the desirability of immigration from that particular category. It was illegitimate to pronounce either the English or Italian immigrant unsuitable simply because large numbers of these immigrants returned to their countries of origin. Instead, the appropriate standard was qualitative, not quantitative—"their manner of assimilation into American life and the contribution which they make to American Welfare."[76]

Economist Isaac Hourwich published the most thorough critique of the opposition between the old and new immigration and, particularly, the economic case against immigration as presented in the recommendations of the Immigration Commission.[77] Hourwich's work was secretly funded by the American Jewish Committee.[78] It provided a comprehensive reexamination and critique of Immigration Commission findings and, in effect, presented a brief against the imposition of additional restrictions on the southern and eastern European immigration. Hourwich took up the challenge issued by Jenks and Lauck that anyone differing from their judgments on immigration "examine carefully the data in an unprejudiced spirit before he condemns the conclusions."[79]

Hourwich refuted pronouncements that the immigrants were negatively affecting the economic well-being of native-born Americans and the old immigrants. The new immigrants were variously charged with displacing American workers, depressing wages and the standard of living, increasing rates of unemployment, and retarding the growth of trade unionism. They were, moreover, regarded as predominantly unskilled in contrast to the old immigrants. Hourwich contended that immigration had not displaced American workers or previous immigrants; it had only responded to labor shortages stemming from a greater demand than domestic labor could supply. Immigration did not bring about unemployment because immigration rates varied with domestic economic cycles. This conclusion had been anticipated in the *Reports of the Industrial Commission on Immigration*.[80] Neither did immigration lower living standards of American workers; eastern and southern European immigrants were not living below the level of their immigrant predecessors. In addition, Hourwich argued that the working day grew shorter as immigration continued, and union activity had grown with immigration.[81] Accordingly, he maintained that a specific immigration problem did not exist; rather the controversial issues were at base those of labor, which itself comprised many subsidiary questions unaffected by immigration. Consequently, solutions to problems about unemployment, labor organization, working hours, and the like did not lie in immigration restriction or its complete prohibition.[82]

Although the Immigration Commission made extensive use of the proliferating economic, social, and demographic data on immigration, the gross dichotomy between the "old" and the "new" immigration persisted in the face of information that should have undermined it. The assumptions underlying the old/new distinction were part of the received wisdom on matters of race difference among Europeans. These assumptions, in turn, constrained the interpretation of the economic and social data examined by the Immigration Commission. Jenks and Lauck cited a racial as well as an economic rationale for the quota law of 1924, the final restrictionist triumph, in the sixth edition of *The Immigration Problem:* "Why do we need permanent restriction of this drastic character? . . . In the first place a conviction has been rapidly growing in this country to the effect that a limit to racial difference has been reached. If not restricted it was felt that immigration of the type coming to this country in such large numbers just before the war would very soon change the entire racial make-up of the American people."[83] Accordingly, Hourwich's conclusion that people in government "took scant notice of the academic disquisitions in the domains of anthropology, ethnology, sociology, eugenics, and political science, which presented the old arguments of the Know-Nothings dressed up in a modern scientific garb" is too facile.[84] The commission remained indifferent to Boas's critique of racial formalism and the putative behavioral correlates of race. Old assertions about race gained uncritical acceptance. Although the commission offered recommendations phrased in terms of the economic and social dimensions of immigration, its indifference to the documented distinctions between groups of old immigrants and to parallels between particular groups of old and new immigrants was dictated by a residue of race-based thinking. Jenks and Lauck had after all provided a racial rationale for their support of restrictionist measures, and their book followed closely on the reports of the Immigration Commision. Despite his own prefatory remarks alleging official indifference to academic debates about race, Hourwich offered an economic critique that nonetheless pointed out problems of interpretation following from the commission's emphasis on the race differences among various immigrants.[85]

For example, the gross characterization of the new immigration held that it was essentially an immigration of unmarried, unskilled mostly illiterate males, who would eventually return to Europe after earning money in the United States. A more refined examination of the old and the new immigration reveals that the German, Scandinavian, and English newcomers of previous decades were more often male than the more recent Jewish, Bohemian, and Portuguese immigrants. More illiteracy appeared among the old Irish and German immigrants than among their new Bohemian and Moravian counterparts. As for the transient status of new immigrants, linked often to the displacement of native-born workers, the Armenians, Dalmatians, Portuguese, and Jews of the new immigration were much more likely to remain in the United States than the English, Germans, and Scandinavians of the old immigration. Except for the Scots, the Jewish immigration included a higher percentage of skilled workers than any group of old immigrants. Also, against the expectation of the old/new dichotomy, the Irish compared with the Italian immigration contained a smaller percentage of skilled laborers.[86]

The amalgam of economic complaint and racial hostility in the prevailing critique of the immigrants distorted many contemporary views of the old immigration. Its seamier aspects, well-documented at the time, were often ignored or shrouded beneath an idealization of hearty, self-reliant farmers and skilled artisans, eager to become Americans and to spurn Old World loyalties and habits. No ghettos or ethnic enclaves—"insoluble clots" in Ross's view,[87]—for these people, much less pauperism and crime, supposedly the twin evils of the new, city-centered immigration. Hourwich described portrayals of the old immigration as "the Golden Age in a modern version."[88] He pointed out the criticisms of the old immigrants at the time of their settlement, when they were regarded by the native-born citizenry in precisely the same terms as the southern and eastern Europeans of a few decades later. Charges of pauperism, congestion, moral decay, illiteracy, resistance to assimilation, and so forth abounded.[89] Even the Immigration Commission acknowledged some of the burdens of the old immigration. In reviewing American immigration law, the Immigration Commission noted the efforts by members of Congress from New York State in the 1870s to press for federal legislation that would secure appropriations to help the state defray the costs of managing the new arrivals in New York City.[90]

Other commentators on the immigration of the 1890s remarked on the similarities between old and new immigrants as well as on the positive contributions of the latter in improving neighborhoods. Kate Claghorn, an economist and a consultant to the Industrial Commission, thus pointed out that recent immigrants

> arrive here at no lower social level . . . than did their predecessors. Their habits of life, their general morality and intelligence can not be called decidedly inferior . . . . The Italian ragpicker was astonishingly like his German predecessor, and the Italian laborer is of quite as high a type as the Irish laborer of a generation ago. In some cases the newer immigrants have brought about positive improvements in the quarters they have entered. Whole blocks have been transferred from nests of pauperism and vice into quiet industrial neighborhoods by the incoming of Italians and Hebrews.[91]

Claghorn's analysis demystified the distinction between old and new immigrants when that race-based dichotomy continued to shape many political, scholarly, and popular attitudes.

Forgotten, too, in the idealization of the old immigration was the Reverend Charles Loring Brace's admonitions in 1872 about "the dangerous classes of New York," formed in no small part by the foreign-born. They constituted a sizable proportion of the city's prison population in 1869 and most of the rest, Brace surmised, were the children of immigrants. Although the "dangerous classes" were mostly born in the United States, their parents were Irish and German immigrants. Seeing these predatory youth as a dire threat to life and property in the city, Brace endorsed "placing out"—the export of impoverished youth from New York to the socially and morally healthier climate of the American West, where they could be adopted. Then the redemptive discipline of farm labor would check the corrosive influence of metropolitan overcrowding, poverty, and vice.[92] Distribution as a response to urban social problems thus antedates post-1881 immigration.

Other critiques of Jenks and Lauck, the Immigration Commission, and the old/new distinction derived from sources not closely identified with the new immigration. Hourwich and the IRO obviously were not neutral observers. Paul Douglas, the economist and later senator, observed that Hourwich's partisan approach to immigration had diminished the persuasiveness of his findings.[93] Still, Hourwich's economic reading of the Jewish immigration found support in the work of scholars removed from the ideological fray. Douglas, for example, presented a statistical and methodological critique, fully consistent with Hourwich's views, of some of the interpretations offered by Jenks and Lauck and the Immigration Commission regarding the skill levels of the immigrants.

Specifically, Douglas took Jenks and Lauck to task for their claim that the skill level of the old immigration (19.5 percent) was more than double that of the new immigration (8.9 percent) based on a sample that excluded Jewish immigrants, the most skilled of the newcomers. The obvious problem of a biased sample was compounded by Jenks and Lauck in comparing the old and the new immigration during a single time period, 1899–1909.[94] By so doing, they made the unwarranted assumption that the skill level of the old immigration had remained unchanged from the time when it was the dominant component of immigration to the United States. Methodologically, the appropriate comparison would have been between the old immigration at the earlier period with the new immigration between 1899 and 1909. Douglas undertook that comparison between the old immigration in the years 1871–1882 and new immigration, first in terms of the percentage of skilled workers out of the total number of immigrants in each category and, second, in terms of the percentage of those with occupations. Douglas's two comparisons show that 11.4 percent of old immigrants and 16.6 percent of new immigrants were skilled—a clear reversal of Jenks and Lauck and the Immigration Commission. When only those with occupations were included, the comparison points to very similar skill levels for the old and the new immigrants in their earliest years in the United States.[95] Skilled workers comprised 22.9 percent of the old immigration and 18.1 percent of the new immigration.

## A Domestic Immigration Policy

The IRO perspective on the relationship between immigrants and the American labor market cuts to the heart of the immigration controversy in the early years of the twentieth century. Hourwich's findings dove-tailed with the IRO position, indeed giving the latter a foundation built on economic research. The very rationale of the organization in fact depended on exposing the proposition, in vogue since the early 1890s, that immigration was outpacing the capacity of the country to employ the newcomers. Restrictionist proposals, such as the literacy test, offered only an arbitrary means for evading the real need; that is, the IRO located the many collateral problems of immigration not in an excess of immigrant labor, but rather in its immobility.[96] "What this country needs is a *domestic immigration policy*, looking to an intelligent distribution and absorption of our immigrants," proclaimed an IRO bulletin.[97]

By contrast, immigrant exclusion would effectively shut off the supply of large numbers of men to areas of the country in need of their labor.[98] The IRO interpreted immigration as a great source of national vitality, a wholly beneficial and economically gainful influence in the life of the country. For the IRO, the notable contribution of American Jewry to the debate about immigration was the promulgation of a "socially constructive immigration policy."[99] The congestion of immigrants in New York, and in Boston and Philadelphia to a much lesser extent, inhibited the full realization of all of the potentialities for national development contained in a vigorous and continuing immigration. At the same time, the failure to match the existing immigrant population to real labor needs would destine people to unemployment and chronic insecurity.

The domestic immigration policy energetically espoused by the IRO aimed to disentangle two key elements of the immigration controversy—

admission of immigrants to the United States and distribution. Too often, these elements were merged, especially by the restrictionists. While sometimes giving lip service to the importance of distribution, they proposed to deal with immigrant congestion in large cities by limiting the admission of new immigrants. Jenk's position is a case in point:

> Some may argue that . . . distributive plans tend to stimulate immigration; but personally I have always favored all reasonable efforts made in this direction, and have frequently publicly urged distribution by either private agencies or proper government measures. In fact I believe it to be one of the most serious problems facing this country. So great has this need become that I feel it would be a good thing to have less immigration for a while until we can make more headway in distributing the immigrants who are now here, and until we work out adequate plans for those who are to come.[100]

The IRO argued that distribution issues fit squarely into domestic policy. An effective program of distribution did not require change in admission criteria and, in fact, could emerge without any reduction in the rate of immigration into the United States. Absorption of immigrants depended only on the resources that the country was willing to commit to the task. Rationality and good planning, not restrictive immigration laws, would effect a satisfactory adaptation of the immigrants.[101]

The IRO's response to Jenks might have convinced skeptics if optimal circumstances had obtained. Under the most favorable conditions, continuing immigration would proceed in tandem with a fully organized, large-scale, government subsidized distribution program. It would be an IRO writ large, so to speak. The government would establish a labor bureau to gather systematic and accurate information about employment needs throughout the country; then it would provide transportation for destitute immigrants to reach the towns and cities where their employment was ensured.

Free and mobile in the United States, immigrants could then turn their shoulders to productive labor in the course of becoming good citizens. However, their labor had to match the needs of particular locales. Distribution was a critical stratagem in promoting the accommodation of all immigrants to the new country and in liberating the considerable energy and enterprise of the newcomers for the ultimate collective good. Although immigration restriction would certainly imperil the beleaguered Jews of eastern Europe, it would also work against the long-term national interest. Restriction would, moreover, compromise the ideal of America as a safe haven for the tormented and oppressed of other lands. In the IRO view, the newcomers and the country at large stood to gain immeasurably, both from resistance to restriction and from a rational plan to pair each newcomer with a job. Liberal immigration policies enabled the United States to live up to its highest ideals while promoting healthy economic and industrial growth.[102] National self-interest and democratic ideology would converge only if immigration was not artificially limited to particular ethnic categories or linked to skills and wealth levels. Unskilled labor and poverty were social debilities of Old World life rather than expressions of inherent temperamental limitations of an entire people.

Ironically, the Immigration Act of 1907, which created the Immigration Commission, also established the Division of Information within the Bureau of Immigration. The division had the potential for realizing the goals of the IRO on behalf of all immigrant groups. It aimed "to promote a beneficial distribution of aliens admitted into the United States among the several States and Territories desiring immigration."[103] Supervised by T. V. Powderly, a former commissioner-general of immigration and long-time labor leader, the division was fiscally restrained from the beginning. Powderly sympathized with the plight of Jewish immigrants, considering them "sober, peaceful, and industrious," an asset to the United States.[104] Moreover, he admired the IRO and, particularly, the fact that Jews more than any other group recognized the pivotal importance of immigrant distribution.[105] Powderly, in turn, was regarded as "a man possessed of a fine social vision and practical capacity and who has for the last seven years been rendering the best possible service within the restrictions that are arbitrarily imposed on his Division."[106] The IRO took particular satisfaction in the formation of the division, although its initial enthusiasm soon waned. The IRO criticized the low level of official commitment to providing the resources essential for a successful dispersion program.

Even before 1907, the Bureau of Immigration had emphasized the importance of distribution in the assimilation process. For example, Frank P. Sargent, commissioner-general of immigration, advocated effective measures of distribution in his annual report for 1903, emphasizing the destructive effects of alien colonies on American soil, which are "a menace to the physical, moral, and political security of the country." Furthermore, such ethnic settlements inhibited the circulation of manpower to areas of the United States most in need of labor and most likely to exercise a beneficial influence on the newcomer.[107] In Sargent's view, distribution would effectively neutralize the single greatest threat of immigration. Bressler commented favorably on Sargent's observations, noting that the establishment of the IRO had foreshadowed them.[108] In fact, the IRO took credit for inspiring government interest in the general problem of distribution.[109] The IRO also expected that the modest distribution model that it had created would stimulate a much expanded version under the auspices of the Division of Information: "Our work is slowly percolating through the minds of legislators and there are hopeful signs that eventually the solution which we have been carrying out in our own limited way and with our limited funds, will be given a much wider scope."[110]

The division set out to collect information from around the country on resources, manufacturers, and the physical features of each state or territory to publish these facts in various languages for dissemination by request among immigrants at various disembarkation points. Many of the positions available through the division were for agricultural workers or unskilled common laborers. Later, the division collected information on "industrial opportunities"—reports on the climate for business formation to distribute among people with some savings. In addition to compiling descriptions about local populations, the characteristics of various cities, taxes, banking, employment possibilities for kin, and so forth, the division also sought information from chambers of commerce and associations of manufacturers. At Ellis Island, the work of the division was publicized in pamphlets printed in the major languages spoken by the arrivals. In addition, the immigrant press published details about the division and the location of its New York office. States and territories were also allowed to maintain agents at immigration stations so that they could immediately present new arrivals with information about the opportunities available in their locales.

Just as the IRO had at times encountered suspicion that it abetted strike-breaking with foreign labor, so too did the Division of Information face the admonition of organized labor along this same line. Labor was prepared to endorse the idea of immigrant distribution if proper investigation of industrial conditions revealed that immigrants would not be sent to jobs embroiled in labor disputes and if job information were also provided to unemployed American workers. Still, the rhetoric of organizations such as the Knights of Labor betrayed the common hostility of unions to the new immigrants. Distribution would scatter newcomers—"the scum of the Old World"—who were crowding urban centers and would prevent or mitigate "hotbeds of anarchy."[111]

Likewise, private employment agencies opposed a competing federal office seeking to match workers with jobs. Shortly after the founding of the division, Powderly reported that one employment agency circulated a rumor, which received wide publicity among unions, that the division had sent workers to replace strikers. The division had not engaged in displacing workers who were idle because of industrial unrest, but the story was damaging. Powderly also criticized private agencies as mercenary and dishonest, believing instead that state and federal level employment bureaus or an enhanced Division of Information would more effectively and honestly cope with unemployment.[112]

Through the division's first two years of operation, 5,008 immigrants found work in 39 states and the District of Columbia. Of this number, 2,565 were employed on farms.[113] Measured against a total European immigration to the United States of 1,891,467 in the same period, the impact of the division on urban immigrant congestion was insignificant.[114] It remained equally ineffective in subsequent years. The necessary organization for an orderly and large-scale plan of distribution and the allocation of resources to support it were never forthcoming.

Immigrant distribution seemed like a very good idea, one that even the restrictionist-minded Immigration Commission could endorse. Notably, only one recommendation of the eight submitted by the commission went beyond measures of exclusion to consider the welfare of the immigrant, and that recommendation supported effective distribution.[115] Economist Frances Kellor pointed out shortly after publication of the *Reports* that the commission's support of distribution through an extension of the work of the Division of Information "is recommended in so colorless a way that it carries little conviction."[116] The division worked with only a small budget and maintained a policy of furnishing labor information only when requested by the immigrant, who in most instances was utterly unaware of this service. Moreover, very few states took advantage of the legal provision sanctioning the placement of state agents at port cities to induce immigrants to resettle in their areas.[117]

What the Division of Information required but never achieved was a well-planned, activist scheme that would direct immigrants to jobs and would, moreover, subsidize their travel from the port city to the inland community where employment was likely. Without adequate financial support, the division could only languish far short of the expectations at its founding. Although the division carried out surveys of employment opportunities around the country and issued information about job opportunities to immigrants, its efforts were not commensurate with the task before it. The commissioner-general of immigration, acknowledging the problematic sources of the new immigration and its less assimilable qualities, wrote hopefully of the Division of Information in 1908: "Had this enterprise been entered upon a decade ago . . . the unequal distribution and consequent incomplete, slow, and unsatisfactory assimilation of foreigners which has been so apparent to all, and which constitutes the chief danger of practically unrestricted immigration, would have been to a large extent avoided."[118] Had it emerged years before in the form it took in 1907, the commissioner-general's prediction would not have been realized. Without an adequate commitment of resources, the division could only remain feckless.

Kellor attributed the encumbrances limiting the division to the same economic fears motivating the restrictionists. Specifically, critics of the division believed that it might encourage immigration and that distribution might additionally bring immigrant workers to places where a glut of labor existed.[119] Suffering the same criticisms from restrictionist quarters, the IRO could only push on, hoping to expand its work on behalf of the immigrants and to demonstrate simultaneously the economic value of immigration to a steadily increasing number of people.[120]

The IRO's critique of the Division of Information appeared in several venues, including Bressler's presentation to the Immigration Commission on behalf of the IRO. In response to the question, "What, in your opinion, can the National Government do to assist immigrants on their arrival at United States ports?" Bressler argued forcefully for the improvement of the division. He recommended enhancement of the labor information that it collected and advancement to indigent immigrants of the cost of transportation to jobs. In this way, even if the government could not fully defray its own costs from the head tax, the immigrants would quickly become an industrial asset to the country. Much was to be gained, even at the small cost of transportation. The most important component of adjustment to the United States was, Bressler argued, economic assimilation, and this vital process could go forth effectively only if workers were able to reach available jobs. Subsidizing travel would also have the added benefit of helping to reduce the general flow of the American population toward large cities.[121]

Gratified that distribution had gained official recognition by the formation of the Division of Information, the IRO was not reluctant to criticize the lack of government support essential to the realization of its enormous potential. The IRO argued that with an additional commitment of resources the division could effect the adjustment of labor to the market far beyond the capabilities of an efficient but small private organization such as the IRO.[122] Reviewing the first seven years of its existence, the IRO lamented that the division had fallen into "respectable mediocrity and a smug conservatism because of the traditions inherited from the past." In its first seven years, when the male immigration to the United States reached 3,164,139, the division provided information to 121,477 job seekers. Of this number, only 25,299 acted on the advice they received and settled beyond the port cities of the east.[123]

In continuing its analysis of the division's work during 1912–1913, the IRO pointed out that the distribution of immigrants was not only very limited but also impermanent in all likelihood. The division received 19,881 requests for information, with the majority represented by unskilled, native-born Americans.[124] Only 5,025 people relocated, and the majority settled in New York State (1,707), New Jersey (1,114), and Pennsylvania (978). The IRO questioned the long-term value of these paltry results for the cause of distribution because immigrants resettled so close to one of the ports of entry could, relatively easily, make their way back to the city.

The underlying problem, the IRO argued again, lay in the failure of the government to subsidize transportation costs. Otherwise, efforts to match workers to labor markets would pivot on the worker's ability and willingness to expend his own meager resources for a distant job, far removed from a more familiar life among immigrant compatriots in the east. The preponderance of relocations to New York, Pennsylvania, and New Jersey likely was related to the same financial considerations; transportation costs from the ports to destinations in these states were more manageable.[125] Agreeing with the division's inspector in charge at New York that "transportation is still the great stumbling block to distribution,"[126] the IRO concluded, "Without the means at its disposal to deflect the stream of immigration by defraying the cost of transportation of worthy immigrants to points in the interior where employment may be found for them, the information it gives and the work it performs becomes [sic] from the practical point of view, of unappreciable value."[127]

Written just before World War I and the cessation of immigration, this assessment pointedly summarized the work of the Division of Information. It would never attain the promise held out for it by the IRO, which emphasized that giving information is fundamentally different from the actual distribution of immigrants and the provision of transportation.[128] The IRO's exasperation at the failures of the "straight-jacketed" division was equally great when the funds collected by the head tax on each arriving immigrant were not directed toward transportation costs. In sum, no effort at assimilation, including immigrant distribution, "will be more than superficially successful unless it results in preparing the Federal Government for the taking over on a larger scale of the work done by the philanthropic agencies at the present time."[129]

The failure of the federal government to take measures that would have enabled the Division of Information to make a decided impact on immigrant concentrations and glutted labor markets continued to rankle the IRO until it suspended operations. In its continuing plea for an engaged, well-planned domestic immigration policy, the IRO found little but frustration in the actual working of the division, promising in its aims but ineffectual owing to its detachment from the specific labor problems of the immigrants. Even in cases in which potential employers, usually farmers, were willing to advance the cost of transportation to the immigrant, few availed themselves of the opportunity. Lacking the network of social support that the IRO provided immigrants traveling to jobs in the interior, the Division of Information, with its poor planning and minimal involvement, could not induce newcomers to leave the eastern ports in large numbers. Even the most pioneering of the immigrants who accepted paid transportation from employers gravitated to jobs within easy access of the familiar cultural milieu of New York.[130]

Once off the boat and cleared by immigration authorities, the immigrant ceased to be of much interest to the various government agencies, except as a possible exemplar of the problems attributed to the new immigration. In one of its final bulletins, shortly after Bressler's resignation and American entry into World War I, the IRO compared its own achievements with modest resources with the pressing needs for distribution on a much greater scale:

> If an institution limited in resources and in scope can accomplish within its field so great and efficient a work, what is there that stands in the way of the nation enlisting its efforts in the work of immigrant distribution on a national scale? With the end of the war, a redistribution of our population will become a necessity. New industries will arise, commerce and trade take on new impetus. . . . Will we then permit the immigrant to waste and squander his ability and energy in crowded tenements and Ghettos?
>
> Let distribution be the key-note of all our future legislation on behalf of immigrant and industry. The citizen of a country as the present crisis clearly shows is a nation's chief asset. The immigrant is America's future citizen. Let us not waste his will, spirit, energy and ability on the desert air. Let us pursue the policy of systematic intelligent distribution. Let this be the knell which summons our "laissez faire" policy to its final resting place.[131]

Befitting the pronouncements of an inspired social movement, the IRO's tone in the face of disappointment remained almost prayerful.

Whereas World War I closed off the European immigration, the crisis atmosphere of American entry into the war stimulated an experiment in distribution that all of the rational argument until that time could not achieve. Ironically, this relatively successful distribution of labor evolved out of the failed Division of Information. Early in 1918, the U.S. Employment Service was founded, when the Secretary of Labor separated the Division of Information from the Immigration Bureau. Prompted by the need for workers in war industries, the service placed five million workers in jobs during the next eighteen months. With a diminished appropriation following the armistice, the service languished, with its functions taken over by state agencies. Its discernible, short-term accomplishments compared with those of the Division of Information were due to a much more active process of job placement, including the receipt of reliable requests from businesses for particular kinds of workers at specified wages and a prompt matching of jobs with job seekers. In other words, the old laissez-faire pattern of the division briefly gave way in crisis to a relatively effective, engaged program to introduce some order and planning into the labor market.[132]

## Conclusion

With the triumph of immigration restriction in the quota statute of 1924, immigration issues faded until the eve of World War II, when relatively small numbers of refugees were able to settle in the United States. Dormant for more than two decades, the idea of distribution as a means of immigrant adjustment surfaced at war's end with the arrival of more refugees. A notable postwar study of the refugee immigration promoted dispersion, rationalizing it in the same terms used by the IRO: "A high degree of concentration draws undue attention to a group, like the Japanese in California and the Jews in New York, often retards assimilation, and sometimes gives rise to fear, dislike, and other unfavorable reactions. A wide distribution . . . facilitates the incorporation of immigrants into American society and lessens the strain on intergroup relations."[133]

As to the post-1965 immigration, new concerns have supplanted some of the old worries about assimilating the immigrants. The pressures of a large influx of newcomers on local schools, medical facilities, welfare budgets, and other community resources now motivate attempts to thin out ethnic enclaves. The clustering of newcomers in areas with scarce housing and few employment opportunities also prompts attempts to distribute the refugees to more suitable places.[134] Despite some new emphases, current dispersion efforts and other policies that might quickly lead newcomers to economic self-sufficiency reinvent in some ways the goals of immigrant distribution articulated in the early years of the twentieth century.

Other shifts regarding the contemporary immigration are also notable, particularly in regard to the role of the federal government and the status of those in flight from political threat. Current social policy on resettlement and distribution focuses on refugees. In American law, refugees are now formally distinguished from other immigrants. Beginning in the early 1960s, the federal government dramatically expanded its prerogatives regarding refugee resettlement. Federal assistance was directed mostly toward Cubans until 1975, when refugees from southeast Asia began to command attention and new legislative initiatives. The Refugee Act of 1980 created the Office of Refugee Resettlement to establish a single, coordinated program joining together all previous federal efforts to assist new arrivals. Before 1960, assistance rendered to refugees was provided by private or religious organizations.[135] Although private institutions no longer play an exclusive role in resettlement, fourteen religious and nonsectarian agencies have received federal grants to aid newcomers in the adjustment process.[136] Nevertheless, residence is not mandated by law and however much immigrant communities are encouraged to disperse, contemporary immigrants, like their predecessors, gravitate to locales that promise cultural familiarity.

# — 3 —

# Internal Debates

The IRO was not only an interlocutor in the rancorous public debate on immigrants and immigration in the early twentieth century; it was also part of an internal Jewish discourse on congestion, unemployment, and the proper relationship of immigrant Jews to American society. The IRO stated its positions through various formal channels that provide an important official view of the organization. The documentary record of annual reports and the like is nonetheless top-heavy, furnishing a restricted version of the encounter between eastern European Jews and their American Jewish benefactors. The statements of IRO officers, especially Cyrus Sulzberger and David Bressler, however, did not in any way dissemble or misrepresent the record. In fact, both Sulzberger and Bressler often provided candid views of the many problems of directed resettlement, and Sulzberger was not reluctant to criticize the arrogance of German American Jews and their institutions. Still, however ingenuous their observations and unusual their empathy and understanding, the IRO leadership spoke in an official capacity that also reflected a personal experience of German American Jewish culture, privilege, and distance from the immigrants.

For that reason, it is necessary to consider other points of view in the Jewish discussion of the IRO itself, the social and economic problems that motivated its founding, and their proposed solutions. These perspectives include those of the Yiddish press; immigrant intellectuals, such as I. M. Rubinow and Boris Bogen; and immigrant clients and ordinary observers of the IRO. Yiddish newspaper coverage and editorials often criticized the attitudes of German American Jews toward the immigrants and also provided a popular forum for letter writers eager to defend or indict the IRO and American Jewish philanthropies. Rubinow joined this very scrappy, left-leaning Yiddish press in that vigorous critique, which also questioned the entire philosophy underlying systematic dispersion. Bogen, by contrast, concurred with the IRO, the UHC, and the Anglo-Jewish press regarding the social pathology of the ghetto and how to treat it. Some clients of the IRO wrote letters directly to the organization or to the Yiddish newspapers about their early attempts at new beginnings in interior communities.[1] Although the immediacy of their own experience provided only a narrow view of the issues, the immigrant letter writers offer revealing glimpses of internal migration in the lives of those most affected by organized immigrant distribution.

There was certainly no singular immigrant view of resettlement schemes in the abstract, and immigrant letters from across the country reflected the course of each individual's effort to fashion a better life. Above all, immigrants were active, vocal, and contentious, whether in opposition to or in support of the IRO and allied organizations. Numerous letters from successful resettlers describe the East Side in terms consistent with those of its harshest critics. These human documents describe the satisfactions of steady work in more congenial settings and recount suffering and despair left behind in New York.

For example, a Mr. Goldstein was sent in 1907 to Columbus, Ohio, "a beautiful and clean city," where he secured a decent job. New York, by contrast, he said, was a "boiling kettle," where a "greener" such as himself could only suffer "hunger, thirst, and insults from all sides." Seeking work from five in the morning at a wage likely to be insufficient to his needs, the writer bemoaned the fact that his only reward was a bench in Hester Park.[2] Such testimonials implied that similarly bright prospects awaited those willing to start anew. A letter written to the IRO and the Yiddish press from "Morris Greenberg, the painter," also condemned New York and urged its abandonment: "Ghetto life in New York is very injurious and abominable whereas here in Toledo we live in clean, sanitary rooms with sunlight and air instead of living in some dingy, dirty rooms on the top floor of a tenement house in Monroe or Cherry Street. My advice is, away from New York, America is big enough where every honest and willing worker has a chance to earn his living."[3] The IRO made abundant use of such commendations in its advertising and exhibitions.[4]

In contrast, some immigrants condemned the IRO. They complained about poor wages, abusive treatment by local agents or employers, and the desperation to which some were believed driven by alleged IRO inhumanity. A letter to *The Jewish Daily News* from Cleveland, for example, implicated the local agent, believed by the writer to be incompetent and heartless, in the suicides of two men sponsored by the IRO.[5] The public complaints intensified the debate and added an emotional element to the intellectual discussion of distribution.[6]

### Philanthropy, Scientific Social Work, and Charity

From the beginning of Jewish immigration out of eastern Europe, the developing relationship between immigrants and German American Jews was discussed extensively in the spirited Yiddish press of the day. The topics for commentary were often variations on the theme of arrogance toward the immigrants. Many took strong exception to philanthropies that assumed that the East Side—the very soul of eastern European Jewish life in the United States—exercised an inimical influence. The sharpest critiques of the ghetto represented fundamental assaults on *yidishkayt* (the culture of eastern European Jewry) itself, and generated an intense reaction in the press. The fundamental cleavages of culture and class between Jews of German and Russian background provided the subtext for all discussions about their relationship. Whatever the press's objection—the rationality of German Jewish reformism set against orthodoxy, the condemnation of immigrant socialists and other radicals, or the distress of German American Jews over immigrant enclaves such as the East Side—the immigrants were not passive before American Jewish action and opinion. Often wry and acerbic, immigrant opinion was a force with which American Jewish philanthropy had to reckon in setting forth its own view of the place of ethnicity, religion, and immigrant culture in American life.

Avoiding elaboration, the 1888 annual report of the UHC executive committee hints at immigrant resistance to the design of German American Jews: "The efforts of intelligent brethren to raise the standard of Judaism have been frustrated by the errors of misguided people who regard all teaching and criticism as an outrage on their suddenly acquired and misunderstood liberty."[7] In a similar vein, the UHC blamed "irresponsible local writers" for the accusation, repeated in the European Jewish press, that the UHC encouraged the emigration commissioners in New York to show prejudice against Jewish immigrants. The UHC parried the charge by pointing out that of the Jewish immigration, which constituted 10 percent of all arrivals at Castle Garden, the emigration commissioners deported only twenty-seven people as paupers.[8]

Still, the UHC's repatriation to Europe of Jewish immigrants deemed unable to support themselves by reason of age, infirmity, or lack of skills did little to diminish its cold-hearted reputation among the immigrants. Always worried about its resources, the UHC felt burdened by the immigrant tide. Immigrants who were unable to support themselves in New York but were capable of working were aided in securing jobs in the interior. Others, whose prospects for self-support were deemed grim at best, were returned to Europe. In its 1886 report, for example, the UHC indicated that 3,036 people had sought assistance in the previous 16 months. The UHC found employment for more than 1,800 immigrants. Of the remaining number, some were judged unworthy of assistance, others did not return to the UHC office, and 744 were returned to Europe because work could not be found for them. The latter lacked special skills and were "physically unable to comply with the conditions demanded in this country."[9] For 79 people regarded as incapable of any kind of work, transportation costs were paid for by the UHC. For the majority, however, the employment committee of the UHC "secured them the privilege of working their way back from here, Philadelphia, and Boston, on freight and cattle steamships."[10] People regarded as physically unfit for American labor demands would not likely have an easier time working off the cost of their trans-Atlantic repatriation on freighters and cattle boats. The continuation of this practice through the 1880s and into the 1890s could only exacerbate the hard feelings held by immigrant critics of the UHC.

Although the UHC espoused the right of immigrants to dignified treatment, it could not escape its own basic paternalistic assumptions. Consequently, a substantial ground of misunderstanding and injured pride lay between the genuine sympathy of established Jewish philanthropy and immigrant sensibilities. A year-by-year reading of the UHC records until the turn of the twentieth century reveals a clear pattern of condescension toward the erstwhile ghetto dwellers of Europe, believed to be in desperate need of the guidance of an enlightened American Jewry. The UHC's relief efforts for the sick, orphaned, or indigent and its work in distribution or finding jobs for immigrants were underpinned by a fundamental belief that the UHC was also engaged in a kind of civilizing mission. Thus, education of the youngest immigrants was especially important "so as to meet every need and insure the proper training of those too young to have succumbed to the influence of foreign ideas."[11]

Within the ideological struggles between differing visions of Jewish life in the United States, some spokesmen of German Jewish background criticized the presumptuous attitude of their confreres toward the immigrants. Sulzberger, for example, reflected on the "normal" Jew in New York:

> A normal Jew in New York is one who either himself or whose father speaks English with a German accent. An abnormal Jew in New York is one who speaks English with a Russian accent. . . . A man who speaks English with a German accent is naturally a native, but a man who speaks English with a Russian accent is a foreigner. Now it stands to reason that the hundred thousand or so native Jews of New York cannot permit the eight hundred thousand or so of foreign Jews of New York to dominate the institutions of New York.[12]

Despite his ironic humor, Sulzberger found more reason for tears than laughter in the relationship he described. More than many German American Jews, he understood that by sheer force of numbers, the eastern Europeans would not accept the effrontery of these self-appointed arbiters of Jewish communal life. Discussing the problem of unifying the institutions of German and eastern European Jews, Sulzberger asked:

> Do we wonder that a rival Jewish hospital is built, when in the Jewish hospital which is being managed by these native born Jews with a German accent, whose religion is so liberal, they offer these foreign Jews with a Russian accent, lobster, oysters and other things which they know is an aversion to the soul of the patient? Is it a wonder that these men will struggle and strive to build themselves an institution where their sick can be treated without having violence done to their conscience? . . . Can these institutions ever be unified, so long as we deliberately show our disregard of the opinions of others by literally thrusting our liberality down the throats of these poor patients?[13]

Notwithstanding the astuteness and sensitivities of distinguished leaders such as Sulzberger, an eastern European Jewish critique of the philanthropy of German American Jews emerged full blown in the pages of the

Yiddish press. It began well before the founding of the IRO and condemned the radical changes that Jewish charity had undergone in the wake
of the immigration wave.

Before the early 1880s, Jewish communities in the United States tended
toward homogeneity because the vast majority of the Jewish population
had derived from the German Jewish immigration of the 1840s and 1850s.
The earlier Sephardim had largely been absorbed, and the eastern European
Jewish presence in the United States was insignificant. Charity within the
homogeneous community was given and received in a universe of common
understanding. Donors and receivers, in effect, shared a culture, including
all that pertained to charitable relief. Membership in the Jewish community
defined one's entitlement to aid. In the Old World, the eastern Jews likewise
were accustomed to an unsystematic, personal form of charity provided to
relieve the immediate suffering of people well-known to the donors, rather
than to help ameliorate broader social problems affecting strangers. Defined above all by personal bonds and the religious value on good deeds, assistance to the needy in the experience of the immigrants aimed to relieve
immediate privation and suffering. Long-term goals of ensuring self-sufficiency, much less investigation of supplicants, were irrelevant.

The inception of "scientific charity" during the last two decades of the
nineteenth century represented, in effect, a move "from the heart to the
brain."[14] That is, professional social work reacted against old patterns of
the giving of alms, motivated only by a desire to relieve temporarily an individual need while perhaps also demonstrating the moral righteousness
of the benefactors. Donations of food or clothing might succeed in helping a person overcome a particularly harsh circumstance, but such obla-
tions had no effect in averting subsequent misfortunes. The young social
service field found the source of individual need in underlying social conditions. If congested immigrant districts were causing distress, then the
proper ameliorative strategy was to thin out these settlements by encouraging people worthy of assistance to live in more wholesome surroundings.

The rhetoric and procedure of "science," "systematic method," "investigation," and so forth could easily offend the sensibilities of the people seeking aid. IRO investigators asked personal questions of friends, neighbors,
and previous employers. Immigrants seeking assistance would often inter-
pret caseworker investigations as skeptical inquiries about their honesty or
veracity, for such questions sought to corroborate the information that
they had already provided on application. Investigation as one of several

"cardinal points" regulating relief was already emphasized by the UHC of New York in 1876.[15] The working assumption of investigation was, of course, that any applicant for aid might well be a schemer, determined to deceive his way into wholly undeserved assistance. The investigative method with its skeptical pose widened the rifts between the charities and their would-be beneficiaries, already degraded by the quest for assistance. In sharp contrast to the personal, religiously sanctioned forms of charity in eastern Europe, professional social service was institutional and impersonal, governed by a formal code of operation and requiring a budget for accountable, paid professionals and office staff. Shortly before the founding of the IRO, the character of modern social work was aptly summed up by Lee Frankel, manager of the UHC: "The art of almsgiving, practiced perfunctorily in many cases, either to remove distress from the sight of the giver or to shrive his soul, has become obsolete. In the enlightened conditions of today, neither mawkish sentiment nor superstitious fear are the impelling forces that make for the relief of the poor and the afflicted."[16]

The influx of eastern European Jews began to force a redefinition of the terms of Jewish charity in the United States and brought to the fore the asymmetrical relationship between German and immigrant Jews. The following description of this change is particularly insightful:

> Assistance was no longer claimed as a fraternal right, nor extended as a kin-like obligation. It was the imperious demand of a stricken humanity. But, as the situation lost its bitter novelty and the burden settled in onerous pressure benevolence waned and something much akin to patronage grew. The charitable association became no longer a semi-social device, whereby the more prosperous members of the community relieved the misfortune of neighbors and associates, but a tax-like charge for the indefinite relief of misery and dependence of a distinct class, different in speech, tradition and origin.[17]

This process prompted Sulzberger's incisive observations about German Jewish attitudes to the more recent immigrants. Although the material largess unquestionably was a boon to many in need of a helping hand, the social organization of assistance and the cultural assumptions implicit in the benefaction of German American Jews patronized the recipients and contributed to the polarization of older and newer Jewish communities.

The prevailing attitude toward immigrant ghettos and the belief that the eastern European Jews constituted a threat to the standing of their established coreligionists rankled greatly because it virtually repudiated an entire way of life, including, of course, the ethnic dimension of eastern European Jewish culture. For the German American Jews, disaster might be avoided if the immigrants would only submit themselves to their prudent guidance. The often superior air of philanthropy created deep resentment among the immigrants, many of whom regarded their patrons as little different from non-Jews. Animus and indignation radiated from letters and columns in the vibrant Yiddish press. Some immigrants had no compunction about trying to take advantage of charitable institutions, which in turn redoubled the commitment of the agencies to case investigation. A writer in the *The Jewish Gazette (Yidishe Gazeten)* went so far as to suggest that some regarded the UHC as a "Gentile institution, which it is a *mizva* [good deed, religiously sanctioned] to exploit."[18]

The conception of scientific charity espoused by German American Jewish organizations coexisted with the more personal, diffuse forms of assistance that the immigrants brought with them from the *shtelekh* of eastern Europe. With its locus in friendships, extended families, or the *landsmanshaft* (an organization of immigrants from the same town or area), charitable assistance among immigrants flourished. This aid received no recognition from the UHC or kindred organizations preoccupied by the financial drain of their immigrant clients. On the contrary, unsystematic personalized forms of giving might very well perpetuate a pauper class so the *shtetl* value on informal assistance, which sometimes was even rendered by the patrons of the UHC, was not desirable. Thus the UHC indicated that by 1883, its office was receiving fewer visits from "beggars and tramps," who had learned that such efforts were fruitless.[19] Nevertheless, the report continued,

[I]mpostors . . . often visit our patrons, and ask for relief, stating falsely . . . that we assist them. It ought not to be necessary to repeat . . . that the small doles which are given by private parties can do little good, and are frequently given to persons wholly unworthy of relief. *Were our friends to refuse aid in all cases at their homes and offices, and send us the money they would thus save, we could give much more substantial aid in many cases, and render outside assistance wholly needless.*[20]

The same report also provides an especially clear expression of condescension toward the newcomers as it explains how a charitable organization renders its greatest service. It was neither by investigating cases nor by providing doles, but rather by "exercising that benign influence which comes from the intermingling of rich and poor, from the sympathetic visits of friends who, though in a higher walk of life, voluntarily devote their leisure to the amelioration of the condition of their poorer brethren."[21]

The relationship between the German American Jews and the eastern Europeans, particularly as it was mediated through charitable institutions, received considerable attention in such publications as the long-running *Jewish Gazette (Yidishe Gazeten), The Jewish Daily News (Yidishe Tageblat),* and *The Jewish Daily Forward (Forverts). The Jewish Gazette,* founded in 1874, was a weekly, publishing the most newsworthy items appearing in *The Jewish Daily News.* During the first years of the century, the *Gazette* had won the largest Yiddish readership not only in New York but also in the rest of the country, where the newspaper had many more correspondents than any other Yiddish paper.[22] Through both its national Jewish readership and its attention to stories of interest outside of New York, the *Gazette* probably attracted a more diverse readership than other Yiddish newspapers. *The Jewish Daily Forward,* founded by Abraham Cahan in 1897, took a social democratic stance. It later became the most prominent Yiddish newspaper in the United States.

Focusing on arrogance and paternalism, *The Jewish Gazette,* in an 1895 issue, addressed matters of class:

> No wonder the Russian poor have come to regard help from a German Reform Jew as charity from a rich *goy* [non-Jew]. . . . All talk of "civilizing and Americanizing" is but exaggerated phrases used to insult us under a mask of friendship. . . . Among the Russian immigrants there are plenty of educated persons whose vice is their poverty and by no means any lack of civilization. The Russian Jews saw that the supercilious attitude of the Reform Jews is nothing more than an indefensible contempt of . . . rich for poor, and it is easy to see why the poor man ceased to regard the Reform Jew as his brother.[23]

*The Jewish Gazette* also countered the image of the Russian Jew as a parasite living off relief from American Jewish institutions by heralding the benevolent activities, personally and humanely rendered, of the immigrants, who were often poor themselves.

Ignored by the German American Jews was the charity of the immigrant benefactors, generous in their support of small congregations, the *landsmanshaftn,* and other seekers of aid. Ten *landsmanshaftn* were said to have supported thousands of impoverished Jews without the latter queuing up in the lobby of "Eighth Street" (the immigrant designation for the UHC) and without having to be "registered in Baron Hirsch's books."[24] The press argued that the charitable efforts by German American Jews paled before the bright image of generosity in the immigrant community.

The Baron de Hirsch Fund was also chastised for penurious, misdirected policies. *The Jewish Gazette* issued an appeal for aid to relieve the suffering and reported starvation of forty-two Jewish farm families in Canada. Although the story contained no indication that the Baron de Hirsch Fund was supporting this Jewish colony, editorial comment about the receipt of more than one hundred dollars in aid nonetheless stated, "Yes, Baron Hirsch can go on making colonies; as long as the divine spark of pity exists in the Jewish people his colonists will not be permitted to starve to death."[25]

The Yiddish press correctly saw the fund as a resourceful instrument of change directed at the immigrants. Of course, the meaning of these accomodating changes for Jewish life in the new country was a very divisive issue, and the immigrants themselves expressed various views. Anticipating a rapid breakdown of customary practice and tradition, many criticized the movement of immigrants from large centers of Jewish life and culture. German American Jews, in contrast, exhorted the immigrants to a rapid acquisition of American values and cultural patterns as the surest course to a new, secure life. A steady attenuation of all differences, excepting religious ones, between newcomers and natives was the ideal. Certainly, many immigrants shared these views or at least a less radical and comprehensive version. Americanization, after all, would entail some kind of break with Old World Jewish life. Others resisted efforts that would seriously interrupt religious or cultural continuity between Europe and the United States.

The Yiddish press remained very critical of the fund's Americanization schemes, for they were at best threatening to the superior values of the Jewish tradition. When two uptown German Jewish clothing manufacturers squared off in a fistfight at the fashionable Delmonico's, an acerbic *Gazette* editorial urged the Baron de Hirsch to initiate an uptown school dedicated to the Americanization of rich Jews. At least when a couple of tailors on Essex or Ludlow Street came to blows, the editorial stated, they fought in the synagogue or in some other Jewish institution away from the disapproving eyes of Gentiles.[26] Likewise, the Gazette reported that two

Jewish notaries publicly fought with each other and eventually went to court, where one accused the other of attempting to take away his customer. In its editorial, the paper asserted, "It would be a very good thing if Baron Hirsch would contribute $120,000 to Judaize these Americanized Jews that they may know their limits. To take earnings or customers away from another man is un-Jewish, and fighting and beating certainly is un-Jewish, for it is said: 'He who raises a hand (against his fellow-man) shall be wicked.'"[27]

## In Defense of the East Side

The Yiddish press regularly questioned the critique of the ghetto and its allegedly inimical influence in the lives of immigrant Jews. Writing in 1896, a correspondent for *The Jewish Gazette* pointed out that the term "ghetto" was never applied to districts populated exclusively by Christians. Each nationality in New York gravitated toward its own distinct neighborhood, and people of the same occupation—actors, musicians, even second-hand dealers—often lived in the same area. He thus noted that Fifth Avenue was really a ghetto of millionaires, and Thirty-Fourth Street was a ghetto of artists. The point was quite clear. People sought out those with similar background and customs, for only then would they feel comfortable and secure in the knowledge that like-minded people would provide the support and sympathy of a community. This principle explained the existence of the Jewish ghetto, not only for the obvious reason that Jews sought out one another but also because Gentiles had abandoned it to live with other Gentiles.[28] Convinced of the enormous attraction of Jews to their religious and secular institutions on the East Side, the *Gazette* reporter argued that the Baron de Hirsch Fund would be unable to "uproot them and put them in hammocks under the trees of Flushing or Bay Ridge."[29] The East Side was not such a terrible place anyway. The streets were by no means the dirtiest in New York, and Jewish homes were probably cleaner than those of other groups. Business on Canal Street was as honest as on Broadway.

The *Gazette* correspondent also pointed out the special perils of small-town life for Jews. Butcheries were nonkosher, and Yiddish speakers would experience enormous isolation. They would be greenhorns to their neighbors, and their children would be "sheenies." Sons and daughters would surely date Gentiles. Cultural practices and religious laws would go by the boards. A small town for the Jew was tantamount to prison, whereas it provided the Gentile a clergyman, a Sunday school, a club, and a saloon. Furthermore, the report argued that Jews then living in small towns looked enviously at people living in big cities. The small-town Jew would be much happier living on the top floor of a tenement on Broome Street than in a cottage in Westchester. Conceding that Brownsville was a suitable place for Jews, albeit the only one outside of New York, the correspondent still added that "one Brownsville was worse than ten New York ghettoes."[30]

In the critical spirit of the Yiddish press but in a different venue, physician-turned-economist I. M. Rubinow objected in more analytical terms to prevailing criticisms of the East Side and the specific plan of the IRO. His critique first appeared in 1903 in two successive installments of *The American Hebrew* and was reprinted soon after in *The Menorah,* the B'nai B'rith monthly.[31] During the same year, the Russian-born Rubinow also published several articles in the Jewish press in Russia assessing the relationship between German American Jews and the immigrants, including the resettlement plan of the IRO.[32] Publication in *The American Hebrew* and *The Menorah* ensured a wide readership, if not a generally sympathetic one, among American Jews, overwhelmingly disposed to accommodation. At a time when the English-language Jewish press was suffused with reports and editorials disparaging ethnic enclaves, Rubinow's article offered a rare and remarkable counterpoint in English to the prevailing wisdom about Jewish life in the immigrant settlement.

Rubinow argued forcefully that the social and economic rationale for the removal work was questionable. In the manner of all immigrants seeking out their compatriots, Jews were finding satisfaction in living among other Jews. Yet where Leo Levi had found this pattern an obstacle to the removal work, Rubinow saw its value as an end in itself: "Here they have their own press, their own theatres, their own clubs, their own atmosphere, all of which harms no one and helps to make them happier and more satisfied beings."[33] The vast majority of Jewish immigrants of the previous twenty-one years, Rubinow asserted, had achieved economic independence on their own, whether as successful businessmen or as ordinary workers. In New York, the UHC, with its "ridiculously small budget," was incapable of touching the lives of hundreds of thousands on the East Side who managed on their own.[34]

As for the use of Jewish agricultural schemes in breaking up the East Side, he found them utterly unrealistic because they contravened the trend toward urbanization and industrialization. At a time when American farmers were abandoning agriculture for the city, Rubinow pointedly remarked, "We want to drive back into the country a people that has for many centuries been devoted to trade and commerce and industry." Successful agriculture also required "money and technical knowledge, neither of which the Jew possesses." This critique was wide of the mark because programs for settling Jews on farms fell not to the IRO but to the JAIAS. Quite unconcerned with the normalization issues occupying German Jewish thought, Rubinow observed, "Value produced in the industrial field is just as much value as when brought forth from the soil by agricultural labor. Shirts, and kneepants are no less useful, no less important than cotton, corn, or wheat."[35]

On the crucial matter of the immigrant's accommodation to American life, Rubinow was direct and unequivocal in his support of "unmelted" Jewish settlements:

> Talk as much as we may about Americanization and assimilation, we have no moral or legal right to force it upon the new arrival. And if he chooses to live out his own life in his own way, without molesting any one else, he is entitled to it. A stranger among strangers in a small town, even if he makes his living, will that make him happy? If the newly-arrived Jew is to feel the difference between the oppression of his old country and the freedom granted in the new, he can only feel it in the large city—in the Ghetto, if you will. There he receives his first political lesson, which is also the most important one, that in this free country of Washington and Lincoln a Jew may look like a Jew, think like one, act like one, pray and speak like one, and yet be a respected and free citizen of the republic![36]

Rubinow's rejoinder to the advocates of removal is utterly free of the kinds of anxieties pervading the recurrent critiques of the East Side in the English-language Jewish press and in the IRO reports. In his praise of ghetto life, he did not share the self-protective posture of established Jews nor their fear that Jews themselves might be perpetuating antisemitism by their failure to alter Old World ways.

Rubinow also disagreed with Sulzberger's contention, regularly reiterated in IRO policy statements, that the Lower East Side was not large enough to contain all of the immigrants and therefore should be reduced in size. He also noted approvingly the continuing growth of the East Side and the power of a large, Jewish population.[37] He thus observed,

We may live to see New York 10,000,000 people strong. And if a large percentage of it will be Jewish, why, in the name of reason and common sense, should the Jew be sorry and worried? Can his own strength grow too heavy a burden for him? Has the Irishman ever regretted that there were too many Irish people in the city? Or has he made as much use of it as he could? Why shouldn't the Jew? Ah, but the Jew is different. Why is he different? Is he? Well, if he is, it is his own fault, for he needn't be; for votes are votes, and political power is political power.[38]

Such unabashed celebration of Jewish political strength was nothing short of extraordinary at a time when the most influential Jews cultivated as much as possible a subdued and unthreatening public image of Jewish communal life. Boasting of Jewish muscle at the ballot box did not figure in that presentation. Jewish support for a diminished ethnic settlement, on the contrary, would attenuate political influence, especially at the local level, where the Russian Jewish vote in New York had by the 1890s become "a factor to be reckoned with."[39] Furthermore, immigration critics had sounded alarms about the corruption of immigrant votes by unsavory machine politicians. Although many Jews did not want to call attention to it, Rubinow unapologetically identified the political force that the newcomers to New York could wield through the sheer power of their growing numbers.[40] In sum, the activist implications of Rubinow's observations and his forthright endorsement of eastern European political leverage and Jewish culture on the East Side stood against the more reactive, conciliatory, and accommodating positions of German American Jews.

Rubinow's views provoked letters to *The American Hebrew* and a critical editorial immediately preceding the second installment of his article. The editorial argued that because the current immigration did not flow from a "natural demand for labor," then the solution to overcrowding did not lie in "natural law." Forced immigration, rather than the ebb and flow of a labor market, governed the movement of people to the Lower East Side. Moreover, Rubinow, the editorial contended, did not consider the "struggling mass with little or no special skill" whose plight grew worse with each increase in the East Side's population. In a reiteration of the *noblesse oblige* woven through the American Jewish response to the immigrants, the editorial argued that amelioration depended on the "more enlightened guidance of men who understand the situation."[41]

Among the most important commentators on Jewish life in the immigrant quarter was, of course, Cahan. Although his newspaper, *The Forward*, publicized the work of the IRO, Cahan felt no sympathy for the East Side's detractors, who saw there only harmful influences retarding the process of Americanization. Not only had his fictional David Levinsky given lie to this claim but so too had thousands of real individuals flooding the night schools in order to learn English: "Surely nothing can be more inspiring to the public-spirited citizen, nothing worthier of the interest of the student of immigration than the sight of a gray-haired tailor, a patriarch in appearance, coming after a hard day's work at a sweat-shop, to spell "cat, mat, rat," and to grapple with the difficulties of 'th' and 'w'.[42]

Relatedly, Cahan pointed out how the Yiddish language did not inhibit the process of adjustment. On the contrary, it was an active part of the Americanization process because the Yiddish press published translations of American stories and original articles on American history and institutions.[43] Furthermore, *A Bintel Brief* (A Bundle of Letters), initiated by Cahan in 1906, featured inquiries to *The Forward* from readers grappling with problems of cultural adjustment to the new country.

### Immigrant Critics of the East Side

The contest between two visions of an appropriate and desirable Jewish life in the United States—the one articulated by Rubinow, the other by the IRO leadership—was to prove decidedly uneven. Many immigrants were quite willing to abandon the East Side for the prospect of economic self-sufficiency elsewhere and entry into a more mainstream life of the sort the German American Jews were defining and living. In their own upwardly mobile quest, many ambitious newcomers enthusiastically emulated their wealthy, Americanized brethren. An undated letter from a successful IRO resettler describes in glowing terms Jewish prosperity in Meridian, Mississippi: "The city of Meridian where I am living consists of about 75 Jewish families which are here for the last 8–10 years and are all well to do. The most part of them are very rich doing business in millions. Three quarters of them are German Jews and the rest of them are Russian Jews, but every one of them is trying get the title of a German Jew." Sharing no common ground with Rubinow, the writer advises "the enslaved Jews in New York to leave the town as quick as they can and come to get the benefit of a good climate and to conduct a good living."[44]

Boris Bogen, also Russian-born and active in Jewish communal affairs and social service, criticized Rubinow's position in economic and cultural terms. He accused Rubinow of disingenuousness, claiming that he knew very well that "the conditions of the Jews in the congested districts are unbearable." Although Bogen agreed with Rubinow that the UHC and all other philanthropies supported only a small minority of the total immigrant population, he believed that the work was important and should not be diminished. As for those who did not seek assistance, their lives were anything but ideal:

> The majority of the immigrant Jews come here with little capital, lose it, as a rule, quite rapidly, and, in the large majority of cases, turn for a livelihood to the machine. Some succeed, by superhuman efforts, in saving a few pennies, in becoming owners of stands, stores, or gain positions as contractors, but this cannot be said of the majority who still work as slaves in sweat-shops and factories.[45]

Because of poor housing and the struggle to eke out a living, Bogen asked rhetorically, "Why not make it possible for some of the East Siders to avail themselves of the opportunities that are not given in large cities?" He was equally critical of Rubinow's positive view of the East Side and its cultural institutions, which Bogen believed inhibited the process of adaptation to the new country:

> It is ridiculous to say that the Jew can display the American spirit in the large citie [sic] only, and in the Ghetto particularly. The preservation of prejudices, the adherence to superstition, the continuation of the life of the Russian and Roumanian [sic] Jew lived in the old country, under suppression and persecution, the maintaining of the downcast posture, frightened look, etc., are not signs of the freedom of this country. People are permitted to live in this country in the manner they desire but the sooner they learn and acquire the habits and customs of this country, the better it is for them and their children.[46]

Although appeals to statistics on unemployment and poor housing could in part objectify the economic arguments pitting Bogen against Rubinow, the contested view of Old World custom and style in the United

States had no resolution except in the choices that people made. The intra-mural battles among newcomers and settled citizens alike over how to be an American and a Jew persisted.

Memoir literature by immigrants offers yet another critical vantage point. In *Out of the Shadow*, for example, Rose Cohen tells with affecting detail her own Dickensian experiences as a child laborer in the 1890s, when the pitiless disregard of health, safety, and human welfare was the norm. She recalled the personal cost of seeking help from the organized charities when she and her father were both put out of work by the depression of 1893. Her mother's illness eventually drove Rose's father to "Eighth Street":

> Monday morning after eating some bread father started for "Eighth Street." He returned in the evening empty handed and sick with humiliation. When he reached the building there was already a long line of people. He stood all day waiting for his turn. He was nowhere near the "window" when the place closed. Next morning, he left at dawn. The day passed and it was dark when we heard his footsteps in the hall. When he opened the door, we saw a pair of chicken feet sticking out of a bag. Father sat down at the table and wept like a child.[47]

Likewise, Michael Gold's angry ghetto portrait, *Jews Without Money*, de-scribes the relentless poverty, exploitation, and crime that motivated his and others' radical politics. Within the Gold family, conflicts over the East Side set mother against father. She is devoted to her neighbors and content with life in the ghetto, whereas he is growing bitter with frustrated ambi-tion. Determined to leave the East Side, Gold's father plans to follow his boss to Borough Park, where, he informs his skeptical wife, they would buy a house and a lot. Mr. Gold approvingly refers to his boss's view that "a man with a future should not live on the East Side."[48]

Many immigrants leaving the ghetto made quite deliberate attempts to efface from their lives the most obvious imprints of the Old Country. Al-though they were unable to alter their accents, they could certainly change their names. Casting off Jewish-sounding names in favor of a mainstream version was part of immigrant upward mobility and connoted a certain respectability, if not refinement. Changing one's name repudiated an obvi-ous and embarrassing symbol of Jewishness and difference. Although some newcomers disparaged any tinkering with names as affectation, it met with the approval of German American Jews, many of whom had al-ready anglicized their original names. American Jewish humor early on found rich material in the rage to camouflage one's background with a new name. Comic narratives inevitably turned on the uncontrollable behaviors and habits of speech that would eventually betray the parvenu's actual origins. Besides their comedic value, these stories provide ironic folk commentaries on the limits of assimilation.

The case of Joseph Lipetz, who was sent to St. Louis in 1903, aptly illustrates the connection between name changing and mobility. After working three years as a laborer, Lipetz moved to Oklahoma City, where he began selling dry goods. Early in 1907, his wife, Anna Lipetz, arrived in New York from Russia and moved in with her sister, whom Lipetz described as "very poor and in miserable condition." Eager to be reunited with his wife but claiming a lack of money, he asked the IRO to provide Anna Lipetz with transportation to Oklahoma City.[49] The IRO demurred, reminding Lipetz that, after waiting three and a half years to send for his wife, he should have allowed a little more time to earn money necessary for her transportation from New York. Having "cheerfully footed the cost" for his resettlement, the IRO declared that he had "no further claim upon us." Nevertheless, the IRO agreed to provide transportation if Lipetz would send a contribution of twenty dollars toward the charges.[50] A little more than a year later, the IRO heard from him once again to acknowledge a letter the organization had sent to Abraham Lipitz, assisted the previous year: "In reply I beg to inform you that Abr. Lipetz is my brother, his name is now Al Lee and a partner in the business conducted by us." The message was written on stationery bearing the letterhead, "Joe Lee, Dealer in Clothing, Shoes, Gent's Furnishing Goods and Jewelry." Lee, né Lipetz, also reminded the IRO that his wife, Anna Lee, "was shipped out by you in 1907."[51]

The Lipetz brothers were not unique among IRO clients in eventually establishing themselves in business. In a number of cases, new merchants who had once sought help from the IRO wrote to the organization with offers of jobs for immigrants who had likewise been beaten down by the East Side. Thus, the brothers' growing business required a shoemaker whom they hoped to procure through the IRO.[52]

### The Jewish Labor Critique

Immigrants active in unions or the socialist movement and sympathetic Yiddish newspapers regarded with suspicion efforts of the Baron de Hirsch

123

Fund and the IRO to procure jobs for immigrants. Labor and union activists believed that organizations dominated by German American Jews lacked genuine sympathy for the economic struggles immigrant working people were waging. After all, German American Jews, often affluent merchants and employers themselves, came from higher economic and social strata. The leaders and patrons of philanthropy, it was believed, were more likely to identify with capital than with labor. Consequently, they could not be trusted to guard the best interests of ordinary working people.

Depending on the cooperation of potential employers, the IRO aroused the suspicion of labor, believing that it was really in league with capitalist interests determined to exploit a large, continuous supply of workers. Ruthless employers helped by the IRO could then hire people for arduous physical labor at substandard wages. The welfare of working people, therefore, could not be safeguarded by the IRO. Under Bressler's leadership, the organization grew very alert to damaging publicity from this sector of opinion. In discussing IRO advertisements, he noted the obstacles to promoting the organization:

> One or two instances tend to show to what lengths those whom we wish to reach will go in their suspicions concerning our motives. A letter was received by one of the Jewish dailies in which the writer calls attention "to the alliance between the Removal Office and cut throat industries in the South and West," and pointing to the advertisements for skilled help as evidence of the understanding between us. The writer asks that every effort be made by the Jewish newspapers to warn its readers against us; that we are sailing under false colors as a philanthropic institution, when we are in effect, nothing less than the paid hirelings of the "persecutors of labor."[53]

Consequently, Bressler regularly answered anti-IRO charges appearing in the Yiddish newspapers or sent directly to the organization itself. Although the latter complaints lacked the public character of the press accusations, they nonetheless reflected disparaging rumors intended to damage the resettlement work and thus had to be addressed.

Press criticism of the IRO first appeared within months of the organization's formation. A particularly scathing account in *The Forward* is illustrative. The IRO papers contain no record of rebuttal, and indeed the article may have passed without much notice owing to the fledgling state of the organization. In addition, Bressler, who took the lead in countering negative publicity, was not yet on the scene. *The Forward* alleged that the IRO was engaged in a slave trade, promoted in advertising in the Jewish newspapers.

> In spite of the fact that we get protests without end from people who have been ruined by the slave trade that is carried on by the band known as the Industrial Removal Office; in spite of the fact that so many letters have been published, written with the blood and tears of family heads and single men sold by the Industrial Office and sent away to the wildest parts of Texas and Alabama, where they are forced to do inhuman labor under the most horrible conditions, where they starve, are beaten, trampled upon . . . starved when they refuse the work that is beyond their strength, not in their line, under unbearable conditions, without getting at least some measurably decent pay—a slave trade that is unheard of—in spite of all this, this band does not stop its dark business.[54]

*The Forward* urged other newspapers, "except the *Tageblatt* which is thoroughly depraved," to refuse IRO advertisements while publicizing "this heinous crime."[55]

A few days later, *The Forward* underscored its claims with the story of Sam Sternberg and some other men in Birmingham, Alabama, where they had traveled as IRO resettlers. The personal account was introduced by a headline reading, "The slave trade of Stanton Street. How the Industrial Removal Office sells into slavery people who are sent into desert and wilderness, do hard prison labor, starve, are brutally beaten and have not even a chance to escape. A letter from a victim." Sternberg and the others went to Birmingham with the understanding that they would earn between two and three dollars a day working at their own trades and that the cost of living and general working conditions were favorable. They found instead a very different, brutal, abusive circumstance. They could not find work using their own skills but instead entered the mines, where the labor required was beyond the capacity of the staunchest among them. They had to depend on the company for room and board, furnished at such exorbitant rates that the workers were paid only two dollars after two weeks of labor. Many ran away, making their way back to New York on foot. Sternberg sold his watch for his return. All of them were starving.[56] Other letters to *The Forward* echoed these grave charges.

How much stock should be put in the anguished immigrant cries about exploitation, maltreatment, and starvation? In describing the work of the

IRO in its first months, Levi had indeed acknowledged that the young organization had made mistakes.[57] In all likelihood, some IRO clients did suffer exploitation and unfair or even cruel treatment at the hands of employers eager to take advantage of a labor market composed of poor and powerless immigrants. There was certainly no want of predatory labor contractors and employers, and the disrepute of the *padrone* system was widely known. Yet, however it may have occurred—through people misrepresenting themselves as IRO staff or errors that the organization itself may have made despite its safeguards—such conduct certainly violated the spirit and intent of the IRO mission to expand the possibilities of decent employment.

For example, the IRO cautiously examined job notices for common laborers. It remained sensitive to the unusual physical demands of some jobs, believing them inappropriate for their clients, however unskilled the latter may have been. In a brief correspondence between a Louisiana cotton grower and the IRO about procuring laborers at the rate of seventy five cents per day for men and sixty cents per day for women for arduous work, Bressler informed the grower that "there are far better opportunities in all parts of the country" and that "the kind of men who apply at our office and whom we send out of town are not men of the calibre [sic] necessary for work on cotton plantation."[58]

Relatedly, Bressler commented unfavorably on an article describing a demand for workers in Indianapolis far beyond their availability. Many of the jobs going wanting were offered by railroads and construction companies seeking hundreds of employees. One employer stated that "Americans think they are too good to wield a pick" and "we can't even get [foreigners] now."[59] Bressler commented that the article described "what is known as gang labor, a condition more or less prevalent throughout the country at this time but of which this office cannot avail itself."[60] Similarly, a Jewish immigrant in the country for three years had become a foreman and interpreter at a quarry and lime plant in Ohio. In soliciting laborers from the IRO, he specified that the work was punishing and that prospective employees must be made to understand its demands.[61] In a brief reply, Bressler explained that "we are not in a position to accept your kind offer, in as much as we doubt very much that our clientele would accept the employment offered and remain satisfied."[62] Despite the charges arrayed against it, the IRO, for reasons of both practicality and principle, did not channel workers into onerous manual labor to which they were manifestly unsuited by reason of disposition or physical ability.

Nevertheless, unskilled workers constituted annually the largest category of IRO applicants, and it was essential that positions be found for them. Early on, then, in response to popular stereotypes and to claims, such as those before the Industrial Commission, that Jews were disinclined to common labor, the IRO declared,

> The charge so frequently made as to unwillingness on the part of Jewish workmen to do manual labor is amply disproved by our experience. We have considerable numbers of men engaged in the breweries, tanneries and tin plate works of Milwaukee, the packinghouses of Omaha and Kansas City, the railroad shops in Omaha, the car shops of Lorraine [sic], Ohio, and in the street cleaning in St. Louis; the uniform testimony of their employers is that their industry and sobriety make them a most desirable class of workmen.[63]

The IRO did not, however, attempt to mitigate unemployment and congestion at any cost. Concern with the welfare of its clients remained a keynote of the organization.

In this light, assessing the veracity of the most serious charges against the IRO requires some consideration of the activities of fraudulent labor agencies in New York that misrepresented themselves to would-be employees. Indeed, the IRO was often mistakenly regarded as a labor or employment agency—a perception at odds with the IRO's operation. Promising well-paying jobs in the South, these agencies charged workers for transportation to their destination and again received money from the employers. Sometimes placed under armed guard in conditions tantamount to peonage, the workers lived in squalor and barely subsisted on the paltry fare provided. The perpetrators of this deception may well have represented themselves as agents or associates of the IRO, the UHC, or other legitimate organizations or philanthropies assisting immigrant job seekers.[64] Consequently, in answering a serious charge of exploitation or deception, the IRO would sometimes find that the complainant had never applied to the IRO.[65] For example, "Mr. Morris Weissman has not been sent by this Office" is a notation appearing at the bottom of the following undated, deeply bitter letter from Birmingham: "No better years should you have and no better chance all your life. A greener is taken and given a job for a day and afterwards he is thrown around. We hope that we shall accomplish much to prohibit people of such murders. People are taken and put in care of robbers. We shall try our best to ruin your entire work. We wish you only ruin and misfortune. You should all take a 'peculiar death.'"[66]

Other letters from Birmingham following the early complaints of ill-treatment there provided a very different picture of the IRO and its agent. In an undated letter probably written in mid-July 1905 when the IRO replied, Sam Segelman challenged the stories of inhumane conduct toward immigrants. He decried allegations circulating in New York that Jewish laborers in Birmingham were forced to work in mines. He observed that each IRO client was employed at his trade, or, if unskilled, in an iron works at a decent wage. Two men, eager to earn more money, went to work in the mines without compulsion. Segelman praised the IRO for its "holy work of spreading Jews in the south and they have a brilliant future before them."[67] Likewise, a Mr. Horsman wrote to the IRO at approximately the same time, echoing Segelman's feelings and praising the attentive and concerned Birmingham IRO agent.[68] Bressler asked the two correspondents to communicate their sentiments directly to the Yiddish newspapers "to give our friends confidence."[69] Many other immigrants, either with the encouragement of the IRO or on their own, wrote to various Yiddish newspapers to praise the organization. Their testimonials were valued as antidotes to the harmful rumors and outright misrepresentations finding their way into print. Still, the damage wrought by various complainants was never severe enough to reduce the numbers of people seeking IRO assistance. Consistently, many more people applied than could be accommodated.

In 1910, Bressler hired an investigator to scrutinize employment bureaus in New York. He visited eighty agencies and concluded that Jewish applicants did not face any serious danger of exploitation as long as the bureaus faithfully represented to their clients the kinds of jobs and wages they might expect. The most onerous jobs—farm labor, tunnel construction, railway or mill work—would likely find few Jewish applicants, even among the unskilled.

Nonetheless, it would have been extremely difficult to guard against the exploitation of individuals by an employment agency determined to misrepresent work conditions and wages.[70] Inflicting the kinds of abuses associated with the worst of the *padrones,* labor agents might induce newly arrived immigrants to accompany them, for a fee, to employment in mines, farms, or other places utilizing gang labor. Agents might collect money at the other end as well from the employer. Fresh from Europe, speaking little or no English, and ignorant of American labor practices and their rights under the law, immigrants were irresistible targets of fraudulent labor contractors. The latter could easily capitalize on the desperation of unskilled eastern and southern Europeans, who accepted the promise of high wages but found only backbreaking work under conditions akin to peonage.

Typical of these cases was the experience of Isaac Cohen, a young Sephardic Jewish immigrant from Monastir, Turkish Macedonia, who disembarked in New York in 1905. Cohen was especially eager to find work quickly to begin accumulating money for the transportation of his wife and children from the Old Country. He and other young Sephardic men with whom he had sailed were recruited almost immediately to work in a West Virginia coal mine. Conditions of work as well as wages fell very short of the agent's promises. Physically isolated, Cohen and his friends had to depend on their employer for food and shelter, provided at exorbitant prices. With steadily increasing debts to their employer and with little expectation that they could pay off what they owed, these young men found themselves in the position of wage slaves. Detained against their will, Cohen and the others exercised their only option, which was escape following a struggle with company guards.[71]

Many others endured a similar fate, but their accusations against the IRO were misdirected. The IRO stood firmly against such practices, never cooperating with enterprises that posed such risks to immigrants nor knowingly directing them to positions that did not meet acceptable wage standards and working conditions. Indeed, local IRO agents and committees served as a check on the possibilities of abuse. Thus immigrants were not sent directly to the places where they would get jobs but rather to IRO operatives, who mediated the relationship between the newcomer and his adopted community, including his employer. The IRO was powerless, however, to prevent the misuse of its name or other misrepresentations. Consequently, the organization frequently restated its intended purpose and denied any connection to dubious commercial or labor practices.

In view of its role in job placement, questions naturally arose about whether the organization was in fact an employment agency. Bressler and his colleagues wanted to correct such impressions, emphasizing the fact that the organization received no commissions from employers and that clients paid no fees. Moreover, the IRO purchased the rail tickets from New York to the immigrant's destination. The Commission on Industrial Relations documented a disgraceful record of deceit and misrepresentation on the part of employment agencies across the country.[72] Abuses of this sort were described by immigrant complainants, providing further grounds for the IRO to distance itself from these shady ventures.[73]

Immigrant labor critics and the Yiddish press directed some of their sharpest diatribes against the IRO's alleged cooperation with employers seeking replacement workers during strikes. The IRO had in fact initially sent men into striking industries before formulating a firm policy against it. Whereas some local agents and potential employers wrote to the main office stipulating that no labor radicals or agitators should be sent to fill particular jobs, there is no evidence that the IRO screened out labor activists from its applicants, much less individuals willing to join a union.

As to the recurrent charge that the IRO was a conduit for scab labor to enter striking factories and industries, it is without foundation, except for some initial instances that were quickly corrected. However, the IRO certainly did not go so far as to maintain a determined ideological stance sympathetic to union positions. Its interest lay in pragmatically abetting immigrant employment beyond New York, which often required a union card. The organization thus remained supportive of immigrants who wanted to join unions by choice or local necessity. Union membership and activity as abstract principles remained quite beside the point, although the promotion of immigrant employment did not extend to strike-breaking. Still, the rumors persisted and were not easily quelled.

Early on, Sulzberger explained before the fourth national conference of Jewish charities in 1906 why the IRO would not send workers into striking industries. He described a meeting of the IRO Executive Committee on 11 February 1902, when it found several hundred men in the application room:

> [U]pon inquiry we learned that these were men who had been sent out by the Removal Office and returned to New York. So we sat down, we four trustees, to inquire why these men had come back, and from 4 o'clock that afternoon until midnight we sat there and listened to the tales of these men, and we found that the story was in almost every instance the same. They had been sent out to take the place of strikers, and when the strike was over the old men were given back their jobs and the scabs were discharged.[74]

In a position dictated only by practical concerns, Sulzberger proclaimed that the IRO was neither pro- nor anti-union. Rather, experience had proved that the goal of decent, self-sustaining employment was much better served when immigrant labor was not directed to striking industries.

Accordingly, the IRO informed its various agents of that policy. Replacing strikers, in Sulzberger's view, would result in undesirable short-term employment and the added burden of such cases reverting to the organization.[75] The policy was purely pragmatic. The IRO's repudiation of activities that would exacerbate labor strife, particularly strike-breaking, also figured in an early annual report of the parent JAIAS describing the resettlement of immigrant workers in Rochester: "Our work in the city of Rochester has been somewhat hampered during the past several months on account of the protracted strike which has existed in the clothing industry there, and in accordance with the well-defined and established policy of the Society, avoiding any interference with the labor question, we have sent to that city only such persons as were engaged in trades entirely alien to that in which the difficulty existed."[76] Relatedly, a simple inquiry in 1905 from Rabbi Feuerlicht, secretary of the newly formed removal committee of Indianapolis, "May I ask whether the Removal Office sent any men from N.Y. to break the Teamsters' Strike in Chicago?",[77] elicited a terse reply:" [I]t has been the strict policy of our Institution to send no people to any place where there are labor troubles."[78] Sounding the same theme, the IRO also reported that its representatives visited large industrial concerns in the Midwest, where they spoke with managers and superintendents about labor available through the IRO. Some of these factories requested that the New York Office send out workers but "before any men were sent . . . the prospective employers were required to give assurances that the men would receive fair compensation for their labor, steady employment in favorable environment, and last, but most important, that the requisition . . . was not made in anticipation of labor troubles."[79]

The IRO's refusal to place men in striking industries was reiterated by Bressler in a letter published in *The Forward* refuting charges of IRO hostility to organized labor. Bressler described as "unalterable" the IRO policy of not sending workers to a city where a strike was in progress. He explained that IRO agents throughout the country had a standing instruction to inform the New York office immediately of strike activity. Any agent attempting to send IRO clients into striking industries would be immediately discharged. Bressler continued, "[W]e welcome applicants who are members in good standing of any labor organization; for we regard the union card virtually as the laboring man's passport, and we find from our experience that it is of invaluable assistance to the man who is seeking

employment in a strange city. You will therefore recognize how utterly unfounded and ridiculous are the charges made against us that we are 'in
league' with Western Railroads and Merchants Associations.[80]

In addition to communications from IRO agents reporting on strike activity, workers or unions in various towns also alerted the main office to
labor actions. A notice from the I. W. W. Press Committee in Akron on 27
March 1913, for example, informed the IRO of the following: "All rubber
raincoat makers out on strike in Akron, Ohio. Request all fellow workers
not to come to Akron. Strike is on in full force, 20,000 out. There has [sic]
been men shipped in from New York employment agencies with expectation there was no trouble here but when they arrived they turned back to
their hometowns. Expect to have all factories tied up at the end of this
week."[81] The following day, Bressler wrote to the I. W. W. Press Committee
that the local IRO agent had already passed the information about the
Akron strike to the main office and requested that no additional workers
be sent to the city. He stated that the IRO was complying with that request
and that any raincoat makers arriving in Akron were doing so without the
sponsorhip of the IRO.[82] On other occasions, Bressler sometimes requested that the correspondent send word when the strike had been settled so that the IRO could again direct workers to that community. The
IRO's final and most public denial of complicity against the interests of
striking workers occurred in Bressler's testimony before the Commission
on Industrial Relations.[83]

The issue of strike-breaking dogged the organization throughout its existence. Although the periodic charges of antilabor bias were without
foundation, a lingering distrust of the UHC may have had a firmer basis.
That in turn reinforced labor's general suspicion of the motives underlying all philanthropy, inevitably reinforcing skepticism about the motives
of the IRO. Unlike the IRO, the UHC did not address allegations of complicity against striking workers, such as the following case:

> In 1894, during the strike of the textile workers in West Hoboken, among
> whom were also a number of Jews, the 8th Street Charities sent in a whole
> contingent of *green* strikebreakers. The entire city was infuriated. The non-
> Jewish strikers shouted, "Shinnies." The Jewish strikers immediately called a
> meeting, sent a delegation to the Charities and waited at the ferry for the
> strikebreakers to explain the situation to them and to ask them to return to
> New York.[84]

Although the source of this information in Epstein's partisan survey of the Jewish labor movement in the United States is not provided, the claim resonates with frequent charges that the UHC lacked compassion.

As to immigrant districts regarded as congested by their critics among German American Jews, Epstein and other labor activists believed that "neither the Jews nor the general public were [sic] any the worse for them."[85] Of the IRO in particular, Epstein derided it as "a total fiasco," resembling similar efforts that "disregarded the reality of Jewish life." In terms reminiscent of Rubinow's defense of the ghetto, Epstein identified its value:

> The great advantage to the immigrant lay in being shielded from losing his identity in the slow and grinding process of acclimatization to a totally strange environment. In the midst of his own kind he was afforded the possibility of gradually shedding his old way of life while adapting the new one. . . . The new "ghetto" discharged a socially useful function by facilitating employment chances and providing a familiar institutional life so indispensable for the dignity of the immigrant. What is of no less importance, the "ghetto" conserved the deeper and more enduring of the cultural values of his heritage.[86]

Likewise, an unregenerate Jewish labor perspective on the IRO and other assistance agencies was articulated by Tcherikower, who criticized the institutional efforts on behalf of the immigrants in pointed, unequivocal terms: "Thus with great sums at their disposal, the leadership of established American Jewry failed in its proposed resolution of the problem of integration of East European . . . immigrants into American society. Control, colonization, distribution, direction—all had proven bankrupt . . . The masses of immigrants, with their own social and cultural needs and aspirations, went their own way."[87] Unwilling even to recognize immigrant success abetted by the IRO or its role in adding to the nucleus of Jewish communities around the country, Tcherikower simply dismissed these efforts as "relatively unsuccessful."[88] Relatedly, the Arbeiter Ring, or Workmen's Circle, a Jewish socialist labor organization, took up the cause of immigrants claiming ill-treatment by employers or IRO agents.[89]

In spite of its scrupulous efforts to run an above-board organization rejecting strike breaking, coercion, cooperation with unscrupulous employers, and the abuses of private labor agencies, the IRO remained vulnerable to criticism from the left.

## Press Cooperation

The early hostility of *The Forward* seemed to diminish in later years. While still publishing letters and articles critical of the IRO, Cahan's newspaper also helped to publicize the distribution program and even referred immigrants to the IRO for assistance.[90] *The Forward* covered IRO exhibitions promoting resettlement, including displays at the Educational Alliance on the East Side and the Educational Alliance of Brooklyn, both held in the latter part of 1906.[91] Yiddish newspapers also carried notices for particular jobs that might be secured through the organization. Writing to *The Jewish Daily News* in 1910, Bressler requested that the paper run the following ad, typical of IRO notices:

> OPPORTUNITIES IN THE WEST
>
> Especially for upholsterers, tinsmiths, carpenters, cabinetmakers, iron molders, machinists, ironworkers, shoemakers and strong able-bodied men without trades. Call at the Industrial Removal Office, 174 Second Ave., Entrance on 11th Street.[92]

Reciprocally, *The Jewish Daily News* in 1906 sought information about job opportunities around the country. The paper planned a campaign urging its readers not to send any money to Russia except for the purpose of aiding Jewish emigration. The editor believed that such details about jobs in greatest demand in the United States would help readers render useful advice to prospective emigrés.[93]

Earlier that year, *The Forward* planned a new feature reporting on Jewish communities outside of New York. Seeking an IRO financial contribution to defray costs, the manager of the newspaper proposed sending a special correspondent around the country to gather material, including information about industries. The paper also planned to name the IRO in the proposed articles "as a proper guide and authority on matters of removal to cities and towns outside of New York." Even in *The Forward*'s proposal, the IRO faced residual doubts about its relationship to striking industries as well as a concern that immigrant Jews were sometimes sent to interior towns deemed unsuitable by some Jewish critics: "You will, of course, understand that considering the purpose of our newspaper, we will not advise workingmen to go to towns where strikes are going on, or to towns which our correspondent does not think well fit for Jewish settlement. We shall always seek your advice on such matters."[94] Despite a wariness borne of its close identification with labor, *The Forward* continued to run IRO advertisements and to print stories that did not disparage its work.

In a similar development, the IRO approved a subsidy for a reporter from *The Jewish Morgen Journal* to travel around the country gathering information on industrial conditions, standards of living, Jewish communities, educational opportunities, and so forth. Reports would appear periodically in the *Journal*, providing "the best possible propaganda in favor of the work in which the Removal Office is engaged."[95] The goal of such sketches was to inform readers about the IRO and to increase support for immigrant resettlement in the interior.

On various occasions, the IRO responded to negative letters in the Yiddish press from aggrieved clients. When Bressler believed that the organization had been represented unfairly, he or the assistant manager wrote to the editors offering evidence for an alternative version of the same story. In *The Forward* of 21 April 1907, for example, Israel Sakin described suffering and hardship following his move to Pittsburgh. Bressler reacted promptly:

Now my dear Mr. Cahan, while I have never had the slightest objections to the truth being printed about us even when it may place us in an unfavorable light, yet I beg to urge upon you the fairness of first verifying the truth of such charges as this man Sakin makes against us and our representative in Pittsburgh before giving them credence. The first principle of justice it seems to me would demand that both sides be heard, and I regret to say that in this instance great prominence has been given to a letter making a fierce attack upon us and which hasn't the slightest foundation in fact.[96]

Bressler then went on to detail Sakin's expectation of continued support for room and board, even after he had begun work in Pittsburgh. As to charges of inhumane treatment leveled against the IRO agent, Bressler defended him as a respected member of the Pittsburgh community who had rendered outstanding service to the IRO for nearly five years.[97]

On another occasion *The Forward* considered publication of a letter seeking advice about "how I should free myself from the swamp into which the Industrial Removal Office has put me."[98] Abraham Berman complained of problems on the job, including a layoff. He came back to

New York, but the IRO had refused to subsidize his family's return to the city. He had pawned jewelry, leaving his wife and children in St. Louis with ten dollars. Before publishing the Berman complaint, Cahan first referred it to the IRO for comment. Bressler explained that Berman worked for more than a year at a good salary, "something which he had been unable to do in the fourteen years that he lived in New York." That he had jewelry to pawn, when in New York he was indigent, gave some indication of the fact that he was able to earn a living in St. Louis. Bressler criticized Berman for not seeking other employment when problems developed. Instead, he chose to return to New York, where he had struggled for so long.[99] A brief response from *The Forward* on 19 June indicates that "the complaint . . . is not well founded, and we will, therefore, not print it."[100]

Aggrieved clients hoping to exercise some leverage sometimes threatened to complain to the Yiddish press if the IRO did not accede to their demands for additional support or transportation back to New York. Many made good on their threats. At times their cases were taken up in editorials or were cited in coverage of the IRO. Other immigrants, successfully resettled, sometimes took up the cause of the IRO by writing letters to the newspapers to counter the various denunciations of the organization.

When the IRO felt itself unfairly treated by the newspapers, it responded in the most measured tones. Always circumspect and diplomatic in its official reports, the IRO at various times acknowledged the assistance and even encouragement rendered by the Yiddish press in publicizing its activities.[101]

## Other Immigrant Correspondence

The sheer volume of applicants for IRO services ensured that the organization would see the entire range of Jewish immigrant life. Hard-working and devoted fathers and husbands with their equally steadfast wives—the stuff of the Jewish familial self-image—were common but by no means universal. Sufficient numbers of problem cases gave clear warrant to the agency's investigative process, however unpopular it may have been.[102] Some immigrants were duplicitous in seeking IRO services when they had the means to help themselves. Typically, the IRO would not support immigrants who traveled to other cities after reaching their destinations nor would the organization aid immigrants who had returned to

New York, only to solicit help once again for transportation to another city.

A few men went so far as to threaten to leave their wives and children in the belief that the IRO would come around to prevent a family from entering the rolls of the Jewish charities. Such efforts came to naught. A Harry Cohen, for example, sought IRO assistance for his wife's transportation from New York to Chicago, where he was located. Employed at twelve dollars per week, Cohen proclaimed, "I will not send one cent" for rent, support, or transportation.[103] He advised that she could seek charity. The IRO was unmoved:

> The reason we refuse to send your family is because they have been in Chicago before and returned to New York without good cause. For that matter you have been traveling between New York and Chicago for some time, and it is not our purpose to assist people who make it a business to travel about as you do. Your threat to leave your family has absolutely no influence with us, as I assure you that so far as we are concerned . . . she will not be supported by anybody here.[104]

In cases in which men abandoned their wives, the IRO and the Jewish press cooperated with the National Desertion Bureau to track them down.[105] Wives and children suffered immeasurably, dependent as they were on male breadwinners.

A Mrs. Balkin of Brooklyn implored the UHC and the IRO for help after receiving no support from her husband. Mr. Balkin, living in Cleveland, had informed her that he was not working and that she would not hear from him again unless he got a job. She sought help from "the Jewish office" (probably the UHC) but was dismissed until she refused to go home. She then received some help with the rent but nothing on which to live. Previously, she had gotten four dollars at the IRO office. Penniless and seeking IRO help once again, Mrs. Balkin indicated that it would be necessary only "until you will find work for my husband."[106]

Bressler detailed the actions of the scoundrel, Balkin. He was working for twelve dollars per week, yet continued to demand IRO subsidies for room and board. Bressler informed Mrs. Balkin that her husband's threat to withhold support if the IRO did not capitulate would be ignored and that he would be prosecuted by the National Desertion Bureau. Regretting Mrs. Balkin's suffering, Bressler remained adamant in refusing assistance either to her or to her husband.[107] Sympathy could provide little comfort to a desperate, powerless woman victimized by a reprobate husband.

While IRO clients often expressed unallayed sentiments, positive or negative, toward the IRO, a few writers conveyed a more mixed reaction to the organization. Some of these tell of the first hints of success yet still criticize the organization. Written in this vein, the following letter is reproduced in full because it conveys exceptionally well and with great dignity the uneasy encounter between proud but destitute immigrants and an impersonal professional agency that assumed a skeptical, investigative pose:

Inclosed please find ten ($10) the ballance of the debt which we contracted for my transportation to this city.

Allow me to thank you for your kind favor, which can really be called "good deeds." You are reputed to be an educated and clever man, therefore you will not resent criticism that is extended to you. I mean to give mine in good intention.

There are different ways of doing things. The most important is courtesy; if the party that is looking for a favor should be refused gently, he will feel better than if he were granted the request and treated as if he was not among those that can be classed as human, and spoken to as if that party did not know the meaning of insult.

When I applied to you for transporation, I told you everything, and the truth only. Yet, it was not enough. You humiliated me by asking why I do not pawn my jelewry which was pawned for the last five years, why I do not sell my furniture, which we did sell to pay my husbands [fare] to Minneapolis. Then you went on asking me, why I do not borrow of friends. . . . At last when I told you I intended to pay it all back as it is only a loan, you made me sign a note for $20. My husband had it all arranged with Miss Foxe [IRO office staff person?] to pay her $15.00 soon as we are in a position to do so.

Sir, I do not complain! In fact, I am very grateful to you. But the reason I mention it all is because, you should not think everyone that comes into the office to ask for aid must be a cheat, a liar and ignorant. The few hours that I sat waiting, I had a chance to study the characters that came in. Some may be such I admit, but there are exceptions and a man like you ought to know the difference.

You will excuse us for not settling the bill as promised. Because we paid the bills in turns. We are now clear from all debts. Nevertheless we are not less grateful to all our friends and good people for their kindness.

Mr. Friedman would like to have the note if possible.[108]

Mrs. Friedman's letter is unusual in two respects. Few women communicated in writing with the IRO, and the letter itself is very well written. The file contains no Yiddish original nor any definitive indication either that Mrs. Friedman penned it herself or received the aid of a sympathetic scribe. It was written on the letterhead of the "Minneapolis, St. Paul & Sault St. Marie Railway Co," perhaps her husband's employer, which might support the latter possibility. In any case, it describes the earliest steps along a route toward a better life, initially charted by the IRO. Mrs. Friedman demonstrates with admirable restraint how human sensibilities were easily offended by well-meaning actions. Like the young Abraham Cahan interviewed by the HEAS representative thirty years before and like untold numbers of others, Mrs. Friedman acknowledged with gratitude the generous motives of her benefactors but not without reproving them for the indignities visited on applicants. Philip Seman, the assistant manager of the IRO, replied in a brief, business-like letter. He returned Mr. Friedman's signed note and thanked Mrs. Friedman both for the ten-dollar check and for "suggestions contained in your letter."[109] The extent to which Mrs. Friedman, as a woman, may have experienced different and less agreeable conduct by staff members more accustomed to dealing with immigrant men cannot be determined. Mrs. Friedman's dissatisfaction was certainly mild compared with other immigrant reproaches coming overwhelmingly from male clientele.

Whereas some complainants found their dignity affronted, others praised the IRO for its tact and understanding in dealing with people in need. Much, of course, depended on the personal qualities of IRO staffers. In a 1912 letter, a Jacob Finkelstein commended the IRO for helping him get to Cincinnati, where he secured a good job at four dollars per day. He expressed gratitude as well for the local office's manner of assisting him with food and lodging. Finkelstein was especially appreciative "because I would have never thought of coming here of my own accord." Hoping to bring his family from New York, he reported:

> I consider it my sacred duty to express you my hearty thanks for what you have done for me. I was thinking all the time and finally came to the conclusion that the work you are doing on behalf of the poor can not be repayed. It is not the free transportation you are giving—no: this is the least. . . . He is taken off the train and given food and shelter with the greatest friendliness. So that he does not feel in the least embaressed—does not feel that he is getting

charity. The main thing, however, is the fact that employment is procured for him and if he is not lazy, he can make a nice living for himself and family.[110]

Other expressions of gratitude took shape in the organization of local IRO committees by former clients. One quarter of a small congregation in Bellaire, Ohio, had settled there under IRO sponsorship. Rising from destitution, "they are all respectable men, each earning his livelihood." Describing themselves as "enthusiastic over your noble work," the former IRO clients committed themselves to helping twelve families a year settle in the community.[111]

## Conclusion

Perspectives on the East Side were indeed contested, even down to the fundamental question of its capacity to absorb economically the many thousands settling there each year. Whereas the East Side provided familiar cultural ground and social networks for the newcomers, claims that employment opportunities were thereby enhanced were simplistic. Critics of the IRO gave short shrift to chronic joblessness, seasonal unemployment in the needle trades, and severe underemployment of large numbers of unskilled immigrants. The challenge of making a living in New York was more formidable than in other major American cities (see Appendix, Table 11). At the same time, Jewish labor activists and critics of American Jewish benefaction ignored the initial self-selection of IRO clients. No one was coerced into applying to the IRO. Likewise neglected in the labor critique were the very real economic opportunities that the IRO quickly afforded to many who were otherwise languishing among the jobless. Consumed with the task of safeguarding Jewish immigrants and immigration, the IRO attended only minimally to the derangement of identity, culture, and tradition that internal migration certainly entailed. Criticism of this feature of immigrant distribution was well placed.

Of those who became clients of the organization, many fulfilled the expectations of themselves and their sponsor in successfully taking the first difficult steps toward building productive lives beyond New York. Others, owing to IRO errors of judgment or to their own truculence or self-seeking, experienced serious problems in the resettlement process. The IRO drew on a self-selected sample of thousands of applicants, yet it would be difficult to reduce the IRO clientele to a single category. Were they only down and out, desperate and despairing people, spiritually broken by their unrelieved privation in New York? Many certainly were. The Jewish activist and playwright Israel Zangwill went further and called them "the failures of New York," much to the chagrin of Bressler.[112] Or were they risk taking and entrepreneurial, eager to leave New York, culturally secure as it was, for the promise of betterment in the hundreds of towns and cities to which they traveled? Many were adventurous and more, whether in settling down in small towns without large Jewish populations or peddling dry goods in the remote countryside. Abram Yaskransky, for example, writing from Marietta, Indian Territory, said simply: "I am sure I can make a living around here for my family."[113] Although the question cannot be answered, one still wonders if the IRO clientele differed in any substantial way from the much greater number of immigrants who left New York on their own. The IRO enabled many immigrants to begin achieving not only their own modest aims but also, in aggregate, the lofty goals of the organization. At the same time, Bressler and his colleagues had their share of setbacks and did not always serve their immigrant clients effectively. Still, the IRO was not the enemy of labor that its most critical detractors among embittered clients and in the press claimed.

# — 4 —

## The IRO at the Local Level

Although the IRO counted more than one thousand towns and cities in its cooperative network, a small number of recurrent conflicts regularly interrupted effective operation of the resettlement process. No problem was unique, and with varying frequency Jewish communities across the country clashed with the main office. The disagreements centered on the numbers of immigrants sent to a community. The IRO agencies and committees wanted to receive only as many newcomers as could be quickly employed, whereas the main office pressured them to receive a steady, if not increasing, volume of immigrants. Immigrants who were sent from New York but who remained unemployed for long periods constituted the single most disruptive and contentious factor in the relationship between the New York office and its constituents. This conflict was particularly intense in agency cities where the IRO tried to persuade the community to receive a monthly quota. When the idle workers were also recalcitrant or unruly, local communities grew even more resistant to pleas from Bressler for greater sacrifices. Other problems entangling the main office and its satellites were largely derivative of the presence of unemployed or uncooperative newcomers.

The cycle of conflict and cooperation was particularly well defined in the Midwest, a focus of IRO activity. Over nearly four months in 1908, Elias Margolis, a graduate of the Hebrew Union College and an IRO organizer, or traveling agent, visited twenty-four cities in Indiana and twenty in Illinois to gauge the prospects of further IRO activity in that area. In his letter to the New York office, Margolis observed the qualities of the region that made it so attractive to the IRO: "The territory I covered is the most prosperous in the United States, agriculturally and industrially. The towns and cities are pretty and clean, rents are low with one or two exceptions, and living expenses moderate. The Jewish workingman ought to be by far happier there, than in the larger cities of the Eastern seaboard."[1]

In 1901, the IRO's first year, the area designated by Bressler as the "central states" region accounted for 43.1 percent of the 1,836 resettled immigrants, most of whom went to Ohio, Illinois, Indiana, Wisconsin, Michigan, and Kentucky. In that year, these states, designated in the IRO classification as the eastern region of the central states, accounted for 31.2 percent of resettlers. In subsequent years, the central states and particularly its eastern region continued to form the mainstay of IRO activity, consistently drawing more than 50 percent of IRO clients in the heyday of the organization's activity between 1902 and 1913. In the latter year, 70.4 percent of accepted applicants relocated to the central states, with 58 percent settling in the six states of the eastern region. Within these states, the IRO by 1913 had established agencies or committees in 345 cities and towns.[2]

Accordingly, IRO activity in this area is representative of the process of organized immigrant dispersal at the local level. This chapter examines how Jewish immigrant resettlement was initiated and sustained through the efforts of local IRO personnel and traveling agents from New York. Typical obstacles are also considered in a number of places, particularly Indianapolis and Terre Haute. The IRO record there also shows that tensions in the relationship between the main office and its constituent cooperators, whether city agencies or committees in smaller towns, were similar, differing only in scale and intensity.

Indianapolis was the site of an IRO agency, whereas Terre Haute could not support as large an operation. Although many of its successes and difficulties resonate with those of Indianapolis and other agency cites, Terre Haute was a considerably smaller stage. That the IRO rarely gave up on a community when serious disagreements arose indicates the perceived urgency of the rising immigrant tide in New York and the determined restrictionist move to staunch it. Although it continually pushed against the chronic resistance of local communities, the organization always remained mindful of the capacity of particular sections of the country to absorb immigrants. Despite its best efforts, the IRO regularly had to deal with local disaffection in Indianapolis, Terre Haute, and other places.

Local communities focused above all on local concerns. They concentrated on the short-term goal of successfully absorbing the immigrants without incurring unacceptably high demands on their own financial and human resources, including their charitable coffers. Conflicts between the long-term aims of the IRO and the more modest goals of local committees would often come to a head when jobs were either unavailable or unacceptable to some of the newcomers. The latter instance occasioned particular rancor because communities had neither the inclination nor sometimes the resources to support people fully capable of supporting themselves. A particular community thus might face the disagreeable prospect of caring for unemployed but able-bodied immigrants looking to it for relief. The IRO consequently engaged in a continuing tug of war with its constituents over the numbers of immigrants sent out. That neither Indianapolis nor Terre Haute could achieve an unbroken record of fully successful placements is not surprising. It could hardly be otherwise, given the extent and urgency of the IRO work, the vagaries of economic and industrial conditions, and the diverse human qualities of the immigrants, agents, and committee members themselves.

### Local Representatives of the IRO

In Indianapolis, when the IRO agency was forming, uncoordinated local Jewish charitable organizations, usually synagogue-based, were federating themselves into a single, overarching organization. It was governed by a prosperous board of German American Jews. A similar process was also occurring in many other cities. Some immigrant eastern European Jews became active participants in these federated institutions and, indeed, IRO local staffs, including agents and committee heads, were composed of growing numbers of the more recent immigrants. In its composition, the Indianapolis IRO agency, including its agent and committee, overlapped to a considerable degree with the executive committee and board of governors of the Jewish Federation. In fact, the agent was also the superintendent of the Jewish Federation. The IRO paid more than one-third of his annual salary. The dual role of agent/superintendent proved very problematic because it invested in a single person responsibilities sometimes at cross purposes—promoting employment and providing relief.[3]

Usually the IRO representative was the first person that the immigrant met on arriving and had the responsibility of initially looking after the newcomer. This task entailed arranging room and board, payable for a week or two by the main office, after which it was expected that the immigrant would be working. The representative directed the immigrant to his new job, sometimes personally accompanying him on the first day, and generally gave him the advice any relocated immigrant required. The representative also served as a kind of cultural broker when the immigrants discovered, soon after their arrival in a hinterland community, that New York and America were not synonymous. In the event of trouble on the job, repeated refusals to accept employment, or travail of any kind resulting from happenstance or the immigrant's own actions, the representative played an active part in trying to resolve the problem and became at times the most visible object of complaint or praise.[4]

Moreover, the IRO representative communicated for as much as a year with the New York Office, keeping the general manager apprised through bimonthly reports of how clients were adjusting to their new jobs and communities. Another obligation was to provide the main office with information about industrial conditions and local needs for skilled and unskilled workers. These reports aided the selection process in New York.

While the IRO at the national and local levels was focused on the plight of eastern European Jewish immigrants, it did not lose sight of the small Sephardic Jewish immigration from the Ottoman territories. In Indianapolis and a few other cities, Sephardic immigrants arrived under IRO sponsorship. The Federation of Oriental Jews of America actively sought the assistance of the IRO in distributing "Turkish Jewish immigrants" beyond New York.[5] Bressler's cooperation resulted in his election to its advisory board.[6] The IRO formed a special section devoted to the Balkan Jewish immigrants and employed an individual fluent in Ladino, the language of most Sephardic Jews. The new section proceeded cautiously.[7] Because these immigrants could speak neither Yiddish nor any other language commonly heard in the United States, it was believed that they would constitute a special problem for the IRO.[8] In Indianapolis, this fear proved groundless as no altercations between the local agent and the main office concerned Sephardic immigrants.

## Problem Cases and Failed Placements

The IRO was particularly eager to find employment for its clientele in Jewish-owned businesses. By restricting immigrant employment to Jewish concerns, the IRO hoped that employers would understand the unique circumstances of the Jewish immigrant worker by taking into account his distinctive culture, language, and outlook. Then the Jewish proprietor might make the kind of allowances that a non-Jewish employer would less likely grant. It was believed that a non-Jewish business would simply regard any problem with immigrant labor as merely an economic matter to be expeditiously resolved by discharging the worker. As Bressler explained, "Their welfare is best guarded by those whom sympathy and racial fellow feeling cause to sacrifice much in cooperating with us, rather than by those whose cooperation is extended essentially in their own interests."[9]

Securing the cooperation of businesses owned by Jews provided no guarantee against failure. Unsuccessful placements, moreover, created a ripple effect by discouraging further cooperation with the IRO, especially if an employer or a community experienced financial loss. The limits of "fellow feeling" sometimes proved exceedingly narrow, and local committees were usually not shy about reproaching the IRO for sending out ill-suited or temperamental immigrants.[10] Later, a more confident IRO, in concert with its local cooperators, established contacts with firms owned by non-Jews.

Sending applicants to fill particular orders for employees early on proved difficult. Bressler explained that prospective immigrant employees often could not speak English or were unfamiliar with local custom, including American methods of work within their own trades.[11] Moreover, the requisitions proved cumbersome, as it was difficult to match workers to jobs at long distance. The time required to secure the request, find an appropriate applicant, and then send him to the community often resulted in cancellation of the requisition. Although the use of requisitions continued to a limited extent, the IRO came to believe that clientele should be sent to communities when only the probability of a position existed. Thus, the IRO plan shifted from finding men for jobs to finding jobs for successful applicants. This strategic change also aimed to increase the numbers of immigrants moving out of New York while placing more responsibility on cooperating committees to canvass their communities for positions. Communities were expected to find positions for immigrants *after* they arrived.[12] IRO cooperators were, therefore, required to tolerate a certain number of newcomers for whom jobs were not immediately available. No longer relying on specific requisitions from employers, the IRO resettled immigrants in places where employment prospects were high but not immediately certain. Sending clients to communities under this new arrangement resulted in numerous conflicts between local committees and the New York office because a failure to locate a newcomer in self-supporting employment placed financial burdens on the communities. Newcomers without self-support turned to the local IRO group for continuing payment of their lodging and board and sometimes did so in a particularly irksome manner.

Other complications further limited the effectiveness of the distribution scheme. Despite the investigative process in New York, deception might enable a man unwilling to work to gain IRO help in leaving the city. In other instances, the IRO sometimes resettled individuals who expressed strong disappointment at the wages offered in the new job. Some claimed that they had left very good jobs in New York to evoke sympathy and financial support from local committees. In practice, immigrants could rarely be guaranteed jobs at a particular wage. Rather, resettlement depended on a willingness to accept the work offered, which at the least was sufficient for earning a very modest living. Once located, they were, of course, free to change jobs or to leave town but without any legitimate claim on further IRO assistance.

In 1902, William Kahn pointed out that some of the immigrants successfully deceived host communities unaccustomed to dealing with wily people. Complaining of poor wages and seeking financial support, they concocted stories about giving up remunerative employment in favor of resettlement.[13] Levi went further in outlining the destructive consequences of such cases:

> Work is obtained for a man. In a few days he becomes dissatisfied and quits; then he is housed, fed and other work sought for him, which he refuses on one pretext or another. Then he tells of friends or relatives in New York or elsewhere who will help him and he demands transportation. He denounces those who sent him, plays the martyr, and makes himself a nuisance. In the end he gains his point and is sent to another community, where he repeats the game. The result is that the various places which he visits denounce one another and all denounce us.[14]

Another reason for investigations came from the antics of "traveling mendicants," who presented themselves as clients of the IRO. Especially vexatious, these people prompted Levi to advise all cooperating communities "to accept no story of hardship or cruelty until it is proven," by wiring to the main office, if necessary. For their part, various communities new to distribution programs too readily accepted the sorrowful stories of immigrants seeking their help. Levi advised a "judicious" rather than "emotional" response; otherwise, the tendency to satisfy complainants as quickly as possible created severe problems because "the appetite for . . . giving is soon satisfied, but the appetite for . . . receiving grows."[15]

Communities feeling themselves beleaguered by schemers and shirkers sometimes relieved the discomfort as quickly as possible by exporting their problem cases to other towns and cities. However expedient the remedy, the IRO, as well as other Jewish institutions, sharply criticized this measure because it "endangers our work, exasperates the next community and every other community to which these men drift, and is of no benefit, in the true sense of the word, to the recipient." To the extent that the IRO was implicated in the travels of such individuals, its task of sustaining support for distribution was more difficult. Therefore, the IRO urged communities to provide no aid whatsoever to people unwilling to support themselves. Kahn argued that every man assisted by the IRO should understand that "he must either work or walk, and that the municipal laws apply to Jewish vagrants as well as to vagrants of any other religion."[16]

If such conflicts festered, the local communities sometimes threatened to suspend their cooperation. As the sine qua non of the entire IRO program, local cooperation had to be preserved. Consequently, either through correspondence or visits from traveling representatives, the main office expended prodigious effort in repairing relationships damaged by difficult cases or recurrent problems.

### Traveling Agents: Maintaining, Restoring, and Expanding the IRO Network

Organizing local IRO activity usually began with traveling agents—individuals from the main office who periodically embarked on tours of the interior to form new committees and agencies or to revitalize stagnant efforts. During their excursions to existing IRO units, they reported on the progress of resettlement in its several dimensions. Whether visiting with IRO clients in their new homes or speaking with committee members, the traveling agents renewed in a personal way the connection between the main office and the community. As a self-styled social movement, the IRO confronted the discouragement or despair of its cooperators and then vigorously tried to renew their commitment to distribution. Direct contact with representatives from the main office often provided the encouragement necessary to restart, sustain, and even to increase, if only temporarily, the level of local work in the face of problems and crises. Then another round of unfavorable results would once again require inspirational letters from Bressler and personal visits by traveling agents. When not visiting IRO communities, most of the agents served as office staffers in New York. They included Morris Waldman (who subsequently would head the Galveston Bureau and, eventually, the American Jewish Committee), Stanley Bero, Philip Seman, Elias Margolis, and Abraham Solomon.

Beyond brief site visits, Bressler also traveled on behalf of the IRO in an early Midwest tour and in an extended trip to the American West in 1909, when the IRO resettled 3,504 people. That relocated population was the smallest since 1902, owing to the suspension of cooperation by some established agencies following the economic depression of 1907. He organized IRO agencies in Los Angeles, Portland, Seattle, and Spokane, hoping that IRO units in these cities might make up for the temporary loss of primary destinations, especially in the Midwest.[17]

The Midwest continued to be a primary immigrant destination during the remaining years of IRO activity. Big cities, such as Cleveland, Detroit, and St. Louis, as well as smaller outlets, including Cincinnati and Indianapolis, were pivotal. The resettlement possibilities within the area were sufficiently promising that the IRO also enlisted the cooperation of very small communities, despite their cultural and economic limitations.

Margolis toured the midwest in 1908 to expand the IRO's reach. He met with representatives of factories and industries to explain the organization and to ascertain the willingness of these businessmen to hire immigrant workers through arrangements with the local IRO representative. Margolis reported that he received an interested hearing from large plants and smaller employers, including merchant tailors, shoemakers, painters, and paperhangers. Noting that the depression of 1907 struck most severely the building and mechanical trades, he found that plumbers, tinsmiths, and carpenters were little interested in the IRO program because these trades would likely remain in low demand until economic and industrial conditions improved. Margolis and his colleagues emphasized that the organization could provide "a sober and industrious class of mechanics and workingmen who could be relied upon at all times" in contrast to "a shiftless and drunken class of workingmen who work three days, spend three more days in a bar room, and then disappear for parts unknown.[18]

That the main office was willing to expend money and effort in cultivating the assistance of small Jewish communities is indicative of several concerns. The IRO's exhortations to multiple small settlements of Jews to assume a fair share of the burden of unemployed immigrants grew in proportion to increasing social and political capital that the immigration restrictionists found in urban congestion and poverty. Also, the unemployment and underemployment of Jewish immigrants in New York was a persistent problem, made more severe by the depressed economic conditions of 1907 and a continuing influx of European Jews. Additional outlets were essential, although the organization had no illusions about the capacity of smaller communities to offset the sharp decline in immigrant resettlement in the bigger cities. Small towns were particularly limited in their capacity to accept unskilled workers.[19]

Many of the communities on Margolis's itinerary indeed sought only skilled labor. The narrow range of employment possibilities was, of course, well known in small IRO outlets. A Mr. Bernstein, the IRO correspondent in Marshalltown, Iowa, in 1904, aptly summed up the difficulty after noting that of five resettlers, one was farming, and four had left, two for Des Moines, one for Chicago, and one for an unknown destination: "It seems there is not much of a show for these people in small country towns. They don't stay, and there is not much work to be had."[20]

In meetings with members of the Jewish community, traveling agents explained the nature and the rationale of the IRO work. They often spoke to groups assembled at a lodge or a religious congregation. A positive, enthusiastic response with pledges of support was sometimes forthcoming. In contrast, Margolis reported that on first raising the question of cooperation with the IRO, he also encountered suspicion, owing to previous community experiences with the *shnorers,* the "traveling mendicants" described by Levi. Margolis's audiences frequently protested that communal financial resources were scarce. He then explained that IRO clientele were not *shnorers* but rather "self-respecting workingmen who were coming, not to look for a job but to fill one."[21]

Margolis tried to put at ease the Jewish communities that he visited, explaining that their cooperation with the IRO did not entail financial sacrifice. To accomplish their task of expanding the range and volume of immigrant resettlement, the traveling agents said little or nothing about the inevitability of problem cases in spite of IRO investigation and screening. From the beginning, the IRO assured communities, with just enough equivocation for honesty's sake, that "they would be held practically free from any financial responsibility."[22]

Newcomers sometimes did become financial burdens to their host communities, which, however, feared the repercussions of cutting off support. One consequence—the adverse opinion that Gentiles might hold of their Jewish neighbors—provided the more venal IRO clients with leverage against the community. The taint of their visibly idle, complaining coreligionists motivated committees to provide money to some willful newcomers, contrary to IRO advice. A few such grudging donations could undermine local commitment to the IRO, even when the community had achieved a record of successful placements..

Accordingly, Margolis's idealized description of the work must be seen as part of the IRO's self-described propaganda campaign to recruit communities, sometimes against considerable inertia or outright resistance. Should some locals remain dubious, Margolis tried to invite their cooperation through moral persuasion of the sort first argued by Levi and then frequently pressed by Bressler and Sulzberger. In Margolis's rendering, "They were not fulfilling their obligations to the Jewish people merely by attending to their parochial duties."[23] In this same vein and recalling his own words to Bressler before embarking on his 1912 tour, Solomon, an idealistic young socialist, wrote from Muncie, Indiana, that "if one is imbued with the broad vision and tackles this work with something of prophetic zeal, then he can overcome prejudice indifference and all objections. Only in addition to being prophetically in earnest, one must be quick and resourceful in refutation."[24]

The traveling agents also visited established agencies and committees to take stock of the IRO work, to offer suggestions, to hear complaints from agency or committee personnel, and to attempt to resolve lingering complaints or misunderstandings. In addition, traveling agents met with IRO clients to gauge their adjustment to their new homes, thus supplementing information that the main office periodically received from the agent or committee head in charge.

Bressler was also very mindful of the problems attending the arrival in a new community of men for whom jobs were not immediately available. Continued cooperation between the community and the New York office was jeopardized to the extent that communities saw themselves as extensions of the Jewish unemployment problem in New York. Although Bressler regularly urged IRO agents and committee members to bear inconvenience on behalf of the larger good, he also wanted to keep the tolerance level of communities within manageable limits by rationalizing as much as possible the selection process. He praised Solomon for his skill in enlisting the cooperation of communities without their limiting the IRO to particular classes of workers who might be sent. He also urged Solomon to consult the Chambers of Commerce, other associations of businessmen, or the most informed members of the IRO committee, so that he might include in his reports a more specific statement about the kind of workers most likely to secure employment. This advice was emphatically tendered: "I cannot too strongly emphasize the importance of complying with this suggestion; since the continuation of cooperation will depend to a considerable extent upon the fairly ready absorption of the men we send by the cooperating communities."[25] Bressler was attempting to steer a middle course between the flexibility that the IRO required in deciding where to send particular workers and the outer limits of community altruism.

The IRO had long known that communal generosity, both in a material and a social sense, would continue only so long as it was not squandered by an excessive number of failed placements. It was precious capital indeed, always at risk in the audacious work of immigrant distribution. But as the main office discovered with annoying regularity, much lay beyond its control as contingent events, eccentric personalities, and local conflicts and rivalries sometimes undercut the most rational plan.

Despite the interest that Margolis aroused among prospective employers, it was still necessary to break through stereotypic thinking, benign or otherwise, especially in small communities. IRO representatives had to be alert to the general level of acceptance that the Jewish citizenry had achieved in midwestern towns and to instances of antisemitism. Having secured a requisition for a painter at twelve dollars per week from a Mr. Long, "a very fine old gentleman of the old school of good Americans," Margolis reported to Bressler from Elwood, Indiana. In that small community, he found reason for confidence in the economic climate, the amenities of the town, and the level of tolerance for the eight resident Jewish families. Living costs were low, and it was possible to rent a spacious house for eight dollars per month. One available rental stood on a triple lot with "fruit trees . . . in abundance which seems a veritable paradise to an Eastside Jew of the tenements."[26]

Although industrial managers acknowledged the superior, generalized skills of European mechanics, they doubted that Jewish mechanics existed at all, for "they imagined all Jews were either storekeepers or junk dealers." To press the point about the range of skills and occupations among immigrant Jews, Margolis provided the list of trades represented by the 7,500 IRO clients in 1907. In addition, he had to confront widespread skepticism about the IRO itself—that it gained no profit from its work and that the organization continued to maintain an interest in the adjustment of the people relocated. He had to persuade prospective employers that the IRO was not engaging in a scam.

In speaking directly with industrial managers and businesspeople, Margolis was undertaking a more aggressive strategy than was usual for the IRO. Job canvasses were normally left to people on the local committee as a way of exercising control over the employment process and protecting the immigrants from abusive labor practices. The overall decline in IRO placements after the 1907 downturn prompted more activist tactics in locating jobs. The main office also sent circulars around the country describing the IRO program to potential employers and inviting requests for workers. While the local representative continued to play his accustomed role, the exigencies of hard economic times and diminished placements compromised the earlier caution.

However pragmatic, there were risks in the new strategy, including, particularly, the exploitation of Jewish immigrant labor. The industrial and business surveys by the traveling agents as well as their visits with IRO clients brought various problems to light. Normally, the local agent or committee member tried to resolve the difficulty, but a traveling agent on the spot would certainly involve himself.

Margolis was called on by the main office to visit Cedar Rapids, Iowa, to look into a dispute between several IRO men and their employer, the Perfection Manufacturing Company, which produced women's clothing. John Taft, the owner, had called on Bressler in New York, having seen an IRO circular. Bressler was favorably impressed, regarding Taft as a "straightforward businessman with good intentions and . . . likely to deal fairly with his employees."[27] Soon after, four IRO men were sent to Cedar Rapids for jobs with Taft's company. The men subsequently registered complaints against the company with the local IRO representative, a Mr. Braverman, a Russian Jewish businessman, and with the main office itself. Seeing justice in the complaints, Braverman demanded that the IRO stop sending immigrants to Taft's firm. He was particularly worried about the families of the men, once they were reunited. If the men were laid off or their wages reduced—a clear possibility in the opinion of Braverman and the men—they and their families would be at the mercy of the company, the only clothing manufacturer in the town. Bressler wrote to Taft for an explanation and asked Margolis to speak personally with him, with the four IRO men, and with Braverman.

Margolis's investigation, predictably, pointed to Taft's desire to minimize wages. One man was denied the overtime he claimed; a second was assigned piecework, enabling him to earn only six or seven dollars rather than fifteen dollars a week; the third complained of low wages in the pressing department; and the fourth wanted some indication about the tenure of his position at eighteen dollars per week. The Perfection Manufacturing Company found itself in serious competition with garment producers in Chicago, Cleveland, and New York and, as a new company, faced the reluctance of retailers to buy goods from a manufacturer outside of the major urban centers of clothing production. Consequently, Perfection had to undersell its better known and established competition, which was possible only if wages were limited. Taft had effectively controlled the wage scale by employing local women until it became apparent that they could not produce the kind of stylish clothing that would enable the company to compete with eastern firms. Taft then decided to bring in the IRO men, skilled in the New York needle trades, but for wages he had paid local women. Margolis described Taft as a good Methodist who "would not regard the exploitation of labor as a serious crime." Likewise, Taft was not the sort of person who could "be accused of any serious lapse into philanthropy."[28] Margolis recommended that future cooperation with Taft's company should be predicated on a written agreement.

The IRO later fine-tuned its methods again. Bressler dissuaded Solomon, from following the tactic Margolis had used in 1908:

> I want to caution you against accepting scattering [sic] requisitions from individual employers. Let your work be confined rather to the concentrated committee plan. If individual members of each community desire special types of workers, let them make request through [the] medium of the Chairman, Secretary or Agent—whichever the case may be—of the committee. My idea of concentrated cooperation of each community . . . is based upon my desire for concentration of authority and consequent responsibility. This should be your policy, subject naturally, to well advised exceptions.[29]

Besides industrial conditions, the IRO and its traveling representatives also had to be alert to the particular outlooks of German and Russian Jews within a community. At the local level, no simple generalization was possible, for supportive or critical stances toward the IRO did not neatly sort themselves along German or Russian lines. Dedicated and unselfish people of both groups added their share to the successes the IRO could claim. By the same token, an indifferent or ungenerous attitude toward the immigrants and Jewish charity was not the monopoly of German Jews, however much some of the latter condescended to or disdained the immigrants. Those who had left czarist Russia only a few years before they were called on to cooperate with the IRO could also be uncaring toward people so much like themselves.

In communities where both German and Russian Jews had settled, the nature of their relationship could affect the internal politics of the Jewish community and hence the quality of participation in the IRO plan. Or, in those communities with no Russian Jewish settlement, the German Jewish attitude toward eastern European Jews could limit participation in the resettlement plan. But so, too, could some of the increasing number of eastern European Jews among IRO cooperators. Samuel Kaufman, for example, the Indianapolis agent after 1908, was Russian-born and often took an extremely critical view of Jewish immigrants—"a stiff necked people"—and at times actively resisted IRO efforts.[30] Consistently, Kaufman and the German American Jews overseeing the IRO agency and the Jewish Federation were in accord on all matters concerning resettlement. Although Kaufman was immediately constrained by the Jewish Federation, which paid the major portion of his salary, no evidence suggests that his recalcitrant and unsentimental attitude toward the immigrants was anything but genuine.

Still, the IRO counted Russian Jews among its most dedicated correspondents. Both Margolis and Waldman praised the efforts of Braverman. Living in a community of approximately forty Russian Jewish families, Braverman strongly supported the IRO work and defended it in print against complaints in the Jewish press.[31] Also, Waldman, after visiting several towns in the Midwest where the IRO received reports of unsatisfactory placements, wrote to Bressler from Cedar Rapids, Iowa, and refuted suspicions that the problems lay in coldness or superciliousness of local IRO committee members. These sorts of charges, usually leveled against German Jews, were unfounded, according to Waldman. Much of the local work in those communities was done successfully by sympathetic Russian Jews.[32]

Likewise, the Terre Haute group consisted of very sympathetic volunteers of Russian background and more hard-headed German American Jews. The Russian Jewish correspondent, S. J. Goldstine, and his committee ally Rabbi Kaplan at one point sought resettlers whom the main office and German American Jews on the committee were unwilling to subsidize. Both Goldstine and Kaplan appealed to Bressler for greater sympathy and charity toward these particular cases.[33]

In other places, a community composed almost wholly of Russian Jews, including people of means, did not guarantee compassionate participation in IRO activity. Finding indifference to each other and to the IRO among German Jews and the more numerous Russian Jews of Marion, Indiana, Margolis wrote, "There is a woeful lack of entente cordiale between the two factions. They do not seem to comprehend . . . the necessity of doing any charity work, and they complain bitterly if they have to raise a paltry $10.00 to help some poor family, in spite of the fact that they (even some of the Russians) have amassed great wealth."[34]

Some communities were marked by an easy accomodation between the German and Russian Jews, thus facilitating their mutual efforts on behalf of the IRO. Margolis wrote the following from Muncie, Indiana: "There are about one hundred Jews in Muncie, the majority of them being Russian. Both classes mingle in their religious and social life. The President of the Reform Congregation is a Russian Jew."[35]

Sometimes, a divide between German Jews and Russian Jews provided a formidable obstacle to IRO work. In South Bend Indiana, Margolis reported in May 1908 on the layoffs at the Studebaker factory, where several IRO men had found employment. Certainly a consequence of the depression, idleness among the workers was interpreted differently by the IRO agent, a Mr. Greenebaum. He believed workers were laid off because of a bomb throwing incident at Union Square (New York). Margolis reported that Greenebaum was especially antagonistic toward Russian Jews, whom he spoke of very disparagingly. To Margolis's astonishment, Greenebaum thought that all orthodox Jews were anarchists. The city's Jewish population of 2,000 was overwhelmingly eastern European, but the wealth and influence of the approximately seventy-five German Jews made their participation in IRO work essential. Margolis described the latter as very rich and "not only do they despise the Russians but they do not even attempt to help them in any way. There is enough antisemitism as it is, and the lot of the Russian Jew is doubly hard."[36] Solomon's humorous summing up of the contentiousness among the various segments of the Jewish community of Youngstown, Ohio, in September 1912 might well be taken as representative of many American Jewish communities of the era: "Youngstown has a Y.M.H.A., three synagogues, two Talmud Torahs, three lodges, and a recently federated Charities. Result: disharmony, jealousy, and all the appendages."[37]

Prejudice on the part of German American Jews toward Jewish immigrants of eastern origin and some disagreeable experiences with IRO men inhibited resettlement activity in Lafayette, Indiana.[38] Against this unpromising record, Solomon reported on his effort to revitalize IRO activity in the city:

> I consider the result here gratifying for it was achieved only after the hardest kind of fighting. The Lafayette Jews are massed into a mountain of indifference. Experience with a few removals prejudiced them. One removal turned out to be a thief and one was an anarchist etc. A gentleman . . . very keen, had the greatest collection of objections imaginable but finally trapped himself. Finally, there is a strong dislike of the Russian Jew, fostered by Russian Jewish upstarts. This attitude I slammed good and hard and finally Zinkin (the Rabbi) was so indignant, he had to do the same thing.[39]

Despite their strong resistance, Solomon generally was favorably impressed with the seven members of the Lafayette committee that he reorganized. But even the rabbi, described by Solomon as an enthusiastic and intelligent young man from whom much could be expected, strongly criticized the IRO regarding one of the men sent to the city.[40]

The new agreement assumed a quasi-legal format, written and signed by the reorganized committee.[41] It pledged to accept a minimum of two IRO men per month after advising the New York office "of the class of removals best adapted to local conditions."[42] In view of Solomon's struggle to reestablish the IRO relationship with Lafayette's Jewish population, the agreement was very precarious. The committee simply had raised too many objections and was clearly on its guard against any repetition of problems or the appearance of new complications. Only six weeks after Solomon's heroic effort, trouble erupted when the committee protested that the main office had sent two men without prior consultation and that no work was available.[43]

Although IRO surveys of towns where committees might be established identified industrial activity as a paramount concern, information was also sought on the quality of Jewish cultural and religious life. The size of the Jewish population and the proximity of the town to a major city usually affected these factors. Margolis had attributed some of problem cases to the lack of Jewish communal life in small towns. He found that fewer men had disappeared from places with organized Jewish communities.[44] Life in small towns sometimes proved extremely difficult for immigrants, although they might have secured decent jobs. In evaluating its applicants, the IRO had to determine the extent to which Jewish institutions and styles of living were important to a prospective resettler.

For example, an immigrant committed to traditional practice, including maintaining a kosher diet, would not be directed to a community where Jewish life was only nascent or where observance of the dietary laws would be impossible. From Bressler's point of view, self-sustaining employment remained the foremost consideration, even if religious and cultural compromises proved necessary. But Bressler did not impose this view on those determined only to settle in a Jewish community capable of supporting the religious and cultural life they required.

After a series of complaints from Joseph Markman and Charles Graff, two IRO men living in Logansport, Indiana, Bressler responded unsympathetically. They were, after all, employed and were not living in New York, where their children could not be properly raised. Logansport had a Jewish population of approximately one hundred, virtually all prosperous German American Jews. A rabbi from Lafayette visited every two weeks.[45] The town would certainly have appeared alien to an eastern European Jew for whom long-term residence in New York would have provided no hint of what to expect. Still, Bressler was unmoved by the complainants because the IRO had informed them in advance about the limitations of the town. He reminded them of their eagerness to leave New York for employment elsewhere, even if their departure required the sacrifice of some familiar cultural amenities.[46] Having settled into a new community and begun work, Markman and Graff had no legitimate claims on the IRO.

A related issue was simply the loneliness the immigrants experienced in a remote place or the personal indisposition, both of which could affect a newcomer's general outlook and the quality of his work. In 1908, the Jewish population of Bluffton, Indiana, consisted of a Mr. Salinger, a proprietor of a clothing store, and his family and the Levensons, of whom

Mrs. Levenson devoted considerable effort to looking after the four IRO newcomers. Three of the latter originally settled in Sheboygan, Wisconsin, where they got work with the King Piano Company. When the company moved to Bluffton, the three men took up the same jobs in the new community. A fourth IRO client, a Mr. Mayers, worked for Salinger as a bushelman. Salinger found him "a first class workingman" but was not especially satisfied with his employee. Mayers seemed interested in the work and complained that he could not subsist on ten dollars per week. Salinger raised Mayers's salary to twelve dollars while remaining unhappy with Mayers's work and his refusal to wait on customers. Margolis apparently was able to exercise some positive influence, despite Salinger's continuing exasperation with Mayers: "When he got his raise he immediately invested in a $34 Victor talking machine on the installment plan and has been spending quite a sum on records since. That disgusts Salinger altogether. I gave Mayers a little lecture and it did some good at least while I was present. He actually waited on the trade and sold things."[47]

### Contradictory Views at the Local Level

The undated IRO informational booklet, *Der Indostrial Revoval [sic] Offis: Zayn Thetigkeyt, Zayn Tsvek un Zayne Oyfgaben* (The Industrial Removal Office: Its Activity, Purpose, and Task), provoked a critical response that revealed disparate local interpretations of the newcomers. Although immigrant clients and the local IRO committee chairmen often presented discrepant views of the removal work, controversy among settled members of the community was less frequently recorded. A letter responding to the IRO booklet reveals cleavages of this sort. The booklet, probably published in 1906 or 1907, described distribution and reprinted Yiddish letters to the organization from successfully resettled immigrants in such places as Wichita, Kansas; Columbus, Ohio; Meridian, Mississippi; Rock Island, Illinois; and Buffalo, New York. Another communication published in the booklet from Rabbi Gershuny, the IRO correspondent in Lafayette, Indiana, described the very successful marriage of a daughter of the Klimovitzky family to a local junk dealer. Following the ceremony at the German Temple, the couple traveled to Waterbury Springs and then on to New York City, where they visited the main office to reimburse the IRO for the cost of the tickets to Lafayette for the bride and her family.[48] Although nothing is said of the other Klimovitzkys, the booklet's report of the marriage of a daughter of recent IRO clients to a prosperous local man must have counted as one more indication of the hopeful prospects that awaited immigrants leaving New York. Marriage in a Reform ceremony also implied that the couple was socially and economically mobile.

A letter to the IRO from Lafayette offers a very different reading of events, including the entire local work of the IRO. A Mr. Rastoff expressed astonishment at the letter from Gershuny. First, he stated that the IRO resettlers, all of whom eventually left Lafayette, "from the first to the last were all a burden to the community." As for the Klimovitzsky family, the community provided them thirty dollars in cash, free groceries for a month, and furnished rooms. Mother and daughter quarreled until the latter left home.

> She was fortunate enough to become acquainted with one named Mendel Rabiner a rags peddler 35 years of age. If he earns a dollar or more he is satisfied. He does not care to become rich and to all this his physiognomy causes people to lock their houses.
>
> The ceremony was performed by Dr. Morganstern of the German Temple and Dr. Gershuny was not even admitted to attend them, because we all know him well here.
>
> To inform you of all scandals that took place on account of the people sent here would be enough to fill a journal. Klimovitzsky left for Columbus, Shapiro for Minneapolis and the 4 young men for Chicago.[49]

Shortly after receiving this letter, Bressler addressed an inquiry to the congregation "to let us know of the situation in your city."[50]

Although no record of a reply to Bressler's inquiry survives, Bero provided additional information about the IRO record in Lafayette. It is neither as grim as Rastoff suggested nor as auspicious as Gershuny's account of the Klimovitzky wedding. In its almost messianic eagerness to publicize organized immigrant distribution and to enhance cooperation with the removal enterprise, the IRO was not given to critical scrutiny of reports of its successes. Agreeing with Rastoff, Bero remarked without elaboration that "Gershuny is no good," while still finding that the prospects for IRO clients, especially skilled tradesmen, remained favorable. Of sixty-five orthodox families in the city, fifteen settled in Lafayette through the IRO and were managing very well in such endeavors as tailoring, dry goods merchandising, peddling, and shoe repair.[51]

## Gauging Success

Of course, many immigrants quickly adjusted to their new homes in the manner envisioned by the IRO. Many resettlers then set out to bring their families and friends from New York or Europe to join them. These were unequivocal stories of success. By contrast, some individuals remaining in the towns where they were sent proved obstinate, refusing to work, moving from job to job, and demanding support. Still others on their own drifted away from their new communities and broke off their contact with the IRO. The organization's representatives simply noted the departure as a final comment on the absent client, although the IRO consistently claimed that the numbers of immigrants remaining at their original destinations were very high. In Bressler's presentation to the Immigration Commission in November 1910, he reported that less than 15 percent of those distributed departed from their new communities and that less than 5 percent had returned to New York.[52] Testifying before the Commission on Industrial Relations in May 1914, Bressler again reported on the staying power of IRO resettlers. He estimated that at least 88 percent remained in the communities where they were sent.[53] Residential stability and self-sustaining employment were important measures of success.

When committees lost contact with those leaving town, it certainly appeared that the IRO could not claim them in the ranks of their successfully resettled clients. It was yet another point of division between the main office and its cooperators. The resettlers' departure from New York, however, counted at the least as a small triumph for the organization, but only if they did not return to the city or again seek IRO assistance. Some so-called successes were, of course, tainted if the immigrants left behind in their host communities unpaid loans or debts. Even if the immigrants owed nothing, their disappearance without notice sometimes provoked criticism. Reports from local committees often indicated that such cases were indicative of a flawed selection process in New York, as indicated in Rastoff's communication from Lafayette.

Characteristically, the main office remained more hopeful, inferring that many of its peripatetic clients were not unsatisfactory placements. In

1902, the New York office accepted 1,451 cases, including families and single men totaling 2,311 people, of whom 503 left their original destination. Virtually all of the departures were by single men. The IRO noted,

> It must not for a moment be imagined because these five hundred and one cases moved from the places to which they were originally sent, that they were all unsatisfactory cases. On the contrary, only a small minority were, their removal from the original point having been due to various causes such as unsuitability of the work offered, or the filling of the position prior to the applicant's arrival, or because better opportunities presented themselves elsewhere.[54]

Despite the absence of records in the New York office on the later course of their lives, many of the people leaving their original destination undoubtedly managed to achieve success. (See Appendix, Tables 7 and 8, for data on client mobility and for IRO estimates of successful relocations and the changing criteria for evaluation.)

The experience of Louis Shapiro, mistakenly reported in the Rastoff letter to have left Lafayette for Minneapolis, is illustrative. Later, Bero correctly informed Bressler that Shapiro had left for Indianapolis.[55] Emigrating from Odessa, Louis and Rose Shapiro arrived in New York early in 1906 with their six children. The Shapiros had owned a grocery in Odessa but decided to emigrate after the 1905 outbreaks of antisemitic violence that injured Shapiro and destroyed his business. Having previously experienced pogroms, Shapiro decided to emigrate after the latest and worst depredation. In Lafayette, he began work in the junk business of a Mr. Spector.[56] The Shapiros came to Lafayette as an IRO request case.[57] That is, they received IRO assistance in reaching Lafayette because they had known Spector, who had assured Shapiro of a job. But not finding that line of work agreeable and hoping to reenter the food business, Shapiro in June 1906 took his family to Indianapolis, where he and his wife opened a store using five hundred dollars they had brought from Russia. Unable to eke out a living in the new venture, Shapiro found work in a dry goods establishment while his wife ran their fledgling business. More bad luck followed when he was injured by a falling packing box. In the course of medical treatment, it was discovered that he had tuberculosis. With assistance from the Jewish Federation of Indianapolis, he was sent for treatment to the National Jewish Hospital for Consumptives in Denver.[58] On returning to Indianapolis, Shapiro rejoined his wife selling coffee and other foodstuffs door to door.[59] Their small business grew, evolving into a highly successful delicatessen. Now owned by a fourth-generation Shapiro, the business is a well-known Indianapolis institution.

## Contesting the Flow of Immigrants

Following the depression of 1907, resistance developed, although not for the first time, against the numbers of workers sent to Indianapolis. The economic slump had a substantial impact on the city's industry and commerce, leading the IRO agent, Samuel Levinson, to oppose the arrival of additional immigrants under IRO sponsorship. Bressler's efforts in late 1907 to enlist the Indianapolis committee in receiving five immigrants landing in Galveston is a case in point. Bressler was the secretary of the recently formed Jewish Immigrants' Information Bureau aiming to send immigrants disembarking at Galveston to communities west of the Mississippi. Not yet equipped to do so but expecting the arrival of an estimated two hundred immigrants at the Texas port, the bureau wanted to use the existing IRO network temporarily. Accordingly, Bressler appealed to Levinson to "obtain employment and . . . make as comfortable as possible five immigrants . . . the Bureau will send you in the course of the next few days."[60] In response, Levinson reported "extremely bad" conditions making it "practically impossible to place men at anything." Many large shops had closed and others had severely reduced their labor force. Moreover, wages were falling. Unable to place IRO men already on the scene and facing requests for assistance from those drifting to Indianapolis from Cincinnati and other cities, Levinson stated that "it would be folly for me to receive any men now."[61]

Bressler accepted Levinson's plea with deep regret, but was persuaded that labor conditions in Indianapolis justified the request for no additional resettlers. He informed Galveston not to send people to the city.[62] As the objective of the removal work was not simply to relocate people to the interior regardless of their economic prospects, their unemployment in Indianapolis would constitute no improvement over their unemployment elsewhere. Bressler trusted the agency's assessment of the city's grim economic circumstances and honored the request to send no one to Indianapolis until he got Levinson's approval. Yet he submitted that "any leniency in this regard that you may feel privileged to extend will be very very much appreciated, because we are in a sadly crippled condition."[63]

The economic stagnation of 1907 rendered even more conservative the Indianapolis agency's view of its capacity to absorb removal clients. Its resistance to the main office's requests was especially distressing owing to the IRO's estimation of the high potential for job placements there. As a rail hub with varied industry, it offered the IRO an excellent prospect for helping immigrants gain economic independence in a congenial community. Bero approvingly remarked, "The rents are low, the district in which they live residential and does not bear the impress of a Ghetto. I find the social life here decidedly good." The traveling agent's report also noted the satisfaction expressed by the IRO clients settled in the city and the "proper spirit" of the removal committee. In the redemptive terms often used by the IRO, Bero praised Levinson because he "not alone understands them but guides them morally, socially and in every other way."[64] Similar views were expressed by other IRO observers. In 1912, Solomon noted, "What a wonderful opportunity this town offers. I have nowhere seen such a wide demand for labor nor such a diversification of industries."[65]

This profile and the agency's good record provided leverage against Bressler's importuning. Although he gave the Indianapolis group some latitude, he did not relent from pressing the agency to receive more newcomers. Not given to false accolades, Bressler still had to temper his more pointed remarks with praise and entreaties, given IRO dependency on the good will of its constituents. The contest over the flow of immigrants came to a head several times between 1912 and 1914 when the IRO threatened to reduce the agent's salary after local resettlement work had waned. It was not the first time. In Bressler's view, the IRO could not continue to pay for services that were not rendered.[66] In each confrontation, Bressler backed down from the Indianapolis committee. Its formidable threat to suspend the IRO relationship should Agent Kaufman's salary be reduced was a price that Bressler was unwilling to pay.[67]

## Not an Employment Bureau

With rapid adjustment and absorption in mind, communities often specified the kinds of immigrants that they wished to receive. Some communities favored single men, either unmarried or initially unaccompanied by their families. Others requested entire families. As to the types of workers sought, the general preference was for skilled artisans, based on the belief that they could more easily be placed. In Terre Haute, an early call for families followed when the community took note of the profound depression and loneliness felt by one of the newcomers. Such men, in the opinion of the Terre Haute correspondent, Harry Schloss, "certainly won't stay away from your city long but will return, and then you are compelled to begin over again."[68] Families would more likely make the long-term adaptation the IRO was seeking, in Schloss's view, because the children might work in addition to the head of the household. Self-support would be virtually certain from the start. Despite a poor early record ("one stayed, the others were no good"), Schloss remained supportive of the work, albeit with several caveats.[69]

The IRO hoped to enlighten Schloss about the broader picture of Jewish immigration so that he could understand the difficulty of complying with his strict specifications. Bressler regretted that the IRO could not undertake work in Terre Haute under Schloss's terms. His response provides a concise early profile of New York's Jewish immigrant population and the problems of resettlement. Writing in 1904, he pointed out that 10,000 Jewish immigrants were arriving each month and that 70 percent remained in New York. The IRO found it difficult to convince families with grown children to leave the city because the sons and daughters were usually able to procure employment, even if the household head could not. Moreover, fear of the unknown and the cultural appeal of the East Side discouraged movement from New York. Bressler, however, proposed sending an interested family composed of parents and six children, four of whom were old enough to work in the way that Schloss proposed. This case was, however, exceptional, and

[A]s far as future co-operation is concerned, we would emphasize the fact that it could not be carried along the lines you suggest. The majority of the immigrants if they are married have their families in Europe. If you could make the heads of these families self-supporting in your City, they could ultimately send for their families from abroad and in that indirect way you could gradually accomplish the very same purpose. We trust you will understand our position. We are anxious to do everything in our power to make the burden of co-operation as light as possible for those who are public spirited enough to assist us and we trust that the communities will appreciate our efforts and will do their utmost to adjust themselves properly to the existing conditions. We have many families who have no grown-up children, who are anxious to be sent out. Efforts must be made for them, especially as the burden of supporting them depends on one individual alone.[70]

That the head of the household described by Bressler had no trade did little to ignite community enthusiasm.

Schloss had approached a Jewish concern, the Ultra Skirt Company, about the possibility of taking workers from the IRO. The company indicated its urgent need, "to splendid advantage to them," of as many as thirty skilled tailors who would earn between fifteen and twenty-five dollars per week. It was essential, however, that the company secure only those tailors "who have had experience on high class work in our line."[71] Considering the wages for common labor, one dollar and ten cents per day or perhaps less, the arrangement Schloss had instigated seemed very promising, "if you can give us the proper people."[72] The company was even willing to place people with lower skill levels. Reluctant to accept twenty-five people at once, Schloss urged Bressler to send a few at a time, until they might be appropriately settled. Schloss believed that the newness of the distribution work required a slow pace, and he also worried about possible hardships on the community:

> We are just like other communities [and] can't bear the entire burden of helpless people; but are very willing to meet half way. We have had a number sent here before and one made good out of six. The six cost us $600 . . . and as I have stated before our people as a whole are unable to stand this burden, and those who are able are the very ones who shirk this duty they owe themselves. Greed for money being a greater theme.[73]

Bressler agreed that it would be precipitous to send twenty-five people at once, even if they had high level skills.

More pertinent to dispersion efforts in the long term, however, was the fact that most IRO applicants had limited occupational abilities, as Bressler explained to Schloss:

> The class of applicants that come to us are essentially men who are not expert mechanics, and while a great many of them have been employed at one time or another in certain trades, they are for the most part recent arrivals in this country, who have not as yet become familiar with the American methods of workmanship. They adapt themselves however, quite readily, so that they be-

166

come very useful, even if they do not attain the highest grade of workmanship. We are therefore hardly in a position to furnish the kind of help that the Ultra Skirt Company is in need of.[74]

In view of these limitations, Bressler urged Schloss to inform him about other opportunities more in keeping with the pool of IRO applicants. Bressler referred to work in the needle trades requiring less than expert proficiency and manual labor that offered some hope of wages reaching beyond one dollar and ten cents per day.[75] It was simply not feasible for a committee to order up the kinds of people it was willing to help. On the contrary, the New York office would call on Terre Haute and other communities to accept people about whom doubts persisted—unaccompanied men of limited occupational skill.

Similarly, Indianapolis agents and their colleagues attempted to maintain cooperation with the New York office on their own terms. Typically, they wanted to participate at the lowest cost to their welfare funds and only to the extent of their personnel's time and patience. Writing to Bressler in 1908, the Indianapolis agency specified "tailors, shoemakers, and other mechanics who can find employment here." The agency believed that it was unfair to the community to take "an arbitrary number of men, without regard to our ability to place them." As to openings in Indianapolis for mechanics and other skilled workers, "New York's inability to fill them ought not be charged against us."[76]

Bressler objected to the term "arbitrary," believing that the main office had respected the Indianapolis agency's wishes to limit IRO clients during the previous year. He was rankled, too, by the charge that the main office could not provide the skilled workers requested:

The Welfare of the unskilled is our concern in even greater degree than that of the skilled. . . . It is the former class to a very large extent . . . that has created the social problems of this community, and . . . it is not less incumbent upon us to bring home to the other communities in the United States that the problem of the unskilled, who are not necessarily incompetent or dependent, is in some degree theirs as well as that of New York. . . . Each community must to a reasonable extent accept its share and that share cannot be confined to skilled workers only. . . . It is the other class that . . . is a constant burden, that becomes a grave problem when it segregates itself to an overwhelming degree in one locality. A thousand such families must in time, because of their bulk become a serious problem, while it has been proved time and again that this thousand divided into very small groups and scattered, will work out their own salvation. It is not to be gainsaid that a large majority of this class, even when scattered will require some kind of assistance at the outset, but then that is only a temporary condition which every community should be willing to accept.[77]

Specifications from communities about acceptable kinds of workers implied that the IRO was a kind of employment bureau filling orders for particular positions. Addressing the National Conference of Jewish Charities in 1904, Bressler found that the cooperating communities at that early point in IRO work were limiting the effectiveness of the organization by agreeing to help only a restricted range of job seekers:

One community will say, you may send us only newly arrived immigrants; another, you may send us only mechanics; another, only laborers; another, only such as speak English, and so on. Such orders would be helpful provided every Jew in New York were willing to leave the city. It must be remembered that comparatively few persons apply at the office, and of them only a part are possessed of handicrafts in which there is a general demand. It can, therefore, be seen . . . that in order that the work may be promoted in the most effective manner, the bureau must not be regarded as an employment agency, whose province it is to cater to the demands of employers. . . . but the cooperating communities must be prepared to take people whether there is a crying demand for them or not.[78]

Bressler believed that if the IRO's purpose had consisted only of supplying workers for waiting positions, then the vast majority of problem cases would not have arisen and there would be no need for a removal office. It would merely be an employment bureau.

It was obvious from the beginning that the easy placement of immigrants would not be a certainty, especially when it came to unskilled workers. In sharing the responsibility of relieving the conditions of indigence and unemployment among the immigrant Jews of New York, communities had to face squarely all of the dimensions of the problem. They would have to undertake the relatively simple task of placing skilled workers as well as the more difficult challenge of absorbing people with few skills. Disputes between the main office and its cooperators waxed and waned as a function of the number of unemployed resettlers in the community. Small communities with unpaid volunteers, although not immune to the problems of IRO city agencies, encountered these difficulties less frequently. The IRO was well aware of the larger proportional burden that problem cases would bring to a small Jewish population. Greater restraint operated in these instances.

### Exporting the Problem: A Rail Ticket out of Town

A nearly irresistible temptation facing a community feeling beleaguered by unemployed newcomers was to return them to New York. Few actions at the local level provoked a sterner response from the main office. A return to New York represented the immediate failure of the person in question and an error in judgment by the IRO in its selection process. Most seriously, it repudiated the organization's very *raison d'être*. The first Indianapolis IRO agent, Samuel Wolf, informed Bressler in the summer of 1905 that the Indianapolis committee had advised him to return three or four men to New York because they refused work paying one dollar and twenty-five cents per day. Bressler sent a pointed telegram to Sol Kiser, head of the Indianapolis Removal Committee, stating, "Under no circumstances return men to New York, letter follows."[79]

Bressler's letter, offering the Indianapolis committee advice on dealing with its problems, explicitly precluded returning idle workers to New York under any circumstances. He reminded Kiser that no individual was ever promised that he would earn more than a dollar a day and overall prospects in the interior were usually understated to diminish any sense of disappointment that clients might feel. Jobs at a dollar a day provided no just cause for complaint, and the disgruntled clients therefore should either work or be left to fend for themselves. Bressler stated that if they had a just grievance, however, then it was the committee's responsibility to set the matter right.[80]

Kiser concurred with Bressler's view. Men unwilling to work should not receive any support from the IRO or from community institutions. Remarking on "quite a little trouble with a few of the last ones sent us," Kiser concluded, "I trust that in the future you will try to be more careful in sending us people who are at least willing to earn a livelihood, and that we will have no more trouble of this kind."[81] It proved a vain hope, but one certainly shared by all IRO cooperating communities wary of expense, inconvenience, or unpleasantness. Less than two months later, Kiser complained about a family of six sent without prior notification. This lapse, Kiser asserted, was especially troublesome because "the husband and father is in such physical condition that he cannot earn enough money to maintain his family."[82]

Men who drifted into a town from their original IRO destination could imperil resettlement work, although the main office and its constituents agreed in broad terms about the appropriate response. The Indianapolis Jewish Federation stated bluntly that the "primary object of our organization is the relief of our home poor, not the wanderer."[83] To the extent that some IRO clients moved about by cajoling communities into support or transportation to another destination, then the reputation of the IRO suffered. The IRO strongly opposed donations to able-bodied men unwilling to work and so advised its correspondents on numerous occasions. No community should abet the movement of immigrants from town to town. The Indianapolis agency acknowledged its agreement with this position and asserted the need for any charitable institution to run "not only on charitable but on sensible and true business principles."[84] Nevertheless, the more trying IRO cases sometimes led the Indianapolis office to capitulate to demands it considered unreasonable. Facing a difficult or a demanding individual, a community might provide a train ticket to New York; to the place from where the person had just traveled; or, in desperation, to almost any destination that an individual specified.

Ticket-giving was the quickest way of disposing of an annoyance. It was condemned by all Jewish social service agencies. Bressler noted a particularly egregious record of ticket-giving in the performance of the committee in Youngstown, Ohio, where Bero found only 20 to 30 percent of IRO men remained in place.[85] Bressler characterized its work as the poorest in the Midwest. Following the 1907 economic decline, when the IRO was especially eager to reenlist inactive committees and agencies, Bressler took the unusual step of abandoning Youngstown as an IRO terminus. He observed that the committee there had chosen to follow the most expedient way of ridding itself of IRO men—providing them with transportation to Cleveland, Dayton, or Cincinnati.[86]

The IRO believed that ticket-giving encouraged pauperism rather than self-support. When some of the first IRO clients were sent back to New York from Terre Haute, Bressler remarked that "this is the very worst thing that could have been done." Their departure from New York in the first place was spurred by their failure to make a living there. Hence, after gaining an opportunity for some slight improvement, they should have been encouraged to seize it. Providing return tickets to people who had a job at hand simply forestalled the day when they would have to be independent and self-reliant.[87]

## "To Hazard the Respect of Their Fellow Citizens"

Rabbi Leipziger accepted Bressler's criticism regarding the return of four men to New York shortly after resettlement work began in Terre Haute. Yet he wanted to remind Bressler of an overriding local concern, for "one thing you forget and it is a condition that perhaps only those in small communities will appreciate. The respected Jewish citizens of the community are unwilling to hazard the respect of their fellow citizens by allowing Jewish riff-raff to remain among them."[88]

While tending their own carefully guarded public standing wherever they resided, American Jews found their reputations particularly vulnerable in small towns. In such communities, missteps among Jews and unwanted public attention were especially liable to the scrutiny of non-Jewish opinion and judgment. In large cities, by contrast, populous Jewish settlements could somewhat mitigate embarrassment by the sheer numbers of people living what was broadly defined as an acceptable, inconspicuous sort of life.

Deflecting possible consequences of the bad behavior of one's coreligionists was highly problematic. Their alleged shortcomings might be nothing more than differences of cultural manner, language, etiquette, and all of the rest of what comprises a tradition or Old Country style. Therein lay much of the criticism by immigrant Jews against the haughtiness of German American Jews who were determined to be arbiters of what was appropriate Jewish comportment. In any case, Jewish communities were determined to control and restrain Jewish differences, perceived as distinct from the values and manners of an American mainstream growing increasingly restive over immigration. Leipziger was reflecting a widely held view that took on a special intensity in cities such as Terre Haute and Indianapolis, where Jews felt especially exposed amid a predominantly white, Protestant, and native-born majority.[89]

The Indianapolis IRO agency feared public embarrassment and rationalized decisions that went against the main office's advice and its own better judgment. At one time or another, gamblers and socialists distressed the Indianapolis group. Agent Kaufman was not hesitant in criticizing what he saw as the corrupting influence that young gamblers, some of whom had been arrested, were exercising on other IRO clients. Such problems seemed particularly nettlesome when exposed to public opinion, both Jewish and non-Jewish. He thus cautioned Bressler, "You will please bear in mind that Indianapolis is a small community, and no matter how good you try to treat a person, he always has something to complain, and, as all the Jews live in one block, it creates a lot of trouble, and for that reason we are sometimes compelled to do things for people who are absolutely undeserving."[90] Some immigrants effectively played on the community's fear of scandal and used it to extract financial support. Many communities quavered when they contemplated the damage that disgruntled newcomers might inflict on the public image of American Jews and their institutions.

Through self-policing, Jewish communities tried to control their collective reputation. Guarding the Jewish public image, moreover, fell not simply to German American Jews but also to many immigrants themselves. The latter adopted equally stringent standards for the way that Jews should present themselves to outsiders. No matter how much respect they might collectively achieve, many Jews felt that the standing of their communities, and indeed their own personal and economic security, was tenuous. This fragile edifice could only be burdened by the considerable weight of even one person's bad public behavior. Jewish communities were thus marked by a defensive vigilance and a chronic nervousness, aptly described as the "*tsitterdik* [trembling] syndrome."[91]

Vociferous public displays within the Jewish community were serious enough but were perceived as even more dire when attracting wider attention. Jewish shame and humiliation were intensified before a non-Jewish audience. The Miller family brought Kaufman this kind of grief. He in turn protested to Bressler for having sent them to Indianapolis. Arriving in Indianapolis in April 1910, Miller, a presser, worked for several months earning nine dollars per week. In early August, his wife complained that her husband was not earning enough money and that they wanted to return to New York. In line with IRO policy, Kaufman informed her that he could not pay for their transportation but would attempt to find another position for Miller. Kaufman continued, "She left the office with the promise that her husband would come to see me. Instead of coming up to see me or looking for another position, they went around from house to house crying and begging that they were starving here and the only thing they wanted was to be sent back to New York."[92]

Likewise, the Adelstein family also wanted tickets back to New York. Adelstein had been discharged from two jobs and continued to get support from the Jewish Federation. Kaufman called him "undesirable," although "he was treated as a perfect gentleman and we did all we could for him to make him feel at home." Instead of going to work at a new job, Adelstein joined Miller in going to the police and complaining "that they were brought here with large families from New York with all kinds of promises that when they arrived they were refused work and assistance."[93]

One member of the agency committee advised Kaufman to press for the arrest of Adelstein and Miller. He demurred, hoping to avoid further publicity while trying to rid himself of the two families "because they incite newcomers to the same action they have taken."[94] In the sink-or-swim view of the IRO, Bressler advised the agent "to let them severely alone if they fail to make good."[95]

The agent was, of course, familiar with the IRO philosophy of minimizing dependency. Immigrants who refused employment should find themselves struck from the rolls of the IRO and its constituents. Still, he was apprehensive about the scene that was unfolding and the opprobrium that might be unleashed within the Jewish community or, worse, from outside of it.

Kaufman's anxiety was all the more intense after the Adelstein and Miller cases came to the attention of the police and *The Indianapolis Star*. The news story appearing under the subheading "Humane Inspector Investigates Complaint Against Federation" provided in embarrassing detail the saga of the two malcontents. The investigation revealed

an attempt by two Jewish men, who came from New York a short time ago, to compel the Jewish Federation of Indianapolis to pay their transportation to New York for alleged failure to comply with the promise of obtaining profitable employment for them. . . . They complained to the police that they had been promised work by the federation and that they have not received assistance. They asserted they were married and had several children to support, which they could not do on $4.50 a week, the earnings they named in the complaint.[96]

The news story also reported the views of the Jewish Federation officials, who denied either sending for the men or promising them jobs. It was also pointed out that the men refused to work. That the Indianapolis police apparently sustained the views of the IRO agency against the charges of Adelstein and Miller in no way diminished Kaufman's concerns about publicity.

The Meyers, parents of seven, also played on the Indianapolis agency's strong desire to avoid a public embarrassment to itself and to the Jewish community of the city. Unable to live at a very high level owing to Meyer's limited skills and small earning capacity, Mrs. Meyer complained publicly and to agent Kaufman, who described her unrealistic aspirations: "Mrs. Meyer wants a house with all modern improvements just on the same style as they are in New York. Unfortunately, the poor people in Indianapolis cannot afford to have such homes, as all our poor districts have no homes with modern improvements." Frustrated that the IRO had presented Meyer as a first-class baster, Kaufman again urged Bressler to take more care in the selection of applicants.[97]

Bressler exhorted local IRO units to remain resolute in the face of unreasonable demands and threats of adverse publicity. At the same time, IRO operatives had to persuade working immigrants that their new circumstances were immeasurably better than the life of unemployment and squalor that they had left behind in New York.[98] With ironic humor, Bressler made this point to Kaufman.

> It is too bad that Mrs. Meyer is not quite satisfied with the housing conditions in Indianapolis. It might be a wise provision in the future to send with each family not only their furniture and belongings, but a well appointed bungalow or mansion with steam heat, hot water, shower bath, telephone and electric lights. . . . I wonder if Mrs. Meyer possessed all these improvement in the New York Hekdesh [hovel; poorhouse]. Perhaps she is lonesome and sighing for the fire escape beds and the sweet savours [sic] emanating from forty kitchens through the tenement airshaft.[98]

Cautioning Kaufman about excessive fear of public and specifically non-Jewish opinion, Bressler urged him to rise above apprehension and insularity.

> The Jews are just as human as the non-Jews and therefore have their failings. If instead of covering up the lapses from rectitude of some of our coreligion-

ists, we openly and frankly sought to punish the wrongdoers and disturbers in general, our Christian friends would not expect perfection from us, and it would not be cause for scandal every time a Jew happened to be human enough to do wrong.[99]

Kaufman thought it far easier to act on such advice in New York than in Indianapolis, and he questioned Bressler's hard-headed recommendation simply to cut off support and contact with those causing trouble.

Kaufman pointed out the likely consequences of Bressler's counsel "to let them severely alone:"

> It is very easy to make such a statement but what would you do if Mrs. Meyer and her seven little children would stand either on a Hester Street corner or on Fifth Avenue of your great metropolis and cry that they were starving and there would be a large crowd around them trying to find out the cause of their distress, and the woman would say she was sent here with her husband by the Industrial Removal Office of Indianapolis; that they promised to be given work and assistance; that her husband cannot find suitable employment; that they have no means of livelihood—Would you say "Let them severely alone if they fail to make good?"
>
> If we would not grant such a family assistance Mrs. Meyer would positively take all her children and walk down to Maple Street, Eddy Street, or South Illinois Street [a neighborhood of the very poor] (Where the "Chosen People" of God reside) and make the above complaint. Believe me all the bystanders would either mob our office or your *office*.[100]

Although he felt that Bressler's urgings might be appropriate for a single man or a family without children, Kaufman believed that his office had to help a large family despite the false information that Meyer had provided about his job skills. Kaufman was convinced that the family would have to be sent back to New York. Bressler responded predictably:

> You ask what would I do if Mrs. Meyer and her seven children would stand on Hester Street or on Fifth Avenue . . . and cry that they are starving etc. I'll tell you what I would do. I would familiarize myself with the facts and act accordingly. Our friends are cleverer than you are. They know that you are afraid of the consequences and they work you accordingly. . . . The way you

describe the case . . . shows that these two families had you thoroughly buf-
faloed . . . I admit that they make your life miserable by such antics but it
will give you only temporary relief to give into them. As soon as they decide
to try their game again they will recall previous results.[101]

Cautioning Kaufman about permitting policy to be dictated by fear of
"what will the Goyim say?" Bressler argued that they will say nothing if
they are fully aware of the facts. In contrast, Kaufman's petulant and demanding clients would always succeed if he permitted fear of public opinion to shape his decisions.[102] Two days later, Kaufman reported that the
Meyer family appeared to have settled down, with Meyer working at a job
that promised support for himself and his dependents.[103] Trouble again
erupted only three days later when Meyer quit his job and left Indianapolis
for Chicago.

Kaufman complained about the money required to provide for the family because the Meyers had arrived without adequate furnishings, clothing
for themselves, and even shoes for the children.[104] Virtually the entire
agent's report for August 1910 was taken up with this family and Meyer's
labor difficulties from their arrival on 3 August.[105] After two weeks at the
Kahn Tailoring Company earning nine dollars and sixty cents per week—a
below-average wage for a baster owing to his working part time and his
lack of skill at custom work—Meyer went to Chicago on 21 August. He remained there for one week. Helped by the Jewish Aid Society in Chicago,
Meyer returned to Indianapolis, where the Kahn Tailoring Company was
persuaded to take him back. Kahn, a prominent member of the Indianapolis Jewish community, could be prevailed on, although within limits.
Kaufman described the family as "uncontrollable" and indicated that
Meyer "caused a great deal of trouble" on the job. The Kahn Tailoring
Company discharged him. Consequently, the executive committee of the
Jewish Federation had decided to return the Meyer family to New York if
there were no improvement and to charge the New York office with the
transportation cost.[106]

Bressler objected to the proposal and refused to subsidize the Meyer
family's return. Such cases, he argued, were to be expected, and for every
irksome experience of this sort that the Indianapolis committee encountered, the New York office faced many more. But should every effort at resolution fail, then Bressler advised again, "leave the family severely alone to
shift for itself, withholding any assistance whatsoever.[107]

Two days later the Indianapolis committee returned the Meyer family and their possessions to New York and presented the main office with a bill for sixty-six dollars and ninety-one cents.[108] Bressler was "grieved" at the action, refusing to reimburse the Indianapolis committee for ridding itself of a burdensome case "by a method most convenient to the community but ruinous to all valuable cooperation."[109] With the Meyer family's return to New York, the case aroused no further exchanges and appears to have ended IRO involvement.

### World War I: The Beginning of the End of Resettlement

The outbreak of World War I severely disrupted all of the IRO's work. The winter of 1913 had brought an economic downturn, and the war exacerbated the declining fortunes of industry. Reports to the IRO from three major outlets for industrial workers—Detroit, Cleveland, and Pittsburgh—all confirmed the increasing difficulty in placing IRO clients. Industrial contraction and job layoffs augured poorly for the immediate future of IRO-sponsored immigrant distribution. In 1913, the IRO managed to resettle 6,469 people, but the number fell sharply to 3,501 in 1914, despite the IRO's receipt of 11,565 applications for resettlement. The hardest blow to IRO activity following the outbreak of war was the sharp reduction in income from the ICA. By the summer of 1914, the curtailment of revenue prevented the IRO even from taking advantage of the labor opportunities that were available.[110]

The chairman of the IRO, Reuben Arkush, wrote to cooperating agencies and committees about the severe constraints facing the organization and appealed for continued cooperation, however limited. Arkush effectively presented a *deus ex machina* for the last and most serious dispute between Bressler and the Indianapolis group over the agent's salary. He asked all IRO agencies to accept a suspension of agents' stipends until the return of normal conditions. Furthermore, he explained the necessity of reducing the allocation for maintenance of newly settled immigrants. Room and board would be provided only when absolutely necessary but for no more than a week. Without specifying any particular number, Arkush appealed to IRO cooperators to accept as many people as possible. His letter tried to make the best of a desperate situation and to keep the "machinery of distribution" intact.

Looking to a future that did not materialize, the chairman believed that the IRO should remain prepared for an efficient and rapid distribution of newcomers once immigration recommenced at war's end.[111]

Arkush's special appeal notwithstanding, IRO activity in Indianapolis and elsewhere never achieved its prewar levels. Instead, it went into sharp decline. By the end of 1913, the IRO had resettled a total 2,661 people in 42 towns and cities of Indiana, or an average of 204 people each year.[112] Between 1914 and 1917, only 239 reached Indiana under IRO auspices, with 1917 marking the lowest point when only 17 people were resettled in the state.[113] Nationally, the resettlement record for 1913 represented one of the organization's high water marks, exceeded only by the 6,922 and 7,586 individuals resettled in 1906 and 1907, respectively.[114] In 1914, immigrant distribution plummeted with the resettlement of 3,501 individuals.[115] For each of the next 3 years, the total number of resettled IRO clients was 1,821, 1,434, and 1,006.[116] Between 1918 and the formal dissolution of the organization in 1922, IRO activity was at a standstill. As for Indianapolis, between 1901 and 1917, approximately 1,475 individuals settled in the city under IRO sponsorship.[117]

## Conclusion

Throughout the Midwest, the experience of local IRO agents and volunteers tells a story similar to those of Indianapolis and Terre Haute, of success mixed with failure, of exemplary workers and burdensome schemers, of self-protective Jewish communities falling short of IRO numerical goals. Unqualified, positive assessments of the immigrants were consistently counterbalanced by impatient reports of petulant newcomers refusing work, demanding financial assistance after quitting a job, espousing socialist or radical ideas, departing town leaving behind personal debts, and so forth. Correspondents protested with monotonous regularity that their towns were unable to absorb as many immigrants as the main office was sending. Locally, IRO correspondents generally did not share the broader vision of the New York leadership or at least could not sustain it against the pressure of those cases draining their time, patience, and resources. Organizing IRO committees and encouraging their continued work on behalf of immigrant distribution called for all of the skills of argument and persuasion that Bressler and the IRO traveling agents could

178

muster. Results always fell short of expectations, given the immense task of safeguarding immigrants and immigration.

Still, thousands of people settled in the midwest to restart their lives and to help realize the IRO's vision of a dispersed Jewish immigrant population. The immigrants constituted the links in a chain of migration drawing an indeterminate number of others, including family and countrymen, out of New York or Europe and into the American heartland, amid an often uneasy alliance among their patrons. The relationship between the local agencies and committees and the New York office is indicative of the enduring tension in those years between immediate but narrow communal self-interest and the developing consciousness of a Jewish community, national in scope and ideologically committed to a broad definition of collective responsibility.

# — 5 —

## Conclusion

The IRO was born amid the controversies over the eastern and southern European immigration to the United States. The organization vigorously defended immigration in a prolonged debate centering on its economic consequences and the repercussions of a steady cultural diversification of the nation. Nearly a century later, when large-scale immigration is again a controversial fact of American life, these twin concerns have reemerged as the dominant themes in the current discussion. Although the numbers of immigrants coming to the United States are to an extent smaller than the annual arrivals in the thirty years before World War I, the arguments remain as acrimonious as any engaged in by the IRO.

More than most issues in contemporary life, immigration encourages reflection about the character of the American nation—not only its composition but also its values. National immigration policy, domestic labor markets, and immigrant enclaves in American cities—all concerns of the IRO—also figure in the discourse about the present condition and future prospects of the country. Although Latin Americans and Asians primarily compose the contemporary immigrant population, the much more numerous Jewish, Italian, and Slavic immigrants of the earlier era were regarded as no less different from the American mainstream—a eugenic nightmare for the legion of xenophobic guardians of American purity. For the latter, the barbarians were not only at the gates; they had also taken over the cities, and prudence demanded an end to it. Unassimilable aliens from the backward parts of Europe obsessed the nativist imagination of one hundred years ago as it conjured a social apocalypse that never materialized.

180

Much to the contrary, those venturesome immigrants from southern and eastern Europe, their children, and grandchildren have given lie to nativist fantasies by the model of their own lives and achievements, whether as ordinary citizens or as notable figures in the professions, politics, science, the arts, and, indeed, every domain of American life. To take only one example, Henry James's foreboding about the English language after his visit to the Lower East Side appears fatuous in light of the stellar literary achievements of many celebrated children of Jewish immigrants—accomplishments so significant that the very character of American letters in this century pivots on their contributions. The forecasts of other immigration naysayers about the imminent desolation of the American social landscape sank into the same oblivion.

Yet prophecies of doom continue as many voices warn of the peril accompanying the current movement of peoples to the United States. Illegal immigrants present the most obvious target for present-day restrictionists, but the latter extend their critique to legal immigrants as well. Whereas the eugenic preoccupations with racial purity have faded in the public conversation, except at the social and political margins, strident nativism and economic nationalism tinged with racial and ethnic animus produce a similar dread. Any student of European immigration who closely attends to the contemporary dispute soon recognizes the recycled apprehensions of the earlier period, including fear of job loss for natives, immigrants on the dole, and linguistic and cultural fragmentation. Some now advise a wide-ranging disengagement that would block immigration and frustrate economic globalization, transnational commercial relationships, and other breaches of the familiar politico-economic boundaries of the nation. In the process, they hope to defuse an economic and cultural "time bomb," in the panicked words of two recent immigration critics.[1]

Current objections to immigration on racial and ethnic grounds are often expressed through a veil of economic argument. They derive from a farrago of early twentieth-century pseudoscience and bigotry, assuming a hierarchical ranking of racial and ethnic groups that also indexes their worthiness as immigrants. Chastened by World War I, America in the 1920s turned inward, severely curtailing immigration in 1924 with the passage of quota legislation based on national origins, thus codifying the racial and ethnic hierarchy. This limitation on immigration effectively ended the large-scale arrival of those regarded as least desirable. Even the rising tide of German antisemitic violence from the 1930s until American entry into World War II could not loosen the irrational immigration strictures used to deny admission to people fleeing for their lives.

The racial and ethnic determination of eligibility for immigration eventually gave way with the Immigration Reform Act of 1965. That legislation set the stage for the large-scale immigration of Latin Americans and Asians that has proceeded during the last thirty years. New eligibility criteria were defined, including prior family ties in the United States and particular occupational and professional skills. It was the very questioning of the uses of race and ethnicity as eligibility categories that animated in part the 1965 revision of the old immigration laws. The national quotas were glaringly out of step with the momentous developments of the 1960s. Then, the movement for civil rights long denied to African Americans awakened the public to yawning disparities between constitutional ideals and the discriminatory reality of race-based public institutions and laws. The nativity quotas of the 1920s seemed of a piece with the retrograde treatment of American citizens based on race or ethnic origin. Ambivalence, contradiction, and uncertainty have nonetheless suffused the American response to immigration, past and present.

In reprise of the anti-immigration arguments in which the IRO engaged, the current dispute about the economic impact of immigration focuses on its consequences for American workers. The income and job security of the native wage earner represent the lightning rods for much of the discussion. Critics charge that legal and illegal immigrants get employment at the expense of the native born and depress wages. The effect of immigration on state and local governments is also a matter of worried concern, especially regarding the impact of needy immigrants on already burdened public social services and welfare agencies, which were nonexistent during the European immigration. Gauging the economic repercussions of immigration is an enormously complicated task that a number of economists have undertaken. Against the more vocal critics of immigration in politics and the popular media, the weight of professional economic opinion falls on the positive side. The United States has gained materially from the post-1965 immigration.[2]

In the earlier era, the economic needs both of newcomers and hosts drove much of the immigration to the United States. As a result, immigrant numbers proved very sensitive to American economic cycles. Periods of increased immigration coincided with industrial and commercial upturns and expansions that stood to benefit from immigrant labor. Likewise, economic stagnation or depression diminished immigration. Although large, concentrated settlements of newcomers aroused the fears of many people personally unfamiliar with cultural and language differences, such derangements of customary experience in neighborhoods and workplaces were insufficient to stifle American immigration policy. Moreover, until the end of World War I, organized labor as well as protectionist and nativist associations eager to close American ports were, despite great effort, unable to counter the economic forces pushing and pulling the immigrants.

Although many of the rationales and criticisms of new immigrants echo the earlier debate, the current immigration differs in important ways from that of a century ago. Its reduced vulnerability to American economic rhythms stems from several factors. Since the 1930s, federal intervention in the economy has effectively limited the depths of the cycle, thereby diminishing the older, self-regulating aspect of immigration. Slowdowns since 1965 do not begin to rival the economic plunges and uncertainties of 1893 and 1907, for example. Because a potential immigrant now gets a place in line, so to speak, an individual determined to come to the United States is unlikely to leave the queue simply because job prospects are dim. Motivated by a desire for family reunification, many present-day immigrants also arrive without any intention of immediately seeking work and are therefore less constrained by the kinds of economic factors that limited the earlier European immigration.[3]

Other differences in the two periods of immigration are noteworthy. The range of cultural and linguistic variation in the cities of a century ago pales before the extraordinary diversity of the present. Port cities, particularly, where newcomers like their earlier European counterparts tend to settle, are more polyglot than ever. Spanish is ubiquitous, and a wide variety of languages are represented from the Indian subcontinent; Southwest, East, and Southeast Asia; the Pacific Islands; and Africa.

Many immigrants, in contrast to the eastern and southern European newcomers, are highly educated professionals. Compared with the unskilled or semiskilled, these individuals are less buffeted by shifts in the postindustrial economy. In addition, physicians, chemists, physicists, computer scientists, mathematicians, and engineers among the immigrants compensate for an insufficient pool of native-born professionals to meet national needs. Relatedly, when native professionals are geographically concentrated, immigrants, trained either abroad or in the United States, fulfill vitally important needs. Medical care, for example, is not well-distributed across the country. People in many communities outside of large urban centers lack reasonable access to physicians. This problem has been ameliorated to some extent by immigrant doctors who set up practice in underserved areas. It is now commonplace to see Indian, Chinese, or Korean names in the medical directories of small-town clinics.

The current immigration also includes many more entrepreneurs than in the past. Immigrants bent on starting businesses have effectively revitalized whole neighborhoods with their enterprises. Like Cubans in Miami or Koreans in Los Angeles, ethnic entrepreneurs are changing the face of many American cities. The new merchants, grocers, hoteliers, and restaurateurs either arrive with some capital or otherwise call on the intense labor of the entire family to accumulate sufficient money for business formation. As taxpayers, employers, investors, producers, and suppliers of goods and services, these businesspeople contribute to local economies in a ripple effect. Indeed, the garment industry in New York since the late 1960s has been profoundly affected by immigrant entrepreneurs able to parlay ethnic resources into high-risk clothing manufacture in a swiftly changing market.[4]

Large numbers of legal and illegal immigrants, in contrast, reproduce the economic patterns characteristic of the European immigration. Today's sweat shops in New York and other places employ immigrants under conditions that yield nothing to the meanness of the needle trades at the turn of the twentieth century.[5] Many people enter the American economy in the secondary labor market, characterized by the lowest pay, the least security, and the most severe working conditions. The news media are saturated with stories of desperate, illegal aliens from Mexico, Central America, and Asia. Often after enduring great physical danger in crossing the border or reaching a port, they take work at the minimum wage or less and labor in bitter, exploitative circumstances to which native workers would not submit. Yet these jobs, usually in crass violation of legal standards of safety and fairness, may provide income in excess of anything available to them in their home countries and a first tenuous step on what they hope is a path to something better. Like the "birds of passage" so characteristic of the Italian immigration of a century ago, some immigrant workers come to the United States temporarily. Their goal is to accumulate enough money before returning to their home countries to begin small businesses. They suffer great hardship, performing work that flourishes on human desperation and the single-minded drive of some employers to cut costs in violation of labor laws.

Proportionately more of the European generation of immigrants entered the American economy at its lowest levels, yet their foreignness and lack of skills and education did not block their cultural and socioeconomic adaptation to the new country. Socialized in American institutions, such as the public school, their children accelerated the process of assimilation and entered the mainstream of American life. These first two generations were hardly the "insoluble clots" that E. A. Ross warned of in 1912.

To what extent does the social trajectory of the European immigrants and their descendants predict that of the contemporary immigration? This question is challenging for several reasons. An ideological fervor attaches to much of the contemporary academic and popular discussion of ethnicity and immigration, inevitably clouding the interpretation of empirical findings. Furthermore, in considering the questions of ethnic continuity or transformation in immigrant communities, it is also important to note that cultural persistence in American cities is partly ensured by a continuing immigration that vitalizes the ethnic community with the addition of active tradition bearers and speakers of the language. Steady immigration, more than a simple weakening of the processes of assimilation, may explain the flourishing of ethnic traditions in large urban immigrant centers.

The relevance of the immigrant experience of a century ago to present immigrant and ethnic trends turns in large measure on the controversial idea of assimilation. Long a part of the conceptual tool kit of the social sciences in explaining the impact of the new country on European immigrant minorities, it also has reflected popular attitudes. The restrictionist legislation of 1924 further entrenched the value of leaving the Old World behind, as immigrants already resident in the United States faced an Americanization movement even more emphatic in its assimilationist credo than anything that had preceded it. Since the 1960s, however, assimilation both as a social science concept and as an American value has come under intense analytical and ideological scrutiny.

The most unequivocal expression of assimilation as a social process occurs in what has been called "straight-line theory," elaborated particularly well by the sociologist Herbert Gans.[6] In his view, the core of ethnic life, including its institutions and obligatory cultural practices and commitments, has withered. Built on assertions about the efficacy of the American melting pot, the theory postulates an inevitable incorporation of ethnic groups into the broader culture. Still, the assimilation process has not run its course, for European-derived ethnic groups persist in spite of strong tendencies toward cultural homogenization. Characteristic ethnic styles, whether of outlook, humor, taste, or the like survive into the third and fourth generations.

Gans suggests that these various expressions of ethnicity do not contradict straight-line theory. Features of ethnicity that do survive represent for Gans a manifestation of "symbolic ethnicity."[7] He notes the attenuation of ethnic institutions and practices, except when they comport with the rhythms and the routines of American life. Then, the accommodation is without cost or sacrifice. No longer exclusive or compelling, ethnic practice becomes optional, a take-it-or-leave-it, leisure-time activity that can appeal to people of various traditions. It is an ethnicity without solid organizational moorings. In New York, everyone, including a black or a Jewish mayor, can be Irish on 17 March. Ethnicity becomes more a matter of feeling and sentiment than of obligatory participation by ethnics in an array of distinctive and exclusive institutions.[8]

Other processes accompany the linear incorporation of mainstream cultural values and institutional practices in the lives of immigrants and their descendants. Sharp declines in native language competence, even between the immigrant and the second generation, provide an especially revealing index of cultural transformation.[9] As broader cultural values are internalized, educational and occupational mobility proceeds, along with increasing cross-ethnic marriage rates and other indicators of weakened barriers between different groups.[10]

Much of symbolic ethnicity is little more than an exercise in low-cost nostalgia—a way of connecting emotionally to the world of the immigrants without enduring the hardship of having to live in it. In Jewish community centers, for example, recreations of Lower East Side life have included warm scenes of pushcart vendors and klezmer musicians. Other characteristic features remain unacknowledged: airless, squalid tenement rooms housing families and boarders too numerous for the space; fetid, trash-strewn streets; meager sanitation; chronic respiratory illness; and early death. In short, a longing for the past filters from collective memory all of the pitiless and grinding oppression of immigrant poverty.

The assimilationist model lends itself particularly well to the experience of American Jews despite efforts at Yiddish revival and a return to orthodoxy by a notable but very small segment of the third and fourth generations. High rates of marriage between Jewish and non-Jewish partners alarm both religious and lay leaders. Some particularly sanguine observers, however, note in all of this assimilation a level of acceptance of Jews hardly envisioned by the immigrant generation or indeed by any Diaspora community outside of the United States. Without fear or self-consciousness, Jews can embrace their religion and culture without defensiveness. They can, moreover, fully participate in all of the institutions of American social and political life.[11] In effect, the American Jewish future that the IRO surmised in its most optimistic moments has been realized.

The IRO firmly believed both in the acculturating power of American institutions and in the capacity of the immigrants to adapt themselves to the laws and customs of their new home. The experiences of four generations of Americans of eastern and southern European origin have fully vindicated that faith. Assimilation has indeed worked its way through those immigrant communities. When Isaac Rubinow defended the Lower East Side in political, economic, and cultural terms against the prevailing perspective expressed by the IRO, assimilationist values were ascendant. Although he found support in a resistant, sometimes churlish Yiddish press, Rubinow was not representing the views of a large, assertive, and self-conscious minority that was intensely aggrieved and politically active. The European immigrants had encountered a dominant discourse on assimilation, and, by and large, accepted its fundamental assumptions, if not always with enthusiasm. Rubinow's was the voice of a minority within a minority. The ideology of cultural absorption suffused the dominant world view, asserting that economic success in the new land varied with the cultural distance that one was willing to travel from the obsolete lifeways of Europe. Irving Howe, in his popular book, *World of Our Fathers*, pithily summarizes the process: "In behalf of its sons, the East Side was prepared to commit suicide; perhaps it did."[12]

For the upwardly mobile, economic achievement severed many strands of ethnic continuity in a remarkably brief time. Of course, every immigrant Jew did not "make it" nor did all of the second generation, as pockets of Jewish poverty have quietly persisted in the shadows of the aggregate statistics on Jewish economic success. Moreover, as Stephen Steinberg has pointed out, poverty has insulated from assimilation segments of even the most successful groups, so that carrying on ethnic traditions and practices is more characteristic of the economically marginal.[13]

Despite the pervasive influence of assimilationist models in social research, notable critiques have emerged in the social sciences over the last thirty years and in recent multicultural discourses about American society.

In the early 1970s, various writers proclaimed the failures of assimilation as evidenced by a revived consciousness of ethnicity. The new ethnic awareness purportedly proved not just that certain symbols of ethnicity had managed to withstand the intense heat of the melting pot but that the melting pot itself was defective. Ethnicity, it was claimed, was flourishing among people two or more generations removed from Europe.[14] Ethnic feeling, despite a weakened nucleus of ethnic institutions, nurtured solidarities that influenced urban politics.[15] The skeptics, however, have pointed out that much of the assertiveness of white ethnics focused on working-class interests. Ethnic concerns were not at issue, although it was ethnicity that mobilized political activity in a defensive reaction against growing black consciousness and political pressure.[16]

The diffuse ethnic feelings that accompany potent expressions of ethnic political power such as those manifested among white ethnics in the 1970s are thus consistent with the phenomenon of symbolic ethnicity. Eating ethnic foods or observing holidays rooted in Europe simply provide the diacritics of group definition and political consciousness without forcing a choice between ethnic symbols and practices, on the one hand, and full participation in American society, on the other. Although the symbols of ethnicity enjoy a broad, undemanding, and affectionate allegiance, a more consequential dimension of contemporary ethnicity is its relationship to malleable interest group politics. An effective means of political self-protection, ethnicity as interest does little, however, to renovate ethnicity as culture.

Although the effort to revive ethnic consciousness was closely associated with rightward shifts in the voting patterns of people historically associated with the Democratic party, the multicultural critique of assimilation is situated on the political left. That critique grows out of the social turmoil and challenges to conventional authority—political and academic—that began in the 1960s. At its best, multiculturalism springs from fundamental democratic values and a desire to promote a broader participation in all levels of American life. It includes several reformulations about the historic and current place of minorities. Segments of the population that conventional views put well to the side of the central stage—immigrants, blacks, Indians, women—began to get long-overdue scholarly and curricular recognition as important actors in the American historical drama. In colleges and universities, substantial curricular changes have led to the development of courses and programs devoted to once excluded segments of the American population.[17]

These concerns have exercised their effect on popular consciousness as well. Along with ethnic festivals and various assertions of ethnic pride through cultural preservation, public conversations about the value of ethnicity in American life are ubiquitous. They enjoy considerably more support and legitimacy than the resistant and marginal discourses articulated by Rubinow and other minority critics of the early twentieth century. A reasoned multicultural critique has called attention to neglected contributions to American life by various groups. Having much to celebrate and therefore to preserve, some anxiously resist any further erosion of tradition. Of course, exposing some American influences as destructive is nothing new.

The inimical effect of crowded cities on immigrants established the *raison d'être* of the IRO, which, however, prescribed resettlement and attendant assimilative change as the antidote. Likewise, Michael Gold's bitter portrait of the Lower East Side angrily repudiated bigoted claims that Jewish gangsterism was the province of low-class immigrants. Contending that Jews have done no killing since the fall of Jerusalem, he asserted, "It is America that taught the sons of tubercular Jewish tailors how to kill."[18]

Assimilation has thus come to represent a problematic process, especially for intolerant varieties of multiculturalism. It is reviled as the outcome of an American cultural hegemony that would continue to diminish the cultural integrity of ethnic groups unless resisted. Cultural or linguistic assimilation is widely opposed, at least rhetorically, bound up as it is believed to be with an historic record of mistreatment and exploitation of people beyond the mainstream. Against the substantial effects of assimilation, native language study and other ubiquitous expressions of ethnic self-assertion are, of course, redolent with psychological meaning, if not cultural efficacy. It is part reclamation and part resistance to a further wearing away of custom—at times fetishizing distinctions that express little more than what Freud termed the "narcissism of petty differences." However passionate the resistance, one cannot easily gainsay the relentless transformative power of American institutions. The blandishments of American culture continue to redirect ethnic communities, if not precisely along the path traveled by the earlier European immigrants.

Native language usage is a case in point. Attempts at various levels of government to declare English the official language of the United States are motivated by fears that the country is well on the road to Babel. Several grass-roots organizations also spread the alarm, mobilizing popular support against bilingual education and similar efforts at language preservation. Any move to sanction multiple languages is seen as a step toward cultural polarization or some variety of schismatic linguistic nationalism. French Canada is the usual exemplar. Notwithstanding the failure of some immigrants to learn English or the crippling excesses of bilingual education that delay for too long the immersion of immigrant children in classes taught in English, the American linguistic reality at the end of the twentieth century does not portend national doom. English is not under siege. The children of immigrants, and many immigrants themselves, learn it. Around the country classes in English as a second language are heavily oversubscribed. Many of the enrollees are little different in their aspirations and outlook from the night school students Abraham Cahan described long ago. After many hours at their jobs, they struggle with the intricacies of English phonetics and grammar. Having cast their lot in the new country and determined to make the best of it, they learn English as part of the bargain. Even in Miami, the American city most fundamentally transformed by immigration since the 1960s, English flourishes. Many of the children and grandchildren of immigrants not only speak the language fluently but also prefer it to Spanish in their daily lives.[19]

Multiculturalism in its narrow-minded forms concentrates on the most troubled features of the relationship between ethnic groups and the United States. It stimulates energetic efforts to shore up the integrity of these groups against assimilation and to beat back the recognition of more universal identities and loyalties as well as common culture. Often defensive and alienated, these regressive multicultural campaigns can encourage their own brand of intolerance and chauvinism, arousing in turn predictable and equally intolerant responses. As civil debate yields to unreason, the constructive and democratic discourse of moderate multiculturalism on campus and beyond is tainted by the parochial and odious claims of others wearing the multicultural mantle.

A resistant and divisive multicultural rhetoric has ignited strong reactions, ranging from the constructive and sensible to the demagogic and opportunistic. A reasoned conception of the American experience appropriately values a comprehensive view of the national past and present. At the same time, that progressive view criticizes retrograde moves toward social fragmentation and polarization; it also stands against any determined opposition to the forging of common bonds across a diverse America. Indeed, a new ethnic tribalism that spurns civic values and common citizenship in self-righteous and intolerant ways is a persistent feature of the current social landscape.[20] The difficult challenge on the cusp of a new century is an old one: to accept differences while standing for the mutual loyalties, values, and obligations of a shared American citizenship, estimable precisely because its rights and guarantees are not dependent on ethnic origin.

Leaving aside the ideological critique of assimilation, a continuing refinement of that concept in light of accumulating empirical investigations is very desirable. It will make possible finer-grained comparisons of the social trajectories of the earlier immigration from Europe with the post-1965 Latin American and Asian immigration.

Economic and cultural components meld together in the conventional, straight-line assimilationist perspective, for, in the experience of the immigrants from Europe, economic mobility and social participation in American life were predicated on the adoption of both English and mainstream values. It is now widely understood, however, that these processes are separable. A knowledge of English and close acquaintance with or even acceptance of the values of the broader society do not necessarily entail access to the full range of economic opportunities or social institutions. Consequently, the experience of the children of the European immigrants does not provide the sole model for the incorporation of other immigrants or ethnic minorities into American society.

Americans of African descent, more than any group, have been shaped by their historical experience in the United States and in turn have enriched American cultural life in countless ways. Yet the legacy of discrimination and legal and customary obstacles to educational and occupational opportunities, housing, credit, and the like have negated assimilation as measured by socioeconomic mobility. The European immigrants and their children, reviled as racially inferior and subject to many social limitations, endured this hostility for a relatively brief time. Economic and residential mobility, education, name changes, and the like effaced the most apparent differences between themselves and their neighbors. The debilities of skin color, in contrast, cannot be overcome in the same ways, and indeed the very value of much immigrant labor historically depended on the exclusion of black Americans from substantial portions of the labor pool.

In Miami, an inner-city black underclass represents a powerful force actively assimilating Haitian young people into American society through a culture of resistance. The world view of native black youth derogates what

191

Haitian parental values extol—education, achievement, and the use of social networks within the immigrant community to promote accomplishment. These values are precisely those that would normally help to preadapt Haitian youth to the American life their immigrant parents are seeking. Assimilation is indeed occurring, but it is propelling youth into a downward socioeconomic spiral.[21]

In contrast to the Haitian pattern of cultural assimilation without socioeconomic mobility, Miami's Cubans have prospered economically and achieved political power without the kinds of cultural sacrifices made by the European immigrants. These gains have come, not in spite of the persistence of ethnic social institutions and cultural practices but because of them. Moreover, these ethnic organizations and behaviors enjoy an equal standing with those of the previously dominant Anglos.[22] Cuban Miami has not had to commit suicide on behalf of its children. In rethinking the models based on the European data, Portes and Zhou have aptly termed the several modes of immigrant incorporation "segmented assimilation."[23] Although the case of Cubans is exceptional and goes against the grain of conventional assimilationist expectation based on the third and fourth generations removed from Europe, the time scale is also very different. Whereas the straight-line assimilationist model of European immigration and ethnicity looks closely at the lives of the grandchildren and great-grandchildren of the immigrants, research on the recent immigration from Asia and Latin America provides a much narrower generational picture. Later generations may experience some of the same assimilationist processes that reshaped the lives of those descended from the southern and eastern European immigration.

At the same time, one must acknowledge that the place of immigrants and minorities is very different from what it was when the IRO was promoting distribution and acculturation. Their undeniable but costly cultural transformation in the course of a generation was matched by the equally extraordinary influence that they wove into the American social fabric. The adjustment of the nation to its newest citizens is now more openly recognized and valued. It is possible to join a self-conscious and unapologetic ethnic affiliation with American citizenship in a way that is more compatible than at any time in the past. The recognition of acculturation as a two-way process grants legitimacy to cultural practices that continue to influence positively the United States at the same time that the newcomers are constrained to reorganize their lives and to act in new ways.

Whatever form it takes, ethnicity is a pervasive fact of American life. It is so much the age of ethnically compounded Americans—African, Chinese, Italian, Irish, Jewish—that other identities often seem secondary. Yet individuals are much more than their ethnicities and, consequently, they share with people of other ethnic groups multiple possibilities for relationships. Religious, political, professional, avocational, and numerous other features of social life are not inevitably enclosed within ethnic group boundaries. However primordial many people may regard ethnicity, we know what the IRO knew and its antagonists resisted: ethnicity is a matter of history and culture, not genetics. Ethnic groups can wax and wane in strength and importance; can be more or less open to external influences; can be more or less exclusive; and, most significant, can represent one among many group associations. When ethnicity alone defines social, economic, and political destiny in pluralistic states, as it continues to do throughout much of the world, the consequences are usually ruinous.[24]

What the IRO asked of the immigrants was that they accommodate themselves to the new country through independent self-supporting labor—the first and most important step in their own salvation. Leaving New York, immigrant Jews could work in a variety of occupations, thus breaking out of the constricted Jewish economic niche that they had been condemned to in eastern Europe. Simultaneously, they would encounter, as one group among many, the broad stream of American life and its inevitable influences. The country in turn would encounter them, emerging the richer for their labor, sobriety, and social participation. So it is for all immigrants in relationship to their adopted land—a dynamic, two-way process of mutual influence in which neither the nation nor the immigrant communities can remain as they were. The IRO expected immigrant Jews simply to observe the expectations of good citizenship and to determine for themselves the extent of their own cultural practices and observances. Ethnic possibility and movement would thus supplant ethnic slotting and stasis.

Horace Kallen's vision of a pluralistic America, noted in Chapter 2, was predicated on the belief that American institutions were freeing up ethnic consciousness. Americanization, in his view, liberated rather than repressed ethnic nationality.[25] The IRO believed that Kallen had overstated Jewish proclivities toward self-consciousness and the preservation of Old Country forms. The organization feared that his critical stance toward the melting pot would be used by immigration opponents to support their claim that the immigrants were resisting incorporation into American society. In rebuttal, the IRO said simply that Jewish immigrants, like all others, assimilated enough to become good citizens. But what was enough?

The IRO wisely left this question unanswered, and it should remain so. Individuals and the ethnic groups to which they belong are the best arbiters of what is worthy of preservation and practice within the framework of American life. Of course, this matter is not wholly one of self-invention and independent preference, given the extraordinary power of acculturation. Nevertheless, there is room for maneuver. Groups and individuals should be able to lay claim to an American entitlement—a tolerant recognition of differences by their fellow citizens—as they determine what to preserve and practice as core expressions of their ethnic selfhood. The continuing American quest for the difficult reconciliation of pluralism and homogeneity, diversity and universalism, ethnicity and common culture remains as formidable and as promising as it was a century ago.

# APPENDIX

Eleven Tables Summarizing IRO Placements, 1901–1917. Compiled from Annual Reports of the JAIAS and the IRO, with Comparative Data from the *Reports of the Immigration Commission.*

Table 1. The distribution of individuals from New York by state,
including Canada and Latin America, 1901–1917

| | | | |
|---|---|---|---|
| Alabama | 934 | Nevada | 20 |
| Arizona | 59 | New Hampshire | 37 |
| Arkansas | 261 | New Jersey | 1,041 |
| California | 4,850 | New Mexico | 56 |
| Colorado | 2,791 | New York . | 3,773 |
| Connecticut | 388 | North Carolina | 113 |
| Delaware | 23 | North Dakota | 597 |
| District of Columbia | 51 | Ohio | 10,017 |
| Florida | 387 | Oklahoma | 311 |
| Georgia | 1,262 | Oregon | 858 |
| Idaho | 17 | Pennsylvania | 3,466 |
| Illinois | 7,534 | Rhode Island | 55 |
| Indiana | 2,900 | South Carolina | 247 |
| Iowa | 1,532 | South Dakota | 89 |
| Kansas | 465 | Tennessee | 1,239 |
| Kentucky | 895 | Texas | 1,560 |
| Louisiana | 680 | Utah | 139 |
| Maine | 89 | Vermont | 95 |
| Maryland | 272 | Virginia | 455 |
| Massachusetts | 577 | Washington | 907 |
| Michigan | 5,735 | West Virginia | 201 |
| Minnesota | 2,497 | Wisconsin | 3,709 |
| Mississippi | 353 | Wyoming | 46 |
| Missouri | 6,627 | Canada | 1,464 |
| Montana | 117 | Latin America | 13 |
| Nebraska | 2,156 | | |
| | | Total | 73,960 |

*Note:* The Boston and Philadelphia branches of the IRO resettled a total of 2,576 and 2,459 individuals, respectively. Most of the work of these IRO offices was accomplished by 1913. Grand total 78,995.

**Table 2.** Marital status of IRO clients and the location of
their families at the time of their departure from New York by year

| Year | Families leaving New York with head | Families sent later to join head | Married men with family remaining in New York | Married men with family in Europe | Unmarried men and women[a] (wage earners) |
|------|------|------|------|------|------|
| 1901 | 89 | 104 | 179 | 269 | 628 |
| 1902 | 118 | 237 | 249 | 545 | 1053 |
| 1903 | 345 | 346 | 318 | 983 | 1328 |
| 1904 | 327 | 400 | 222 | 2081 | 1082 |
| 1905 | 374 | 406 | 144 | 1706 | 1354 |
| 1906 | 604 | 423 | 167 | 1264 | 1628 |
| 1907 | 635 | 424 | 243 | 1369 | 2178 |
| 1908 | 451 | 428 | 202 | 511 | 1195 |
| 1909 | 321 | 311 | 96 | 292 | 689 |
| 1910 | 363 | 345 | 114 | 389 | 761 |
| 1911 | 366 | 377 | 107 | 288 | 618 |
| 1912 | 352 | 589 | 456 | 493 | 1401 |
| 1913 | 288 | 614 | 597 | 912 | 1707 |
| 1914 | 186 | 376 | 307 | 350 | 806 |
| 1915 | 106 | 227 | 149 | 96 | 406 |
| 1916 | 127 | 170 | 101 | 43 | 189 |
| 1917 | 60 | 125 | 63 | 10 | 153 |
| Total | 5,112 | 5,902 | 3,714 | 11,601 | 17,176 |

| | | |
|---|---|---|
| Total number of families resettled | 5,112 + 5,902 | 11,014 |
| Number of individuals comprising 11,014 families | | 41,469 |
| Persons per family | | 3.76[b] |

[a]At a time when concerns were rife about the dangers that cities posed to women, single or unaccompanied immigrant women and girls were regarded as especially vulnerable. Organizations such as the National Council of Jewish Women provided assistance at Ellis Island to ensure that women and girls traveling without male kin would safely reach their destinations in the city, usually the homes of relatives or friends.

Applicants classified as direct or original removals (i.e., individuals willing to travel as strangers to a town or city selected by the IRO) were exclusively men. The second category of client, the reunion case, usually included women and their children seeking to join the household head after he had begun working in the new location. In other instances, reunion cases might bring a sibling or other relative to a previously settled client. The third category, the request case, represented individuals seeking IRO assistance to enable them to join relatives or friends who had not been IRO clients. Sometimes, these relatives or friends applied to the IRO on behalf of the person whom they wished to sponsor.

The discrepancy between the grand total of people distributed from New York (73,960), listed in Table 1, and the total (41,469), listed in Table 2, is due to the exclusion of request cases from the latter table.

[b]An average family size of 3.76 persons, including parents, points to the relatively young age of IRO clients. Table 3 provides more concrete data on this point.

**Table 3.** Age profile (in years) of 6,469 IRO clients in 1913,
comprising 3,382 men, 1,132 women, and 1,955 children

| Under 16 | 16–21 | 21–25 | 25–35 | 35–40 | 40–45 | 45–50 | 50+ | Total |
|---|---|---|---|---|---|---|---|---|
| 1,955 | 823 | 1,135 | 1,703 | 453 | 202 | 97 | 101 | 6,469 |
| 30% | 13% | 18% | 26% | 7% | 3% | 1% | 2% | |

*Note:* The 1913 *Annual Report* offers the first IRO quantitative assessment of the ages of people leaving New York in a particular year. The figures indicate that the successful applicants for IRO assistance tended to be individuals at the peak of their productive lives—a point often made by the IRO on the basis of qualitative evidence. Here, 64 percent of IRO clients in 1913 comprised people ranging in age from 16 to 40.

Table 4. Types and frequencies of IRO Cases, 1906–1917

| | 1906 | 1907 | 1908 | 1909 | 1910 | 1911 | 1912 | 1913 | 1914 | 1915 | 1916 | 1917 |
|---|---|---|---|---|---|---|---|---|---|---|---|---|
| Original[a] | 2,648 | 3,410 | 1,733 | 1,412 | 1,621 | 1,458 | 2,348 | 2,604 | 786 | 303 | 182 | 83 |
| | 38% | 45% | 34% | 40% | 40% | 37% | 39% | 40% | 22% | 17% | 13% | 8% |
| Reunion[b] | | | | | | | | | | | | |
| To join family head | 801 | 492 | 357 | 159 | 210 | 187 | 598 | 914 | 444 | 164 | 135 | 79 |
| | 12% | 7% | 7% | 5% | 5% | 5% | 10% | 14% | 13% | 9% | 9% | 8% |
| To join friends or kin | 916 | 707 | 379 | 156 | 211 | 180 | 459 | 551 | 200 | 72 | 64 | 30 |
| | 13% | 9% | 7% | 4% | 5% | 4% | 8% | 9% | 6% | 4% | 5% | 3% |
| Request[c] to join friends or kin | 2,557 | 2,977 | 2,639 | 1,777 | 2,001 | 2,125 | 2,620 | 2,400 | 2,071 | 1,282 | 1,053 | 814 |
| | 37% | 39% | 52% | 51% | 50% | 54% | 43% | 37% | 59% | 70% | 73% | 81% |
| Annual totals | 6,922 | 7,586 | 5,108 | 3,504 | 4,043 | 3,950 | 6,025 | 6,469 | 3,501 | 1,821 | 1,434 | 1,006 |

*Note:* Original cases regularly comprised less than half the annual total because the initial settlement of the breadwinner represented the most formidable challenge in the process of distribution. Once that placement had occurred, the resettled immigrants could send for wives, children, or other kin, often enlisting the help of the IRO. Among the repercussions of the 1907 depression was a decline in original cases. The IRO had greater success, even in times of economic slowdowns, in helping people reunite with kin or friends in interior communities. This record is reflected in the consistently high percentage of request cases. Likewise, amid a serious absolute decline in IRO activity following the beginning of World War I, most placements involved settled immigrants sending for friends or kin.

[a]Sent to destination chosen by IRO.

[b]Sent to already settled former client—Household Head, Friend, or Kin.

[c]Sent to friends or relatives at their request, if they could guarantee support or assistance; guarantors were not former IRO clients.

Table 5. Client and family resettlement in
relationship to length of residence in New York, 1908–1914

| Resettled clients | Year | In New York <3 years | | In New York >3 years | | Total | | |
|---|---|---|---|---|---|---|---|---|
| | | Families | Persons | Families | Persons | Family | Persons | Percent |
| Families | 1908 | 185 | 643 | 266 | 1,101 | 451 | 1,744 | 34 |
| sent with | 1909 | 86 | 294 | 235 | 965 | 321 | 1,259 | 36 |
| head | 1910 | 65 | 216 | 298 | 1,230 | 363 | 1,446 | 36 |
| | 1911 | 65 | 214 | 301 | 1,255 | 366 | 1,469 | 37 |
| | 1912 | 62 | 203 | 290 | 1,221 | 352 | 1,424 | 24 |
| | 1913 | 57 | 184 | 231 | 967 | 288 | 1,151 | 18 |
| | 1914 | 46 | 143 | 140 | 523 | 186 | 666 | 19 |
| Families | 1908 | 151 | 433 | 277 | 1,023 | 428 | 1,456 | 28 |
| sent to | 1909 | 63 | 203 | 248 | 965 | 311 | 1,168 | 33 |
| join head[a] | 1910 | 40 | 139 | 305 | 1,194 | 345 | 1,333 | 33 |
| | 1911 | 34 | 117 | 343 | 1,351 | 377 | 1,468 | 37 |
| | 1912 | 79 | 233 | 510 | 2,018 | 589 | 2,251 | 37 |
| | 1913 | 108 | 285 | 506 | 1,817 | 614 | 2,102 | 33 |
| | 1914 | 72 | 200 | 304 | 1,172 | 376 | 1,372 | 39 |
| Married | 1908 | | 65 | | 137 | | 202 | 4 |
| men, | 1909 | | 13 | | 83 | | 96 | 3 |
| family in | 1910 | | 6 | | 108 | | 114 | 3 |
| New York | 1911 | | 7 | | 100 | | 107 | 3 |
| City | 1912 | | 53 | | 403 | | 456 | 8 |
| | 1913 | | 105 | | 492 | | 597 | 9 |
| | 1914 | | 56 | | 251 | | 307 | 9 |
| Married | 1908 | | 481 | | 30 | | 511 | 10 |
| men, | 1909 | | 262 | | 30 | | 292 | 8 |
| family in | 1910 | | 361 | | 28 | | 389 | 10 |
| Europe | 1911 | | 269 | | 19 | | 288 | 7 |
| | 1912 | | 434 | | 59 | | 493 | 8 |
| | 1913 | | 857 | | 55 | | 912 | 14 |
| | 1914 | | 337 | | 13 | | 350 | 10 |
| Unmarried | 1908 | | 941 | | 254 | | 1,195 | 23 |
| men | 1909 | | 418 | | 271 | | 689 | 20 |
| | 1910 | | 448 | | 313 | | 761 | 19 |
| | 1911 | | 349 | | 269 | | 618 | 16 |
| | 1912 | | 741 | | 660 | | 1,401 | 23 |
| Unmarried | 1913 | | 1,109 | | 598 | | 1,707 | 26 |
| men and | 1914 | | 543 | | 263 | | 806 | 23 |
| women[b] | | | | | | | | |

Note: There is a relationship among length of time in New York, resettlement, family status, and location of the family. The resettlement of families from New York to other communities—sent with the head or sent to join the head—is weighted toward those residing in the city for three years or longer. Also, married men resettling in the interior but leaving their families in New York tended to be long-term residents of New York. No data exist on the length of residence in New York of all of the applicants to the IRO, so it is not possible to compare those numbers with figures in the table, which represent only accepted applicants. It is possible that the distribution in part reflects a much greater number of applications from long-term residents frustrated by years of partial employment. Always a strong counterweight to leaving New York, the cultural magnet of the East Side proved insufficient in these cases. It may have exercised its greatest pull on the short-term residents who were still willing to struggle economically in the city. Given the highly selective IRO process, this distribution also represents an IRO preference in favor of the long-term and probably more desperate residents.

The pattern is different for men unbound by marital or family ties in the United States. Accepted applicants in this category tended to be short-term residents of the city. Once again no record exists on the residential histories of all of the applicants to determine if the distribution is in part an artifact of a greater number of applications from short-term residents. Without immediate obligations to spouses or children, such men could be more mobile and venturesome. But the same qualities, especially in single men, could also mean less staying power in their new communities, leading the IRO to express its preference for men obligated by family ties. Overall, approximately twice as many long-term residents of New York were resettled during the years under consideration.

[a]Family head may or may not have been an IRO "original removed."

[b]The category "Unmarried men" appearing in the 1908–1912 reports changes to "Unmarried men and women" in 1913. This alteration does not represent any change in policy, for IRO assistance to unmarried women occurred from the earliest days of the organization but only under the request and reunion categories; that is, unmarried women would not be assisted on their own as "original removals" to travel to communities where they had no bonds. In 1913, when the third highest number of people was resettled, the altered designation may only have represented a different way of tabulating the annual data, enumerating unmarried women along with unmarried men instead of counting them among the people within the various family categories. "Original removals" numbered 2,604 (see Table 4), all of whom were considered wage earners. Although women wage earners in these categories appeared in IRO lists of occupations of people distributed (e.g., nurses, midwives, saleswomen,, stenographers), the records are silent on the question of whether they were actually rendered assistance in finding positions, once resettled.

The male focus of the IRO in job placement was unequivocal, also exemplified in its consideration of the 1,707 individuals in the "Unmarried men and women" category. The category is explained as if it comprised only men. The 1913 *Annual Report* thus describes this figure as "interesting insofar as it shows the preponderance of removals who were married over those who were single. Of this latter class, there were only 1,707 individuals. Experience has shown the greater desirability for removal purposes of men with family obligations. They are able to confront new conditions with greater perseverance, having a goal in mind which the unmarried man lacks" (*Annual Report of the Industrial Removal Office, 1913,* 13). If a wife were to remain in New York after her husband's application was accepted, she had to sign a consent form indicating that she approved of his departure.

Once the resettler had begun work, the IRO believed that he was on his own, fully responsible for his own support and, if he were married, for his family. Applicants were thus asked to sign the following pledge, in English or Yiddish:

"I, the undersigned, having been unemployed for _____, do hereby agree in consideration to accept such employment as may be obtained for me by the local society. Realizing that I have no other claim upon this society or any of its co-operative agencies, I obligate myself to depend upon my own energies for the support of myself and family after being placed at work."

As various cases in this study make clear, this pledge did not inhibit complaints and demands for support from the disaffected.

Table 6. Number of people resettled by year and
proportion of short-term (less than three years) to long-term
(more than three years) residents leaving New York, 1908–1914

| Year | In New York City <3 years | In New York City >3 years |
|------|---------------------------|---------------------------|
| 1908 | 2,563 (50%) | 2,545 (50%) |
| 1909 | 1,190 (34%) | 2,314 (66%) |
| 1910 | 1,170 (41%) | 2,873 (59%) |
| 1911 | 956 (24%) | 2,994 (76%) |
| 1912 | 1,664 (28%) | 4,361 (72%) |
| 1913 | 2,540 (39%) | 3,929 (61%) |
| 1914 | 1,279 (37%) | 2,222 (63%) |
| Total | 11,362 | 21,238 |

*Note:* Although length of residence in New York varied among types of
IRO clients, the overall pattern of annual resettlement favored long-term
residents of the city. This table expresses the relative proportions in each
category as a percentage of the total number of resettled immigrants for
each year.

Noting the diminishing number of short-term residents among IRO
clients, the *Annual Report* for 1912 stated: "These figures are significant because they bring into relief the lack of stimulus and opportunity in the metropolis. The majority of 1912 removals were persons who presumably had
some knowledge of the English language; who, by reason of familiarity
with conditions, should have found it relatively easier to procure employment; but the reverse is true." In addition, the report argued that "a continued residence in the metropolis, far from discouraging the immigrant's
initiative, only acts as an increased stimulant to his pioneer spirit—not so
much because he desires an individual betterment, but because he wishes
to insure his dependents against being confronted with the same adverse
conditions which he encountered." (*Annual Report of the Industrial Removal Office, 1912*, 11–12).

Table 7. Location of clients up to one year after leaving
New York and IRO estimation of satisfactory resettlement, 1906–1911

| Estimation[a] | 1911 | | 1910 | | 1909 | | 1908 | | 1907 | | 1906 | |
|---|---|---|---|---|---|---|---|---|---|---|---|---|
| | Number | % | Number | % | Number | % | Number | % | Number | % | Number | % |
| Satisfactory | | | | | | | | | | | | |
| Still there | 2,365 | 59 | 2,681 | 63 | 2,086 | 62 | 4,090 | 74 | 5,606 | 74 | 4,949 | 75 |
| Left for known place | 21 | <1 | 29 | <1 | 10 | <1 | 13 | <1 | 65 | <1 | 135 | 2.1 |
| Total | 2,386 | 60 | 2,710 | 64 | 2,096 | 62 | 4,103 | 74 | 5,671 | 75 | 5,084 | 78 |
| Doubtful | | | | | | | | | | | | |
| Still there | 29 | <1 | 49 | 1.2 | 18 | <1 | 3 | <1 | 57 | <1 | 60 | <1 |
| Left for known place | 21 | <1 | 32 | <1 | 16 | <1 | 8 | <1 | 54 | <1 | 54 | <1 |
| Total | 50 | 1 | 81 | 2 | 34 | 1 | 11 | <1 | 111 | 1.4 | 114 | 2 |
| Unsatisfactory | | | | | | | | | | | | |
| Left for unknown place | 41 | 1 | 33 | <1 | 11 | <1 | 2 | <1 | 59 | <1 | 61 | <1 |
| Back to New York | 16 | <1 | 38 | <1 | 9 | <1 | 4 | <1 | 34 | <1 | 62 | <1 |
| Total | 57 | 1 | 71 | 2 | 20 | <1 | 6 | <1 | 93 | 1 | 123 | 2 |
| No information | 11 | <1 | 52 | <1 | 19 | <1 | 15 | <1 | 52 | <1 | — | — |
| No information sought (family members) | 1,473 | 37 | 1,319 | 31 | 1,203 | 36 | 1,423 | 26 | 1,662 | 23 | 1,234 | 19 |
| Grand totals | 3,977 | | 4,233 | | 3,372 | | 5,558 | | 7,589 | | 6,555 | |

[a]The criteria defining "satisfactory" narrowed over time. Starting with the 1903 report of the JAIAS, satisfactory resettlement meant that the client still resided in the community or had left town without making trouble. An unsatisfactory resettlement meant that the client was troublesome, regardless of whether he remained in the new community. This classification attends more to individuals than to social outcomes.

By 1908, a satisfactory individual was unproblematic and either remained in the new community or left for a known place, where he might still be tracked. Unsatisfactory cases were represented by individuals, however agreeable, who had either left for unknown destinations or had returned to New York. The new classification shifted from a concern with the qualities of the client to the accomplishment of the goals of the IRO. A return to New York marked a palpable failure; a departure for some unknown place, though a less stunning defeat, still showed the inability of a community to accomplish its task or even to keep track of a client. An intermediate category, "doubtful," also added in 1908, included problematic individuals who either remained in the new community or left for a known destination.

Table 8. Location of clients up to one year after leaving
New York and IRO estimation of satisfactory resettlement, 1913

|  | Wage earners | Percent |
| --- | --- | --- |
| Satisfactory | 2,368 | 88 |
| Left for places known | 122 | 4 |
| Left for places unknown | 46 | 2 |
| Doubtful | 17 | <1 |
| Unsatisfactory | 56 | 2 |
| Returned to New York | 93 | 3 |

*Note:* There was a shift to a more narrow definition of satisfactory resettlement.

No tabular summary was provided in the 1912 *Annual Report*, although data are given indicating a high rate (92 percent) of satisfactory cases. In that year, 4,560 people were distributed, of whom 2,473 were wage earners. The report states that 2,282 were satisfactory, twenty-three left for places unknown, the fate of seventy-four was uncertain, and ninety-four were unsatisfactory. It goes on to say that "this is a striking indication of the stability and efficiency of the vast majority of our removals, for under 'satisfactory,' we not only included economic progress and satisfactory employment, but that these wage earners remained where they were originally sent." The report concludes its assessment by asserting that "the percentage of satisfactory wage earners of the removals of 1912, is not abnormally high, and is in keeping with the previous high standard of efficiency attained by removals in the preceding eleven years. The sharp increase in the percent of satisfactory cases in 1912 and 1913 (92 percent and 88 percent, respectively) over the figure for 1911 (60 percent) reflects another change in the calculation. The percentage of satisfactory cases increased sharply as the new tabulations were based on the number of wage earners rather than on all individuals (including spouses, children, and other nonworking kin of the household head). At the same time, satisfactory resettlement included only those unproblematic individuals who remained in their new communities.

Although IRO reports point to a high rate of successful placements, the difficult cases tend to garner a disproportionate amount of attention locally and in the main office. Except for proclaiming success stories, there was little need for the IRO to attend to those people working satisfactorily or moving upward. (No note was taken of Harry Cohen's move upward from "junk" to "junk director," as indicated in the 1911 and 1912 Indianapolis City Directories.)

Raphael and Rockaway have challenged the accuracy of the official IRO figures on the stability of placements. By comparing the names of IRO men sent to Columbus and Detroit with city directories in the years following their arrival, Raphael and Rockaway independently claim that the IRO figures on men remaining at their original destinations are much too high. See Marc Lee Raphael, *Jews and Judaism in a Midwestern Community: Columbus, Ohio, 1840–1975* (Columbus: Ohio Historical Society, 1979), 154, note 20; and Robert A. Rockaway, *The Jews of Detroit, From the Beginning, 1762–1914* (Detroit: Wayne State University Press, 1986), 118, note 49.

A similar procedure was used for Indianapolis. City directories provide a tabulation of male adults residing at a particular address. (Women were listed only if they had occupations or were heads of households.) Using city directories for Indianapolis, available data on IRO placements were checked for each of the two years following the arrival of an IRO newcomer in the city. The record of those remaining in Indianapolis appears dismal, thus confirming the doubts

# APPENDIX

raised by Raphael and Rockaway. Of forty-five men in the 1907 sample, eight appear to have remained in the city in 1908, six of whom appear in the 1909 listing. In the 1910 sample, forty-three men arrived, with nine of them appearing in 1911, and four appearing in 1912. Of thirty-seven arrivals in the 1912 sample, nine are present in 1913, five of whom are listed in 1914.

Although Raphael and Rockaway acknowledge the possibility of errors in the directory canvass, they have overestimated the reliability of city directories as sources for tabulating the staying power of IRO men at their destinations. Immigrants inhabited the social periphery of cities and, when they were newcomers in a community, they were further marginalized. Other factors also limited the accuracy of directory canvasses, including language barriers and variations in the names by which an immigrant might be known. The latter is quite evident in the IRO records.

Of three Jewish immigrants (Joe Glazier, Louis Shapiro, and Sam Weinstein) known to the author to have resided in Indianapolis in the years 1909–1913, one appears in four of the five directories, a second in three of the five, and a third in four of the five. Sam Weinstein appears in the 1907 directory but not in the 1908 edition. The directories are spotty at best. A fourth man (Morris Rosen), known to have lived in Indianapolis beginning in 1911, does not appear in the directories of 1911–1913. Although the IRO figures may be generous, a radical revision downward based only on the use of city directories is unwarranted.

Table 9. Summary and classification of occupations of IRO clients, 1902–1914

| Industry | | Wage earners | Percent |
|---|---|---|---|
| Manufacturing | | | |
| Woodworking | | 3,300 | 9.5 |
| Metal | | 3,408 | 9.8 |
| Building | | 2,783 | 8.0 |
| Printing and lithography | | 358 | 1.0 |
| Needle trades | | 7,828 | 22.5 |
| Leather | | 2,470 | 7.1 |
| Tobacco | | 240 | .7 |
| Miscellaneous | | 782 | 2.2 |
| | Total | 21,169 | 60.8 |
| Nonmanufacturing | | | |
| Miscellaneous | | 775 | 2.2 |
| No trade and peddlers | | 10,105 | 29.0 |
| Farming | | 468 | 1.3 |
| Small dealers in food | | 1,146 | 3.3 |
| Office personnel, professionals, etc. | | 1,140 | 3.3 |
| | Total | 13,634 | 39.1 |
| | Grand total | 34,803 | |

*Note:* The JAIAS and IRO reports from 1902 until 1914 contain a breakdown of the occupations of people distributed over the years. By 1914, a total of 361 different occupations was represented among those resettled by the IRO. An individual moving to an interior community did not necessarily take a job in his previous occupation, although the IRO attempted initially to place its clients in the trades that they had practiced. Nonetheless, local circumstance and changes in the labor market sometimes necessitated that an immigrant take a job in an endeavor new to him. Relatedly, some vocations were not in demand and could not be filled through the IRO network of cooperating agencies and committees. The single Jewish immigrant aviator among all of the IRO clients is the most extreme case.

Consistently, the largest number of IRO clients was in the category of workers without trades, which included unskilled laborers and peddlers. Workers in the needle trades constituted the second largest group of clients year by year. Although New York was the heart of the garment industry, seasonal unemployment, or what the IRO termed "underemployment," drove large numbers of clothing workers to the organization. Likewise, but on a much smaller scale among all IRO clients, men in the building trades faced seasonal unemployment.

The IRO saw the importance of the needle trades among immigrant Jews in New York as a special problem of the congested city. Writing in the 1904 *Annual Report* (p. 6) Cyrus Sulzberger, Chairman of the IRO, estimated that at least 50 percent of the residents of the East Side worked in some capacity in the needle trades. The large number of people in this occupational category was not necessarily because they brought these trades from Europe, where many were unskilled, but because "the subdivision of labor which is practised [sic] in these industries enables unskilled hands speedily to become skillful." As a result, the clothing workers suffered a two-fold economic vulnerability: competition for work was especially severe and economic downturns in the clothing industry afflicted a disproportionate number of people. By resettling immigrant Jews in the interior, the IRO believed that it was preventing the drift to the needle trades and hence toward a tenuous economic future of East Side Jews: "The industrial onesidedness which exists among the Jews in the large

206

cities is thus being counteracted, and while . . . every effort is made to fit a man into the vocation for which he is best qualified, in the event of inability to do this, we can at least prevent his getting into the one calling least desirable hygienically and economically."

Table 10. Occupations of all Jewish immigrants, 1899–1910

|  | Number | Percent of those reporting employment |
| --- | --- | --- |
| Professional | 7,455 | 1.3 |
| Skilled | 395,823 | 67.1 |
| Farm labor | 11,460 | 1.9 |
| Unskilled labor | 69,444 | 11.8 |
| Other occupations | 106,085 | 18.0 |
| Without occupations[a] | 484,175 | 45.0[b] |
| Number reporting employment | 590,267 |  |
| Total number of immigrants | 1,074,442 |  |

*Note:* Derived from *Reports of the Immigration Commission,* 1 *Abstracts* 100–101, Table 12. Although the occupational categories of the IRO and the Immigration Commission differed, some approximate comparison of the IRO figures with those of Jewish immigrants as a whole is possible. The IRO had its greatest impact on unskilled workers, who constituted the largest group of clients. A disproportionate number of the unskilled were represented—29 percent as opposed to 11.8 percent among all Jewish immigrants.

[a]Including women and children.
[b]Percentage of the total immigration.

Table 11. Comparison of native white and Jewish household heads providing entire family income in New York and six other cities

| Nativity of family head by city | Percent | Number of families in sample |
|---|---|---|
| New York | | |
| Native-born white of a native father | 63.8 | 69 |
| Russian Jewish | 20.3 | 296 |
| Chicago | | |
| Native-born white of a native father | 45.5 | 22 |
| Russian Jewish | 29.7 | 91 |
| Philadelphia | | |
| Native-born white of a native father | 77.0 | 37 |
| Russian Jewish | 59.0 | 58 |
| Boston | | |
| Native-born white of a native father | 70.4 | 79 |
| Russian Jewish | 57.7 | 157 |
| Cleveland | | |
| Native-born white of a native father | 52.4 | 21 |
| Russian Jewish | 46.5 | 43 |
| Buffalo | | |
| Native-born white of a native father | 70.6 | 45 |
| Russian Jewish | 56.2 | 36 |
| Milwaukee | | |
| Native-born white of a native father | 79.7 | 101 |
| Russian Jewish | 59.3 | 40 |

Note: Derived from Reports of the Immigration Commission, Vol. 26, Immigrants in Cities, Tables 71 (232), 73 (321), 62 (405), 62 (485), 67 (580), 52 (660), and 67 (741).

The data in this table, although based on very small samples, are suggestive of immigrant economic problems frequently discussed in qualitative terms. The inability of Jewish immigrant household heads to support their families fully was most severe in New York. There and in the other six cities, wives contributed very little, as they remained outside of the formal labor market. This pattern marked a retreat from engagement in the Old Country of married Jewish women in work and breadwinning. See Susan Glenn, Daughters of the Shtetl (Ithaca, N.Y.: Cornell University Press, 1990), 66. When the household head alone could not support the family, the remainder was largely contributed by working children and/or by boarders and lodgers.

Although Boston and Philadelphia were IRO distribution points, the Immigration Commission data suggest that Jewish immigrant household heads in those port cities were doing about as well as their counterparts in Buffalo and Milwaukee and better than those in Cleveland. Each of these three cities was an important IRO terminus. In Chicago, a minority of household heads, including native whites, could support their families unassisted. Recognizing that Chicago presented many of the same problems as New York, the IRO closed its office there in 1903, after only one year of operation.

# Notes

## Introduction

1. Ralph K. Andrist, *The Long Death: The Last Days of the Plains Indians* (New York: Macmillan, 1964), 352–354.

2. David F. Burg, *Chicago's White City* (Lexington: University Press of Kentucky, 1976), 2–3.

3. Ray Ginger, *Altgeld's America: The Lincoln Ideal Versus Changing Realities* (New York: Funk and Wagnalls, 1958), 22–34.

4. Compiled from the *Abstract of the Eleventh Census, 1890* (Washington, D.C.: Government Printing Office, 1894), 34.

5. Compiled from the *Abstract of the Twelfth Census, 1900* (Washington, D.C.: Government Printing Office, 1902), 103–104.

6. Compiled from the *Abstract of the Thirteenth Census, 1910* (Washington, D.C.: Government Printing Office, 1913), 95.

7. C. Wright Mills analyzed the rural, anti-urban biases of sociological commentators on city life. See "The Professional Ideology of Social Pathologists," *American Journal of Sociology* 49 (September 1943): 174–175. This excursion into the sociology of knowledge laid bare the same provincialism suffusing the alarmist forecasts of the immigration critics, including Mills's former University of Wisconsin professor, Edward A. Ross. As Mills pointed out, rural society was the wellspring of American democracy and Jeffersonian ideals.

8. John Higham, *Strangers in the Land: Patterns of American Nativism 1860–1926*, 2d ed. (New Brunswick, N.J.: Rutgers University Press, 1988). Students of American nativism during the era of mass immigration continue to rely on Higham's definitive classic, which was first published in 1955.

9. Morrell Heald, "Business Attitudes Toward European Immigration, 1880–1900," *Journal of Economic History* 13 (Summer 1953): 291. At various times between the end of the Civil War and the panic of 1893, organizations ranging from business leagues to factories supported increased immigration to fill labor shortages. Advertisements promoting

immigration appeared in Europe, and some states established commissions on immigration. See Esther Panitz, "The Polarity of American Jewish Attitudes toward Immigration (1870–1891)," *American Jewish Historical Quarterly* 53 (December 1963): 100–104.

10. Higham, *Strangers in the Land*, 51.

11. John Higham, *Send These to Me: Immigrants in Urban America*, rev. ed. (Baltimore: Johns Hopkins University Press, 1984), 42.

12. H. G. Wells, *The Future in America* (London: Chapman and Hall, Ltd. 1906), 2, 195–196, 200–201, 203, 262–267.

13. Henry James, *The American Scene* (New York: Harper and Brothers, 1907), 127, 129, 135.

14. Hutchins Hapgood, *The Spirit of the Ghetto*, ed. Moses Rischin (Cambridge, Mass.: Belknap Press, 1967), xxxi.

15. Jacob Katz, *Out of the Ghetto: The Social Background of Jewish Emancipation* (New York: Schocken Books, 1978), 20–23.

16. Alexander Altmann, *Moses Mendelssohn: A Biographical Study* (Tuscaloosa: University of Alabama Press, 1973), 16.

17. Ibid.

18. Moses Hadas, ed., *Solomon Maimon, an Autobiography* (New York: Schocken Books, 1967), 96.

19. *Jewish Messenger*, 8 Sept. 1882, 2.

20. Ibid., 20 May 1881, 4.

21. *American Israelite*, 14 May 1891, 1. Reprinted from *The Jewish Messenger*.

22. *American Hebrew*, 4 July 1884, 122.

23. Abraham Cahan, *The Education of Abraham Cahan*, trans. Leon Stein, Abraham P. Conan, and Lynn Davison (Philadelphia: Jewish Publication Society of America, 1969), 217, 218–219.

24. Abraham Cahan, *The Rise of David Levinsky* (New York: Harper and Brothers, 1960), 530.

25. *Jewish Messenger*, 5 Sept. 1890, 4.

26. Steven E. Aschheim, *Brothers and Strangers* (Madison: University of Wisconsin Press, 1982), 12.

27. "The Discovery of America," *Menorah* 13 (October 1892): 233. The B'nai B'rith was a well-established fraternal organization in the United States founded in 1843 by German Jews.

28. Ibid., 224; K. Kohler, "The Discovery of America: Its Influence upon the World's Progress, and Its Especial Significance for the Jews," *Menorah* 13 (October 1892): 241.

29. *Jewish Messenger*, 11 Feb. 1881, 4.

30. United Hebrew Charities, *Seventh Annual Report, 1881*, 9.

31. Ibid., *Thirteenth Annual Report, 1887*, 17, 28, 36–37; Samuel Joseph, *Jewish Immigration to the United States* (New York: AMS Press 1967), 189.

32. Yehezkel Wyskowski, "The American Hebrew: An Exercise in Ambivalence," *American Jewish History* 76 (1987): 344–346.

33. United Hebrew Charities, *Thirteenth Annual Report, 1887*, 36.

34. Ibid., *Tenth Annual Report, 1884*, 14. Italics in original.

35. Ibid.

36. Ibid., *First Annual Report, 1875*, 4.

37. Morris D. Waldman, "Artificial Distribution of Immigrants," *University Settlement Studies 2* (October 1906): 16.

38. Oscar Handlin, *Immigration as a Factor in American History* (Englewood Cliffs: Prentice Hall, 1959), 146.

39. *American Hebrew*, 16 Dec. 1910, 198.

40. *JAIAS Annual Report for the Year 1901*, 34.

41. Ibid., *Annual Report for the Year 1906*, 17.

42. Cyrus L. Sulzberger, "The Year," *The American Jewish Yearbook* (Philadelphia: Jewish Publication Society of America, 1904), 38.

43. Waldman, 15.

44. *Seventeenth Annual Report of the Industrial Removal Office for the Year 1917*, 6.

45. IRO Records, General Manager to the *American Hebrew*, 26 March 1914. Box 21.

46. Samuel Joseph, *Jewish Immigration*, 155.

47. This defensive attitude was very apparent until World War II and manifested itself in various efforts of Jewish communities to police themselves. See, for example, Jack Glazier, "Stigma, Identity, and Sephardic-Ashkenazic Relations in Indianapolis," in *Persistence and Flexibility: Anthropological Perspectives on the American Jewish Experience*, ed. Walter P. Zenner (Albany: State University of New York Press, 1988), 48; and Ande Manners, *Poor Cousins* (Greenwich, Conn.: Fawcett, 1972), Part II.

48. *Proceedings of the Third National Conference of Jewish Charities of the United States* (New York: Philip Cowen, 1904), 140–141.

49. Esther Panitz, "In Defense of the Jewish Immigrant (1891–1924)," *American Jewish Historical Quarterly* 5 (Sept 1965): 57–97.

50. *Jewish Messenger*, 7 March 1884, 4. Various Jewish institutions in New York had to accommodate themselves to the growing influence of Russian Jews and their leaders. The Educational Alliance, for example, originally took a dim view of Yiddish as well as other expressions of immigrant Jewish life that would disagreeably set the community apart. Only English or German conversation was permitted. When David Blaustein became the head of the alliance in 1898, a friendlier attitude toward eastern European Jewish culture took over. The prohibition of Yiddish ended, the library introduced Yiddish books and newspapers, and the premises were made available for the meetings of various Yiddish-speaking organizations. The liberalization of the alliance came in the wake of a growing understanding by enlightened German American Jews of the complexity of eastern European Jewry, which was not all orthodoxy and obedience to ancient custom but also lively and sophisticated secular concerns. See Adam Bellow, *The Educational Alliance: A Centennial Celebration* (Arlington, Va.: Keens, 1990), 77, 83–84.

## Chapter 1. Jewish Immigrant Distribution

1. United Hebrew Charities, *First Annual Report*, 1875, 7.

2. Ibid., *Third Annual Report, 1877*, 23; Rose Margolis, "History of the Industrial Removal Office, and a Study of Its Work as Revealed in Selected Correspondence 1906–1922," (Masters thesis, Graduate School of Jewish Social Work, 1936), 65–73.

3. Margolis, "History of the Industrial Removal Office," 65–66.

4. H. S. Henry, "Hebrew Emigrant Aid Society der Vereinigten Staaten." *Bericht des Prasidenten un Schatzmeisters für das Jahr 1882* (New York: Druckerei des judischen Waisenhauses, 1883), 5.

5. United Hebrew Charities, *Eighth Annual Report, 1882,* 12.

6. Henry, "Hebrew Emigrant Aid Society," 9–10.

7. Gilbert Osofsky, "The Hebrew Emigrant Aid Society of the United States (1881–1883)," *Publications of the American Jewish Historical Society* 49 (March 1960): 178.

8. Henry, "Hebrew Emigrant Aid Society, 6–7.

9. Osofsky, "The Hebrew Emigrant Aid Society," 177.

10. Henry, "Hebrew Emigrant Aid Society," 8–9; Esther L. Panitz, "The Polarity of American Jewish Attitudes toward Immigration (1870–1891)," *American Jewish Historical Quarterly* 53 (December 1963): 112; Myron Berman, *The Attitude of American Jewry toward East European Jewish Immigration, 1881–1914* (New York: Arno Press, 1980), 50–51.

11. Henry, "Hebrew Emigrant Aid Society," 9.

12. Zosa Szajkowski, "The Attitude of American Jews to East European Jewish Immigration (1881–1893)," *American Jewish Historical Quarterly,* 40 (March 1951): 236.

13. *Jewish Messenger,* 24 Oct. 1884, 5.

14. Ibid., 30 June 1882, 2.

15. Osofsky, "The Hebrew Emigrant Aid Society," 182.

16. Ibid., 176.

17. *Jewish Messenger,* 30 June 1882, 2.

18. Ibid., 27 May 1881, 4.

19. United Hebrew Charities, *Fifteenth Annual Report, 1889,* 20–21.

20. *New York Times,* 14 Jan. 1884, 4.

21. United Hebrew Charities, *Fourteenth Annual Report, 1888,* 18.

22. *American Israelite,* 26 March 1891, 1.

23. Ibid.

24. David M. Bressler, "Dispersion," in *The Russian Jew in the United States,* ed. Charles S. Bernheimer (Philadelphia: John C. Winston Co., 1905), 369.

25. Joseph Brandes, *Immigrants to Freedom* (Philadelphia: University of Pennsylvania Press, 1971), 126.

26. David Philipson, "Jews and Industries," *Menorah* 4 (February 1888): 100.

27. Ibid., 101, 107.

28. Aaron David Gordon, "People and Labor," in *The Zionist Idea,* ed. Arthur Hertzberg (New York: Atheneum, 1984), 372, 374.

29. Uri Herscher, *Jewish Agricultural Utopias in America, 1880–1910* (Detroit: Wayne State University Press, 1981), 38–39.

30. Shlomo Avineri, *The Making of Modern Zionism* (New York: Basic Books, 1981), 153.

31. *Fourteenth Annual Report of the Industrial Removal Office for the Year 1914,* 11.

32. *Fifty Years of Social Service: The History of the United Hebrew Charities of the City of New York* (New York: Jewish Social Service Association, 1926), 53.

33. Sophie Trupin, *Dakota Diaspora* (Lincoln: University of Nebraska Press, 1984), 15.

34. Like Trupin, Brenda Weisberg Meckler recalls her family's life on the land and their lack of farming experience. See her memoir, *Papa Was a Farmer* (Chapel Hill, N.C.: Algonquin Books, 1988), 125–134.

For an exploration of the dynamics of community life among Jewish immigrants on the land, see Kenneth L. Kann's oral history, *Comrades and Chicken Ranchers: The Story of a California Jewish Community* (Ithaca, N.Y.: Cornell University Press, 1993). Settling in Petaluma, California, Kann's informants describe a vigorous community of political radicals. They recreated *shtetl* life in some respects, but its staying power sharply diminished across three generations.

Another recent study of Jews on the land traces the course of Jewish farming in New York State from the beginning of the century through its post–World War II decline. See Abraham D. Lavender and Clarence B. Steinberg, *Jewish Farmers of the Catskills: A Century of Survival* (Gainesville: University Press of Florida, 1995).

35. John R. Commons, *Races and Immigrants in America* (New York: Macmillan, 1907), 133.

36. Prescott F. Hall, *Immigration and Its Effects upon the United States* (New York: Henry Holt, 1906), 303.

37. Samuel Joseph, *History of the Baron de Hirsch Fund* (Fairfield, N.J.: Augustus M. Kelly, 1978), 19, 278, 279.

38. *American Israelite,* 17 April 1890, 4.

39. James H. Hoffman and Arthur Reichow, *Vereinigte juedische Wohlthaetigkeits-Gesellschaften, Bericht der Abtheilung fuer Arbeitsvermittelung* [United Hebrew Charities, Report of the Committee for Employment], 1890, 9.

40. United Hebrew Charities, *Sixteenth Annual Report, 1890,* 23.

41. Brandes, *Immigrants to Freedom,* 69–72; Joseph, *History of the Baron de Hirsch Fund,* 48–53.

42. Eugene Benjamin, "The Baron de Hirsch Fund," *Jewish Immigration Bulletin* 5 (May 1915): 9.

43. Leonard G. Robinson, "Agricultural Activities of the Jews in America," in *The American Jewish Yearbook, 1912–1913* (Philadelphia: Jewish Publication Society of America, 1912), 68–69.

44. United Hebrew Charities, *Sixteenth Annual Report, 1890,* 17–19.

45. The German-born Wolf was an influential Washington attorney, one-time consul general to Egypt, former vice president of the B'nai B'rith, and an activist in Jewish affairs.

46. *Official Correspondence Relating to the Immigration of Russian Exiles* (Washington, D.C.: George R. Gray, 1891), 3–4.

47. Ibid., 7.

48. Ibid., 6, 7.

49. The Jewish Alliance of America was founded in Philadelphia in February 1891 to ameliorate "the grave problems presented by the enforced emigration of Hebrews." Composed of representatives from Jewish organizations throughout the United States, the alliance supported instruction of immigrants in the duties and obligations of American citizenship and encouraged their self-support. The latter was promoted by directing immigrants to rural areas and industrial vocations and by emphasizing agri-

culture as the most desirable occupation. Jewish Alliance of America, "Inaugural Report, 1891;" *New York Times,* 16 Feb. 1891, 1.

50. *Official Correspondence,* 12–20.

51. Hoffman and Reichow, *Vereinigte juedische Wohlthaetigkeits-Gesellschaften, Bericht,* 14.

52. *Official Correspondence,* 8–9.

53. "Testimony of Mr. Simon Wolf," *Reports of the Industrial Commission on Immigration* 15 (Washington, D.C.: Government Printing Office, 1901), 245.

54. *Reports of the Industrial Commission On Immigration* 15 (1901), 29.

55. "Testimony of Joseph H. Senner, Former Commissioner of Immigration at the Port of New York," *Reports of the Industrial Commission on Immigration* 15 (1901), 167.

56. Eugene S. Benjamin, "The Baron de Hirsch Fund's Activities," *Menorah* 40 (April 1906): 214.

57. Commons, *Races and Immigrants,* 107.

58. Henry P. Fairchild, "The Restriction of Immigration," *American Economic Review* 2 (Suppl.) (March 1912): 54.

59. Maldwyn Allen Jones, *American Immigration* (Chicago: University of Chicago Press, 1960), 188–190, 192.

60. *Reports of the Immigration Commission* 12 (Washington, D.C.: Government Printing Office, 1911), 65, 66, 67.

61. William Kahn, "Jewish Agricultural and Industrial Aid, Society, New York," in *Proceedings of the Second National Conference of Jewish Charities in the United States* (Cincinnati: C. J. Krehbiel and Co., 1902), 83.

62. Ibid., 85.

63. Benjamin, "The Baron de Hirsch Fund," 9–11.

64. Gertrude Wishnick Dubrovsky, *The Land Was Theirs* (Tuscaloosa: University of Alabama Press, 1992), 21–23.

65. *Reports of the Industrial Commission on Immigration* 15 (1901), 515.

66. Joseph, *History of the Baron de Hirsch Fund,* 129–130.

67. Kahn, "Jewish Agricultural and Industrial Aid Society, New York," 83.

68. United Hebrew Charities, *Thirteenth Annual Report, 1887,* 36–37.

69. Joseph, *History of the Baron de Hirsch Fund,* 25–26.

70. *Fifty Years of Social Service,* 57–58.

71. Mark Wischnitzer, *Visas to Freedom* (New York: World Publishing, 1956), 65–66.

72. *Thirteenth Annual Report of the Industrial Removal Office for the Year 1913,* 11.

73. Wischnitzer, *Visas,* 66.

74. Samuel Joseph, *Jewish Immigration to the United States, 1881–1910* (New York: AMS Press, 1967), 167.

75. *JAIAS Annual Report for the Year 1901,* 32.

76. Joseph, *Jewish Immigration,* 172. Joseph's study remains the standard statistical source on Jewish immigration to the United States between 1881 and 1910. Before 1899, when official statistics listed immigrants by country, Jews were not tabulated separately but instead were counted as "Russian," "Rumanian," and so forth. For figures on Jewish immigration before 1899 Joseph derived his statistical information from the

records of Jewish societies caring for immigrants arriving at the eastern ports of disembarkation. See pages 87–94.

77. Leo Levi, "Removal and Distribution of Poor Jews," *Report of the Executive Committee of the Constitution Grand Lodge. Independent Order of B'nai B'rith (1901–1902)*, 21. (Bulletin No. 3, 1 July 1901), 19–23.

78. *Reports of the Industrial Commission on Immigration*, 15 (1901), 46.

79. *Report of Proceedings of District Grand Lodge No. 2*, 17 May 1902, 69.

80. Levi, "Removal and Distribution," 19.

81. Ibid., 22.

82. Berman, *The Attitude of American Jewry*," 209–230. The growing strength of nativism in the early twentieth century emboldened numerous efforts to pass legislation restricting immigration. Berman argues that American Jews by and large remained passive until the formation of the American Jewish Committee in 1906. Although the founding of the American Jewish Committee is a noteworthy event in the American Jewish confrontation with the forces of restriction, the stirrings of that engagement occurred fifteen years before. Wolf's representation to Secretary Foster, with little equivocation, advocated liberal American policy toward eastern European Jewish immigration.

83. *Reports of the Industrial Commission on Immigration*, 15 (1901), 245, 249.

84. Ibid., 251.

85. *Second Conference of Jewish Charities*, 68.

86. Ibid., 65–82.

87. Ibid., 66–67.

88. Leo Levi, "The Modern Dispersion," in *Memorial Volume: Leo N. Levi* (Chicago: Hamburger, 1905), 29.

89. *Second Conference of Jewish Charities*, 70, 71.

90. Ibid., 71, 72.

91. David M. Bressler, "The Industrial Removal Office," *Menorah* 35 (November 1903): 277.

92. *Second Conference of Jewish Charities*, 72–73.

93. Ibid., 94.

94. Ibid., 69.

95. David Bressler, "The Industrial Removal Office," 283.

96. IRO Records, Industrial Removal Office to Jewish Colonization Association, 27 Jan. 1904, Box 86. Either Cyrus Sulzberger or David Bressler was the probable author of these remarks.

97. Ibid.

98. Ibid.

99. IRO Records, Morris Loeb to Cyrus Sulzberger, 26 Oct. 1907, Box 91. Loeb had previously served on the Executive Committee of the IRO.

100. *JAIAS Annual Report for the Year 1901*, 32.

101. IRO Records, Industrial Removal Office to the Jewish Colonization Association, 27 Jan. 1904. IRO and Jewish Colonization Association Correspondence, Box 86.

102. IRO Records, M. M. Feuerlicht to David M. Bressler, 22 Jan. 1906. Box 38.

103. IRO Records, Industrial Removal Office to the Jewish Colonization Association, 24 March 1903. IRO and Jewish Colonization Association Correspondence, Box 86.

104. *Proceedings of the Third National Conference of Jewish Charities in the United States* (New York: Philip Cowen, 1904), 140–141.

105. *Proceedings of the Sixth National Conference of Jewish Charities in the United States* (Baltimore: Press of Kohn and Pollock, 1910), 153.

106. *Twelfth Annual Report of the Industrial Removal Office for the Year 1912*, 5.

107. David M. Bressler, *The Distribution of Jewish Immigrants in Industrial and Agricultural Pursuits, Agencies and Results* (New York: n.p., 1907), 6.

108. For a study of the Galveston Movement, see Bernard Merinbach, *Galveston: Ellis Island of the West* (Albany: State University of New York Press, 1983).

109. David M. Bressler, "Immigration Distribution," *Jewish Charities* 5 (September 1914): 34.

110. Ibid.

111. Ibid., 32.

112. Israel Zangwill, the son of Russian immigrants who had settled in London, wrote *The Melting Pot* (1908), a play that helped popularize that assimilationist image. At the seventh Zionist Congress in Basel in 1905, a heated debate broke out over the British proposal for a Jewish homeland in a portion of Uganda (now a part of western Kenya). Zionist delegates for whom Palestine represented the only conceivable territory for a Jewish homeland successfully defeated the plan. Advocates of Jewish political autonomy in any suitable locale either accepted defeat or joined Zangwill and his allies in founding the ITO, which then sought to accept the British plan. But the British offer was withdrawn, and the ITO continued to investigate without success an array of territorial possibilities for the founding of a Jewish homeland. In the frustrated aftermath of these efforts, the ITO collaborated in Schiff's scheme for Jewish immigration to Galveston. See Marinbach, *Galveston*, 6–9.

113. Bressler, "Immigration Distribution," 34.

114. Jacob H. Schiff, "The Galveston Movement," *Jewish Charities* 4 (June 1914): 5.

115. David M. Bressler to Jacob Billikopf, 14 June 1914. American Jewish Archives, Mss. Col. 13, Box 3.

116. Schiff, "The Galveston Movement," 6; Marinbach, *Galveston*, chap. 4.

117. Bressler, "Immigration Distribution," 32.


## Chapter 2. Confronting Immigration Restriction

1. David M. Bressler, "The Industrial Removal Office," *Menorah* 35 (1903): 280.

2. *The American Jewish Yearbook* (Philadelphia: Jewish Publication Society of America, 1906), 268.

3. *Eleventh Annual Report of the Industrial Removal Office for the Year 1911*, 5.

4. *New York Times*, 12 Oct. 1919, sec. 3, 6.

5. *Monthly Bulletin* 1 (October 1914): 1–2.

6. IRO Records, David M. Bressler to Reuben Arkush, 20 Oct. 1916. Box 1.

7. "Statements and Recommendations Submitted by Societies and Organizations Interested in the Subject of Immigration," in *Reports of the Immigration Commission* 41 (Washington, D.C.: Government Printing Office, 1911), 141–157, 329–334, 337–339.

8. Henry B. Leonard, "Louis Marshall and Immigration Restriction, 1906–1924," *American Jewish Archives* 24 (April 1972): 11–12. The National Liberal Immigration League began at the instigation of American participants in the Alliance Israelite Universelle. Although the league was nonsectarian and multiethnic, its leadership was primarily Jewish. See Rivka Shpak Lissak, "The National Liberal Immigration League and Immigration Restriction, 1906–1917," *American Jewish Archives* 47 (Fall/Winter 1994): 207, 213–215.

9. Mark Wischnitzer, *Visas to Freedom* (New York: World Publishing, 1956), 72.

10. David M. Bressler, "Work with Immigrants," *Jewish Charities* 3 (February 1913): 9.

11. Horace Kallen, "Democracy Versus the Melting Pot: A Study of American Nationality," Part 2 *The Nation* (25 Feb. 1915): 218.

12. John Higham, *Send These To Me*, rev. ed. (Baltimore: Johns Hopkins University Press, 1984), 208.

13. *Monthly Bulletin* 1 (April 1915): 3, 4.

14. Roy Garis, *Immigration Restriction* (New York: Macmillan, 1927), 143, 171.

15. *Reports of the Immigration Commission* 1 (1911), 23, 48.

16. David M. Bressler and Abraham Solomon, "Immigration Snapshots," *Jewish Charities* 4 (April 1914): 5.

17. *Monthly Bulletin* 1 (February 1915): 2.

18. Ibid.

19. *Monthly Bulletin* 1 (March 1915): 1.

20. *Distribution* 3 (January 1917): 4–5.

21. Ibid.

22. *Distribution* 2 (May 1916): 7, 7–8.

23. *Distribution* 3 (January 1917): 4.

24. Ibid., (March 1917): 5.

25. *Reports of the Immigration Commission* 41 (1911), 109, 107.

26. Ibid., 5 (1911), 3.

27. Madison Grant, *The Passing of the Great Race in America* (New York: Scribner's, 1923), 90.

28. Edward A. Ross, *The Old World in the New* (New York: Century Company, 1914), 256. Ross was a professional sociologist, at one time serving as president of the American Sociological Society. He was also a member of the Immigration Restriction League. Ross could not come to terms with the enormous changes coursing through post–Civil War America. He found deeply troubling the growth of cities, both through immigration and the steady move from farm to factory. Constricted by the biological substrate of his social analysis, Ross was eventually eclipsed when a new sociology emerged, unburdened by the dead weight of racial and Darwinian explanation. Kallen's article in *The Nation* of 18 and 25 Feb. 1915 was provoked by Ross's book.

29. Edward A. Ross, "Significance of Emigration—Discussion," *American Economic Review* 2 March 1912: 87.

30. Ibid.

31. Ross, *The Old World in the New*, 207–213, 144–145.

32. *Monthly Bulletin* 1 (October 1914): 2, 3.

33. John Higham, *Strangers in the Land: Patterns of American Nativism, 1860–1926*, 2d ed. (New Brunswick, N.J.: Rutgers University Press, 1988), 153.

34. George W. Stocking, Jr., *Race, Culture, and Evolution* (New York: Free Press, 1968), 49–50.

35. *Reports of the Immigration Commission* 5 (1911), 1.

36. Ibid., 38 (1911), 1–7, 55–64, 99–115, 127.

37. Ibid., 1 (1911), 44.

38. Ibid., 1 (1911), 43–44.

39. *Monthly Bulletin* 1 (May 1915): 2.

40. Ibid., 3, 3–4.

41. Ibid., (January 1915): 1.

42. George Stocking, ed. *The Shaping of American Anthropology, 1883–1911: A Franz Boas Reader* (New York: Basic Books, 1974), 190.

43. Maurice Fishberg, "New York," in *The Russian Jew in the United States*, ed. Charles S. Bernheimer (Philadelphia: John C. Winston, 1905), 282; "Materials for the Physical Anthropology of the Eastern European Jews," *Memoirs of the American Anthropological and Ethnological Societies*, 1 (Part 1 1905): 39–45.

44. Franz Boas, "The Question of Racial Purity," *American Mercury* 3 (October 1924): 169.

45. *New York Times*, 28 April 1903, 8.

46. *Reports of the Immigration Commission* 1 (1911), 13, 9.

47. Ibid., 47–48.

48. Jeremiah W. Jenks and W. Jett Lauck, *The Immigration Problem: A Study of American Immigration Conditions and Needs*, 6th ed. (New York: Funk and Wagnalls, 1926), xx.

49. Ibid., 3–4.

50. *Reports of the Immigration Commission* 1 (1911), 23.

51. Ibid., 422–426.

52. Ibid., 474, 482.

53. Ibid., 24.

54. Ibid., 180–182.

55. Ibid., 4 (1911), 39–40, 41.

56. Simon Kuznets, "Immigration of Russian Jews to the United States," *Perspectives in American History* 9 (1975): 40.

57. *Reports of the Immigration Commission* 4 (1911), 40.

58. Published in the wake of the *Reports of the Immigration Commission*, Samuel Joseph's *Jewish Immigration to the United States, 1881–1910* (New York: AMS Press, 1967) is one of the first scholarly examinations of the statistical profile of the Jewish immigrants. Permanence of settlement is an important feature. The question of return migration to Europe has been raised most recently by Mark Wyman in his book, *Round-Trip to America: The Immigrants Return to Europe, 1880–1930* (Ithaca, N.Y.: Cornell University Press, 1993). The high return rates for a number of European

groups led Wyman to challenge the notion of American "exceptionalism"—that immigration to the United States was fundamentally different in character from other places, where temporary sojourn was for economic purposes. Significantly, Jews do not figure prominently in his discussion because Jewish returnees to Europe in the period 1908–1923 constituted only 5 percent of the total Jewish immigration in those years. That figure is the lowest of twenty-six groups cited by Wyman from Labor Department statistics (p. 11).

59. *Reports of the Immigration Commission* 4 (1911), 271–281.

60. Through its efforts to record ethnic data in response to the proliferating new immigration, the government encountered opposition only from American Jews. Simon Wolf objected to the new classification in 1901 before the Industrial Commission on Immigration. The issue arose again in the lengthy exchange between Simon Wolf, joined by Judge Julian Mack of the American Jewish Committee, and Senator Lodge during the hearings of the Immigration Commission on the question of whether Jews constitute a categorically distinct racial group. Arguing that the Jews of all religious groups had been singled out for racial categorization, Wolf objected strongly to the separate listing of Jews, or "Hebrews" as they were designated, in national immigration statistics after 1899. In Wolf's view, which represented the thinking of American Reform Jews, the Jewish people were defined only by religion, not by race or nationality. Identifying immigrants specifically as Jews, Wolf believed, would encourage prejudice, antisemitism, and restrictionist sentiment by providing these forces a clear target. See *Reports of the Industrial Commission on Immigration* 15 (Washington, D.C.: Government Printing Office, 1901), 66; *Reports of the Immigration Commission* 41 (1911), 265–279; Esther L. Panitz, *Simon Wolf* (Rutherford, N.J.: Fairleigh Dickinson University Press, 1987), 124–126.

61. Joseph, *Jewish Immigration,* 87, 176–177.

62. Ibid., 176.

63. Ibid., 176–177.

64. Calculated from the Annual Reports of the United Hebrew Charities, 1885–1899.

65. Bressler prepared the statements submitted in the name of each organization. His submission on behalf of the Jewish Immigrants' Information Bureau consisted of an address, entitled "The Removal Work Including Galveston," that he had delivered at the National Conference of Jewish Charities in 1910. *Reports of the Immigration Commission* 41 (1911), 304–321, 336–340.

66. Ibid., 332.

67. Ibid., 154–155.

68. Prescott Hall insisted that other issues beyond economics were significant. In a review of Hourwich's important rebuttal of Immigration Commission findings, *Immigration and Labor: The Economic Aspects of European Immigration to the United States* (New York: Putnam, 1912), Hall asserted, "A large part of the restrictionist propaganda is based on the view that the Mediterranean, Asiatic, and African races are not fitted by inheritance and training to take part in a democracy requiring an intelligent, self-reliant, and homogeneous citizenship." *American Economic Review* 3 (June 1913): 422–427.

In the early years of the Immigration Restriction League, the race argument against immigration was subdued. But early in the new century with the growth of the eugenics movement, Hall's smug racialism became more prominent. See Higham, *Strangers in the Land,* 152, 272.

69. *Final Report of the Commission on Industrial Relations* 1 (Washington, D.C.: Government Printing Office, 1916), 144–145.

70. Ibid., 225.

71. *Distribution* 2 (July 1916): 6.

72. *Eleventh Annual Report of the Industrial Removal Office for the Year 1911,* 6–7. The figures on the number of wage earners resettled and estimated wages average out to a weekly income in 1911 between $9.61 and $11.53 for IRO clients. At about the same time, the Immigration Commission provided data on weekly incomes, which averaged $14.37 and $12.71, for native-born whites with native-born fathers and Russian Jewish immigrants, respectively (Vol. 1, Table 22, 367.) Commission data on immigrant Jews were occasionally divided into the categories, "Hebrew, Russian" and "Hebrew, Other." The latter, mostly from Rumania and Austria-Hungary, areas noted by the IRO as producing more skilled and highly trained workers, averaged weekly incomes of $14.37, precisely the same as those of native whites with native-born fathers. One cannot, however, discern a diachronic dimension in most of the data, so that it is impossible to determine if the greater average wage of Jewish immigrants from outside of Russia was partly related to longer residence in the United States. Likewise, the data on Russian Jewish immigrants are not broken down by length of American residence.

73. Joseph, *Jewish Immigration,* 153.

74. *Monthly Bulletin* 1 (December 1914): 4.

75. Ibid., (May 1915): 1–2.

76. Ibid., (June 1915): 2–3.

77. Isaac A. Hourwich, *Immigration and Labor: The Economic Aspects of European Immigration to the United States* 2d ed. (New York: B. W. Huebsch, 1922).

78. Higham, *Strangers in the Land,* 421–422.

79. Jenks and Lauck, *The Immigration Problem,* xx.

80. Unsympathetic to immigration, the commission nonetheless observed that immigration since the Civil War was in large measure a function of American business cycles and industrial conditions. Commons prepared the section on the economic effects of immigration. He regarded the European newcomers as a menace to American labor. Commons saw a polyglot immigration of diverse ethnic groups as diminishing the condition of native workers. It would inhibit labor organization and weaken the capacity of organized labor to resist machinery and new methods, resulting in a lowered standard of living in machine industries. Without unions, most laborers could not share in prosperity nor protect themselves from downturns in the business cycle. Where unions exist, the integrity of the organization based on the strike, is threatened by cheap, non-union labor. *Reports of the Industrial Commission on Immigration* 15 (1901), 308; 312–315.

81. Hourwich, *Immigration and Labor,* 19–20, 34.

82. Ibid., 34–35.

83. Jenks and Lauck, *The Immigration Problem,* 460.

84. Hourwich, *Immigration and Labor,* iii.

85. Ibid., 52–60.

86. Maldwyn Allen Jones, *American Immigration* (Chicago: University of Chicago Press, 1960), 180–181.

87. Edward A. Ross, "Significance of Emigration," 86; Higham, *Send These to Me,* 194–195. Higham identifies a relationship between restriction and the concern about purity during the Progressive era. Whether it was personal hygiene, wholesome foods, safe drugs, sanitation, disease prevention, or prohibition, crusades against contamination and decay were the order of the day. Anti-immigration sentiment was easily assimilated into this pattern. Ross's image of the abnormal physical body representing the corrupted social body is telling.

88. Hourwich, *Immigration and Labor,* 62.

89. Ibid., 2–3, 62–81.

90. *Reports of the Immigration Commission* 39 (1911), 30–31.

91. *Reports of the Industrial Commission on Immigration* 15 (1901), 491.

92. Charles Loring Brace, *The Dangerous Classes of New York* (New York: Wynkoop and Hallenbeck, 1872), 35, 27, 223–233; Marilyn Irvin Holt, *The Orphan Trains: Placing Out in America* (Lincoln: University of Nebraska Press, 1992), 39–40.

93. Paul H. Douglas, "Is the New Immigration More Unskilled than the Old?" *Journal of the American Statistical Association* 16 (June 1919): 393.

94. Ibid., 394.

95. Ibid., 394, 395, 398–402.

96. Bressler, "The Industrial Removal Office," 287.

97. *Monthly Bulletin* 1 (February 1915): 2. Emphasis in original.

98. Ibid.

99. Ibid., (December 1914): 2.

100. IRO Records, Jeremiah Jenks to the IRO, 28 May 1915. Personal Correspondence, Box 91. Jenks's letter was prompted by the IRO's response, published in its May 1915 *Monthly Bulletin* to his interview with *The New York Evening Post.* Complaining that the IRO had misrepresented his attitude toward immigrants, Jenks requested that the views set forth in his letter be put before the readers of the *Monthly Bulletin.* An edited version of his letter appeared in the June 1915 issue.

101. *Monthly Bulletin* 1 (June 1915): 3.

102. The IRO's double-edged rationale for continued immigration was consistent with many other efforts to combat restriction. Higham, *Send These to Me,* 44.

103. Department Circular No. 156, 25 Sept. 1907, F.P. Sargent, Commissioner-General of Immigration, Department of Commerce and Labor.

104. *Jewish Charities* 2 (December 1911): 6.

105. *Eleventh Annual Report of the Industrial Removal Office for the Year 1911,* 6.

106. *Jewish Charities* 4 (March 1914): 3.

107. *Report of the Commissioner General of Immigration for Year Ending June 30, 1903* (Washington, D.C.: Government Printing Office, 1903), 60.

108. David M. Bressler, "Distribution," in *The Russian Jew in the United States,* ed. Charles S. Bernheimer (Philadelphia: John C. Winston Co., 1905), 370.

109. *Eleventh Annual Report of the Industrial Removal Office for the Year 1911*, 5; IRO Records, Chairman of the IRO to the American Jewish Committee, 14 Oct. 1913. Outside Organizations, Correspondence, Box 21; "The Industrial Removal Office's First Decade," *Jewish Charities* 9 (April 1911): 7–8.

110. *Monthly Bulletin* 1 (July 1914): 1.

111. J. W. Hayes, General Master Workman of the Knights of Labor to Charles Nagel, Secretary of Commerce and Labor, 27 April 1909.

112. *Final Report of the Commission on Industrial Relations* 2 (1916), 1309–1313.

113. "Report of the Chief of the Division of Information," in *Annual Report of the Commissioner-General of Immigration to the Secretary of Commerce and Labor for Fiscal Year Ended June 30, 1909* (Washington, D.C.: Government Printing Office, 1909), 217–227.

114. Immigration totals for 1907–1908 compiled from *Reports of the Immigration Commission* 1 (1911), 95.

115. *Reports of the Immigration Commission* 1 (1911), 46.

116. Frances A. Kellor, "Needed—A Domestic Immigration Policy," *The North American Review* 193 (April 1911): 562. Kellor, managing director of the North American Civic League for Immigrants, urged reform of the Division of Information. Eager to separate strict immigration issues, such as admission and exclusion, from problems of assimilation once the immigrant was admitted, she recommended severing the division from the Bureau of Immigration. She suggested calling the new office, the "Bureau of Distribution" and investing it with a greater range of responsibilities than those weakly discharged by the Division of Information. See Frances A. Kellor and Joseph Mayper, *Recommendations for a Federal Bureau of Distribution* (New York: North American Civic League for Immigrants, n.d.), 1–6.

117. Ibid., 565.

118. *Annual Report of the Commissioner-General of Immigration to the Secretary of Commerce and Labor for the Fiscal Year Ending June 30, 1908* (Washington D.C.: Government Printing Office, 1908), 120.

119. Kellor, "Needed—A Domestic Immigration Policy," 565.

120. *Eleventh Annual Report of the Industrial Removal Office for the Year 1911*, 6.

121. *Reports of the Immigration Commission* 41 (1911), 38–39.

122. *Thirteenth Annual Report of the Industrial Removal Office, for the Year 1913*, 7–8.

123. *Jewish Charities* 4 (March 1914): 4.

124. Ibid.

125. Ibid.

126. "Report of the Chief of the Division of Information," in *Annual Report of the Commissioner-General of Immigration to the Secretary of Commerce and Labor for the Fiscal Year Ending June 30, 1912* (Washington, D.C.: Government Printing Office, 1912), 208.

127. *Jewish Charities* 4 (March 1914): 6.

128. *Monthly Bulletin*, 1 (June 1915): 5.

129. Ibid., (January 1915): 8.

130. IRO Records, Philip D. Bookstaber to David M. Bressler, 30 Sept. 1912. Correspondence of Immigrants, Box 91.

131. *Distribution* 3 (May 1917): 7.

132. William M. Leiserson, *Adjusting Immigrant and Industry* (New York: Harper and Brothers, 1924), 55–59.

133. Maurice Davie, *Refugees in America: Report of the Committee for the Study of Recent Immigration from Europe* (New York: Harper and Brothers, 1947), 77.

134. Jeremy Hein, *From Vietnam, Laos, and Cambodia: A Refugee Experience in the United States* (New York: Twayne Publishers, 1995), 52.

135. Reubén G. Rumbaut, "The Structure of Refuge: Southeast Asian Refugees in the United States, 1975–1985," *International Review of Comparative Public Policy* 1 (1989): 101.

136. Hein, *From Vietnam, Laos, and Cambodia*, 51.


## Chapter 3. Internal Debates


1. The letters of immigrants quoted in this chapter are based on translations prepared at the time of receipt by the IRO. The quotations are minimally edited for intelligibility. Most errors of spelling and grammar are reprinted without a *sic* notation. The vast majority of immigrant correspondence to the IRO was, of course, written in Yiddish. When the letter arrived in New York, the staff arranged a prompt English translation and filed it with the original. Yiddish competence in the IRO office varied from person to person. The translations therefore must be considered the primary documents to which the IRO responded. Many fewer letters were written in German and Russian, but they too were quickly translated into English. In its early years, the IRO also received a few letters in Rumanian. Other letters were written in English, and many appear to have been prepared by the immigrants themselves. The letters in Yiddish show a considerable incorporation of English, written in transliteration, even when equivalent Yiddish terms existed. Sometimes, immigrants would ask relatives, friends, or others to write in English on their behalf, although the identity of the scribe is not always provided.

2. IRO Records, M. Goldstein to the IRO, 13 Oct. 1907. Correspondence of Immigrants, Box 114.

3. IRO Records, Morris Greenberg to the IRO, no date. Correspondence of Immigrants, Box 115.

4. *JAIAS Annual Report for the Year 1905* (19–23), for example, is mostly devoted to the successes of IRO clients who left New York for such places as Ripon, Wisconsin; Birmingham, Alabama; South Bend, Indiana; Buffalo, New York; Cleveland, Ohio; and Detroit, Michigan. Often quoting from the letters of immigrants, the report conveys a set of similar stories depicting long periods of unemployment in New York followed by well-paying jobs in the interior. Some of the writers were able to start their own businesses rather quickly and to buy homes.

5. IRO Records, Extract of letter from S. Klein to *The Jewish Daily News*, no date. Correspondence of Immigrants, Box 114.

6. The Galveston Movement also generated controversy and sensation in the Yiddish press, both through the letters of distressed immigrants and in editorials denouncing their alleged exploitation. See Bernard Marinbach, *Galveston: Ellis Island of the West* (Albany: State University of New York Press, 1983), 34–39.

7. United Hebrew Charities, *Fourteenth Annual Report*, 1888, 18.

8. Ibid., *Twelfth Annual Report,* 1886, 15.

9. Ibid., 32.

10. Ibid., 34.

11. Ibid., *Twentieth Annual Report,* 1894, 18.

12. *Proceedings of the Fifth National Conference of Jewish Charities in the United States* (Baltimore: Kohn and Pollock, 1908), 63–64.

13. Ibid., 64–65.

14. Morris D. Waldman, "Family Desertion," in *Proceedings of the Sixth National Conference of Jewish Charities in the United States* (Baltimore: Kohn and Pollock, 1910), 57.

15. United Hebrew Charities, *Second Annual Report,* 1876, 5.

16. Ibid., *Twenty-Fifth Annual Report,* 1899, 37.

17. Jacob H. Hollander, "The Unification of Jewish Communal Activities," in *Proceedings of the Fifth National Conference of Jewish Charities in the United States* (Baltimore: Kohn and Pollock, 1908), 54.

18. Abraham Ehrlich, *Yidishe Gazeten,* 12 Dec. 1890. Cited in Elias Tcherikower, *The Early Jewish Labor Movement in the United States,* trans. and ed. Aaron Antonovsky (New York: Yivo Institute for Jewish Research, 1961), 107.

19. United Hebrew Charities, *Ninth Annual Report,* 1883, 18–19.

20. Ibid., 19. Emphasis in original.

21. Ibid.

22. Harold Silver, "Some Attitudes of the East European Jewish Immigrants Toward Organized Jewish Charity in the United States in the Years, 1890–1900," (Masters thesis, Graduate School of Jewish Social Work, 1934), 2.

23. *Jewish Gazette,* May 1894, 1. Cited in Silver, 26. Silver states that *The Jewish Gazette,* which began publication in 1874, emphasized a traditional orthodox point of view yet also included other perspectives. An editorial in October 1890 states in truly liberal spirit: "*The Jewish Gazette* is not sold to any political or religious party. Its duty is to hear all sides on every important issue. It will print anything worthwhile, be the writer a rabbi, a doctor, a poet, a socialist, a philosopher, or a crank. Let each one say what he feels; this hurts no one and is sometimes very interesting." (1–2)

24. *Jewish Gazette,* February 1892, 1. Cited in Silver, 33.

25. Ibid., November 1893, 3. Cited in Silver, 71.

26. Ibid., November 1890, 1. Cited in Silver, 62.

27. Ibid., January 1891, 2. Cited in Silver, 64.

28. Ibid., December 1896, 1. Cited in Silver, 126–128.

29. Ibid., 126.

30. Ibid., 128.

31. I. M. Rubinow, "Concentration or Removal—Which?" *American Hebrew* (17 July 1903): 271–272; I. M. Rubinow, "Concentration or Removal—Which?" (Conclusion), *American Hebrew* (24 July 1903): 303–304. Both installments reprinted in *The Menorah* 35 (August 1903): 70–78.

32. "The Jewish Question in New York City," *Publications of the American Jewish Historical Society* 49 (1959): 90–136. This article was originally published serially in the Russian Jewish monthly, *Voskhod,* in 1903.

33. Rubinow, "Concentration or Removal—Which?" 272.

34. Ibid., 271.

35. Ibid., 272.

36. Rubinow, "Concentration or Removal—Which?" (Conclusion), 303.

37. Ibid., 303–304.

38. Ibid., 304.

39. Emmanuel Hertz, "Politics," in *The Russian Jew in the United States,* ed. Charles S. Bernheimer (Philadelphia: John C. Winston, Co., 1905), 258.

40. Rubinow, "Concentration or Removal—Which?" (Conclusion), 304.

41. "To Be Crowded or to Disperse?" *American Hebrew* (24 July 1903): 302.

42. Abraham Cahan, "The Russian Jew in the United States," in *The Russian Jew in the United States,* ed. Charles S. Bernheimer (Philadelphia: John C. Winston, 1905), 32.

43. Ibid., 33–34.

44. IRO Records, Leo Stamm to IRO, n.d. Correspondence of Immigrants, Box 103.

45. Boris Bogen, Letter to the *American Hebrew* (21 Aug. 1903): 438.

46. Ibid., 439.

47. Ruth Cohen, *Out of the Shadow* (New York: Doran, 1918), 168–169.

48. Michael Gold, *Jews Without Money* (New York: Liveright, 1932), 215.

49. IRO Records, Joseph Lipetz to the Industrial Removal Office, 4 May 1907. Correspondence of Immigrants, Box 116.

50. IRO Records, General Manager to Joseph Lipetz, 10 May 1907. Correspondence of Immigrants, Box 116.

51. IRO Records, Joe Lee to the Industrial Removal Office, 30 June 1908. Correspondence of Immigrants, Box 116.

52. Ibid.

53. IRO Records, David M. Bressler to Mark Hyman, 14 Aug. 1906. Personal Correspondence, Box 91.

54. *Jewish Daily Forward,* May 1901, 1. Cited in Silver, 165.

55. Ibid.

56. Ibid., Cited in Silver, 167–168.

57. Addressing the Jewish Chautauqua, Bressler commented on the allegations that the IRO "engaged in slave traffic" and that "the men are sent to the coal mines for such work as cannot command a living wage." He attributed these rumors to disgruntled clients seeking transportation to places the IRO deemed inappropriate for them. Others returned to New York, unhappy about what they had encountered and blamed the IRO. Bressler acknowledged IRO errors in resettling some men who should never have been taken on as clients. Others, he admitted, had been ill-treated by IRO agents to whom they had been entrusted. See David M. Bressler "The Industrial Removal Office," a paper read before the Jewish Chautauqua, July 1903.

58. IRO Records, David M. Bressler to Julius Weis and Co., 31 Aug. 1903. Correspondence of Immigrants, Box 99.

59. *Indianapolis Star,* 30 Sept. 1909, 1.

60. IRO Records, David M. Bressler to Dr. Herbert Friedenwald, 4 Oct. 1909. Personal Correspondence, Box 91.

61. IRO Records, Max Frons to David M. Bressler, 20 Feb. 1910. Correspondence of Immigrants, Box 115.

62. IRO Records, David M. Bressler to Max Frons, 23 Feb. 1910. Correspondence of Immigrants, Box 115.

63. *JAIAS Annual Report for the Year 1903*, 19–20.

64. IRO Records, A. J. Hoyt to David M. Bressler, 19 June 1906; David M. Bressler to A. J. Hoyt, 26 June 1906. Personal Correspondence, Box 91.

65. *JAIAS Annual Report for the Year 1903*, 19.

66. IRO Records, Morris Weissman to the Industrial Removed Office, no date. Correspondence, Box 24.

67. IRO Records, Sam Segelman to David M. Bressler, no date. Correspondence of Immigrants, Box 92.

68. IRO Records, A. Horsman to David M. Bressler, no date. Correspondence of Immigrants, Box 92.

69. IRO Records, General Manager to Sam Segelman, July 17, 1905; General Manager to A. Horsman, 17 July 1905. Correspondence of Immigrants, Box 92.

70. IRO Records, S. Bloch to David M. Bressler, 16 June 1910. Personal Correspondence, Box 91.

71. Reported by Cohen's son, Ben, in Indianapolis, 18 April 1981. Cohen and his friends fled to Chicago. He eventually settled in Indianapolis, where he worked as a tailor. Early on, he sent for his wife and children. Jewish Federation of Indianapolis, Superintendent's Report, 3 July 1907.

72. *Final Report of the Commission on Industrial Relations* 1 (Washington, D.C.: Government Printing Office, 1916), 110. The commission noted, "There are many private employment agents who try to conduct their business honestly, but they are the exception rather than the rule. The business as a whole reeks with fraud, extortion, and flagrant abuses of every kind."

73. *Final Report of the Commission on Industrial Relations* 2 (1916), 1214. The commission amassed information pointing up other important differences between labor agencies and the IRO. The former showed no concern in relieving unemployment but rather exacerbated labor market congestion and joblessness. Motivated solely by fee for service, the agencies would never hesitate to bring workers to cities that were already overcrowded. By the same token, agencies readily filled positions with individuals who were already employed.

The IRO would not accept employed individuals as clients. Although it remained a vociferous critic of dense ethnic settlements, suitable employment—even in New York, Philadelphia, or Boston—remained paramount. Limited resources were to be used on behalf of the chronically unemployed.

74. Cyrus Sulzberger, "Address," in *Proceedings of the Fourth National Conference of Jewish Charities in the United States* (New York: Stettiner Bros., 1906), 39.

75. Ibid., 43.

76. *JAIAS Annual Report for the Year 1903*, 20.

77. IRO Records, M. M. Feuerlicht to David M. Bressler, 7 June 1905. Morris Feuerlicht File, Box 38.

78. IRO Records, David M. Bressler to M. M. Feuerlicht, 12 June 1905. Morris Feuerlicht File, Box 38.

79. *Tenth Annual Report of the Industrial Removal Office for the Year 1910*, 10.

80. IRO Records, David M. Bressler to Abraham Cahan, 8 Feb. 1910. Outside Organizations, Correspondence, Box 25.

81. IRO Records, Notice from I. W. W. Press Committee, Local 470, 27 March 1913. Outside Organizations, Correspondence, Box 21.

82. IRO Records, David M. Bressler to I. W. W. Press Committee, Local 470, 28 March 1912. Outside Organizations, Correspondence, Box 21.

83. *Final Report of the Commission on Industrial Relations* 2 (1916), 1216.

84. Melech Epstein, *Jewish Labor in U.S.A.: An Industrial, Political, and Cultural History of the Jewish Labor Movement, 1882–1914,* 2d ed. (Hoboken, N. J.: KTAV, 1969), 48.

85. Ibid., 46.

86. Ibid., 47.

87. Tcherikower, *The Early Jewish Labor Movement,* 112–113.

88. Ibid., 111, note 36.

89. IRO Records, Report and Resolutions of Branch 248, Arbeiter Ring, Los Angeles, n. d. Outside Organizations, Correspondence, Box 23.

90. IRO Records, Abraham Cahan to David M. Bressler, 14 Dec. 1909. Outside Organizations, Correspondence, Box 25.

91. IRO Records, David M. Bressler to Abraham Cahan, 20 Dec. 1906. Outside Organizations, Correspondence, Box 25. The JAIAS, the IRO, the Baron de Hirsch Fund, and the Educational Alliance organized an agricultural exhibit, held in October 1906 at the Educational Alliance Building. It featured produce from Jewish-owned farms in New Jersey as well as photographs and information about farming and industrial opportunities in other parts of the country. Judging it an enormous success for having attracted almost 50,000 visitors and large numbers of applicants for resettlement, the joint committee of sponsoring organizations arranged for the exhibition to be presented in Brooklyn and Boston. See JAIAS *Annual Report for the Year 1906,* 8.

92. IRO Records, General Manager to *The Jewish Daily News,* 13 July 1910. Outside Organizations, Correspondence, Box 25.

93. IRO Records, Ezekiel Sarasohn to David M. Bressler, 28 June 1906. Outside Organizations, Correspondence, Box 25.

94. IRO Records, M. Jaffee, Manager, *The Jewish Daily Forward,* to the IRO, 2 Aug. 1906. Outside Organizations, Correspondence, Box 25.

95. IRO Records, Board of Directors Minutes, 14 May 1907. Box 1.

96. IRO Records, General Manager to Abraham Cahan, 25 April 1907. Outside Organizations, Correspondence, Box 25.

97. Ibid.

98. IRO Records, Abraham Berman to *The Jewish Daily Forward,* n.d. Outside Organizations, Correspondence, Box 25. Translated either at the office of *The Jewish Daily Forward* or the IRO, this letter was written in Yiddish and appears undated without the original. Accompanying letters about Berman indicate that it was written in the spring of 1912.

99. IRO Records, David M. Bressler to Abraham Cahan, 29 May 1912. Outside Organizations, Correspondence, Box 25.

100. IRO Records, *The Jewish Daily Forward* to David M. Bressler, 19 June 1912. Outside Organizations, Correspondence, Box 25.

101. [*Fourth*] *Annual Report of the Industrial Removal Office for the Year 1904*, 7; *Tenth Annual Report of the Industrial Removal Office for the Year 1910*, 14.

102. IRO Records, Chairman, Industrial Removal Office to the Editor, *Jewish Daily News*, 27 Aug. 1907. Outside Organizations, Correspondence, Box 25.

103. IRO Records, Harry Cohen to the Industrial Removal Office, 17 July 1909. Correspondence of Immigrants, Box 96.

104. IRO Records, General Manager to Harry Cohen, 19 July 1909. Correspondence of Immigrants, Box 96.

105. Ari Lloyd Fridkis, "Desertion in the American Jewish Immigrant Family: The Work of the National Desertion Bureau in Cooperation with the Industrial Removal Office," *American Jewish History* 71 (December 1981): 285–299.

106. IRO Records, Mrs. Balkin to David M. Bressler, 23 Sept. 1914. Correspondence of Immigrants, Box 108.

107. IRO Records, David M. Bressler to Mrs. Balkin, 24 Sept. 1914. Correspondence of Immigrants, Box 108.

108. IRO Records, Mrs. Samuel Friedman to David M. Bressler, 15 Sept. 1912. Correspondence of Immigrants, Box 102.

109. IRO Records, Philip L. Seman to Mrs. Samuel Friedman, 19 Sept. 1912. Correspondence of Immigrants, Box 102.

110. IRO Records, Jacob Finkelstein to the IRO, no date. (Letter received in New York, 6 Aug. 1912.) Correspondence of Immigrants, Box 113.

111. IRO Records, H. Zazipinsky to the IRO, 3 Nov. 1907. Correspondence of Immigrants, Box 113.

112. *New York Times*, 3 July 1907, 3. Bressler took the strongest exception to this characterization, asserting instead that "the Removal Office has uniformly rejected every person whose failure, if such it may be called, was due to anything else than lack of employment. In every instance the persons removed by us were possessed of sufficient wage-earning capacity to earn their livelihood. All they needed was opportunity, and to get that they applied to us. The fact that the great majority of persons sent by us were quickly employed in gainful occupation and earning a decent livelihood for themselves and their families would hardly bear out Mr. Zangwill's statement that they were failures. I can only deplore Mr. Zangwill's unhappy characterization of our work, because coming from such an authority it can only do us harm." IRO Records, David M. Bressler to Jacob Schiff, 3 July 1907. Personal Correspondence, Box 91.

Bressler also brought Zangwill's remarks to the attention of Cyrus Sulzberger. (IRO Records, David M. Bressler to Cyrus Sulzberger, 3 July 1907. Personal Correspondence, Box 91.) He hoped that either Schiff or Sulzberger might be able to exercise some influence in preventing Zangwill from repeating his intemperate remarks. Schiff suggested that Bressler not take great exception to any statement made by Zangwill for, like Sulzberger, Schiff had long since learned that Zangwill "cannot guard his mouth." IRO Records, Jacob Schiff to David M. Bressler, 5 July 1907. Personal Correspondence, Box 91.

113. IRO Records, Abram Yaskransky to the Industrial Removal Office, 13 Nov. 1906. Correspondence of Immigrants, Box 116.

## Chapter 4. The IRO at the Local Level

1. IRO Records, Elias Margolis to David M. Bressler, 7 Aug. 1908. Traveling Agents, Box 19.

2. *Thirteenth Annual Report of the Industrial Removal Office for the Year 1913,* 11–12.

3. IRO Records, David M. Bressler to Abraham Solomon, 23 Sept. 1912. Traveling Agents, Box 20.

4. Ella Auerbach, daughter of Esau Fleishman, an IRO committee member in Omaha, has reflected on her father's considerate service on behalf of the newcomers. See Carol Gendler, "The Industrial Removal Office and the Settlement of Jews in Nebraska, 1901–1917," *Nebraska History* 72 (Fall 1991): 133, note 15.

5. IRO Records, Joseph Gedalecia to David M. Bressler, 7 May 1912. Outside Organizations, Correspondence, Box 22.

6. IRO Records, Joseph Gedalecia to David M. Bressler, 3 Sept. 1912. Outside Organizations, Correspondence, Box 22.

7. IRO Records, David M. Bressler to the Jewish Colonization Association, 4 March 1913. IRO and Jewish Colonization Association Correspondence, Box 87.

8. *Twelfth Annual Report of the Industrial Removal Office for the Year 1912,* 7.

9. David M. Bressler, "The Industrial Removal Office," *The Menorah* 35 (November 1903): 284.

10. William Kahn, "Jewish Agricultural and Industrial Aid Society, New York," in *Proceedings of the Second National Conference of Jewish Charities in the United States* (Cincinnati: C. J. Krehbiel, 1902), 88.

11. David Bressler, *The Distribution of Jewish Immigrants in Industrial and Agricultural Pursuits: Agencies and Results* (New York: n.d.), 8.

12. *JAIAS Annual Report for the Year 1902,* 16–17.

13. Kahn, 90.

14. Leo Levi, "Removal and Distribution of Poor Jews," *Report of the Executive Committee of the Constitution of the Grand Lodge, Independent Order of B'nai B'rith (1901–1902),* 21. (Bulletin No. 3, 1 July 1901).

15. Ibid., 20.

16. Kahn, 87.

17. *Ninth Annual Report of the Industrial Removal Office for the Year 1909,* 4–5.

18. IRO Records, Elias Margolis to David M. Bressler, 7 Aug. 1908. Traveling Agents, Box 19.

19. *Ninth Annual Report of the Industrial Removal Office for the Year 1909,* 5.

20. IRO Records, Placement Records from Cities (Marshalltown, Iowa), 31 Oct. 1904, Box 15.

21. IRO Records, Elias Margolis to David M. Bressler, 7 Aug. 1908. Traveling Agents, Box 19.

22. *JAIAS Annual Report for the Year 1902,* 16.

23. IRO Records, Elias Margolis to David M. Bressler, 7 Aug. 1908. Traveling Agents, Box 19.

24. IRO Records, Abraham Solomon to David M. Bressler, 20 Sept. 1912. Traveling Agents, Box 20.

25. IRO Records, David M. Bressler to Abraham Solomon, 23 Sept. 1912. Traveling Agents, Box 20.

26. IRO Records, Elias Margolis to David M. Bressler, 5 May 1908. Traveling Agents, Box 19.

27. IRO Records, David M. Bressler to Elias Margolis, 26 June 1908. Traveling Agents, Box 19.

28. IRO Records, Elias Margolis to David M. Bressler, 4 July 1908. Traveling Agents, Box 19.

29. IRO Records, David M. Bressler to Abraham Solomon, 23 Sept. 1912. Traveling Agents, Box 20.

30. IRO Records, S. B. Kaufman to David M. Bressler, 14 Feb. 1910. Local Agents (Indianapolis), Box 37A.

31. IRO Records, Morris Waldman to David M. Bressler, 27 July 1907. Correspondence of Immigrants, Box 98; IRO Records, Elias Margolis to David M. Bressler, 4 July 1908. Traveling Agents, Box 19.

32. IRO Records, Morris Waldman to David M. Bressler, 27 July 1907. Correspondence of Immigrants, Box 98.

33. IRO Records, Jacob Kaplan to Removal Society, 7 May 1915. Local Agents (Terre Haute), Box 39; IRO Records, S. J. Goldstine to David M. Bressler, 10 May 1915. Local Agents (Terre Haute), Box 39.

34. IRO Records, Elias Margolis to David M. Bressler, 8 May 1908. Traveling Agents, Box 19.

35. IRO Records, Elias Margolis to David M. Bressler, 5 May 1908. Traveling Agents, Box 19.

36. IRO Records, Elias Margolis to David M. Bressler, 22 May 1908. Traveling Agents, Box 19.

37. IRO Records, Abraham Solomon to David M. Bressler, Sept. 1912. Traveling Agents, Box 20.

38. IRO Records, Abraham Solomon to Industrial Removal Office, 11 Oct. 1912. Traveling Agents, Box 20.

39. IRO Records, Abraham Solomon to David M. Bressler, 11 Oct. 1912. Traveling Agents, Box 20.

40. Ibid.

41. The Lafayette case is not unique. Solomon in his tour certified new arrangements explicitly and in writing, naming committee members and officers and numbers of people to be accepted each month. Solomon then forwarded the signed document to the New York Office. While the IRO employed this formal mechanism to firm up local commitment and to bind communities to their pledge of cooperation, it is abundantly clear that these written "contracts" did nothing to inhibit breaches in the agreement whenever a community believed itself ill-used.

42. IRO Records, Abraham Solomon to Industrial Removal Office, 11 Oct. 1912. Traveling Agents, Box 20.

43. IRO Records, Placement Records from Cities (Lafayette, Indiana), 22 Nov. 1912, Box 17.

44. IRO Records, Elias Margolis to David M. Bressler, 7 Aug. 1908. Traveling Agents, Box 19.

45. IRO Records, Elias Margolis to David M. Bressler, 11 May 1908. Traveling Agents, Box 19.

46. IRO Records, David M. Bressler to Joseph Markman and Charles Graff, 24 July 1908. Correspondence of Immigrants, Box 97.

47. IRO Records, Elias Margolis to David M. Bressler, 21 Dec. 1908. Traveling Agents, Box 19.

48. *Der Indostrial Revoval [sic] Offis: Zayn Thetigkeyt, Zayn Tsvek un Zayne Oyfgaben* (New York: Accurate Printing, n.d.), 13–14.

49. IRO Records, Sam Rastoff to the Removal Office, 18 March 1907. Correspondence of Immigrants, Box 97.

50. IRO Records, David M. Bressler to Congregation B'nai Abraham, 26 March 1907. Correspondence of Immigrants, Box 97.

51. IRO Records, Stanley Bero to David M. Bressler, 9 Nov. 1907. Traveling Agents, Box 18.

52. *Reports of the Immigration Commission* 41, *Statements and Recommendations Submitted by Societies and Organizations Interested in the Subject of Immigration* (Washington, D.C.: Government Printing Office, 1911), 337.

53. *Final Report of the Commission on Industrial Relations* 2 (Washington, D.C.: Government Printing Office, 1916), 1216.

54. *JAIAS Annual Report for the Year 1902,* 15.

55. IRO Records, Stanley Bero to David M. Bressler, 9 Nov. 1907. Traveling Agents, Box 18.

56. Interview with Fanny Shapiro Katzow, age 81 years, 15 Oct. 1980. The third child of Louis and Rose Shapiro, Fanny recounted some Shapiro family folklore regarding Louis Shapiro's first day on the job with Spector. Spector and Shapiro knocked at the door of a house to inquire if the residents had any scrap to sell. Spector negotiated a price for two or three items in the backyard. When he and Shapiro went around the house to put the items in their wagon, Spector loaded the designated pieces and proceeded to take a number of other articles as well. Shapiro pointed out that the lady of the house had not sold them the extra scrap they had just loaded. Spector replied, "Now you're learning the junk business."

57. Stanley Bero to David M. Bressler, 9 Nov. 1907. Box 18.

58. Jewish Federation of Indianapolis, Industrial Removal Office Records, Louis Shapiro, 31 Oct. 1907; IRO Records, Stanley Bero to David M. Bressler, 9 Nov. 1907. Traveling Agents, Box 18.

59. Although the Shapiro saga after leaving Lafayette was lost to the New York Office, his health problems and the early struggle to establish a food business were certainly known to the Indianapolis operatives of the IRO. The local IRO agent was also the superintendent of the federation. He arranged assistance for Mrs. Shapiro and their six children following Louis Shapiro's hospitalization in Denver.

60. IRO Records, David M. Bressler to Samuel J. Levinson, 11 Nov. 1907. Local Agents (Indianapolis), Box 37A.

61. IRO Records, Samuel J. Levinson to David M. Bressler, 13 Nov. 1907. Local Agents (Indianapolis), Box 37A.

62. IRO Records, David M. Bressler to Samuel J. Levinson, 14 Nov. 1907. Local Agents (Indianapolis), Box 37A.

63. IRO Records, David M. Bressler to Samuel J. Levinson, 15 Nov. 1907. Local Agents (Indianapolis), Box 37A.

64. IRO Records, Stanley Bero to David M. Bressler, 7 Nov. 1907. Traveling Agents, Box 18.

65. IRO Records, Abraham Solomon to David M. Bressler, 1 Oct. 1912. Traveling Agents, Box 20.

66. IRO Records, David M. Bressler to G. A. Efroymson, 17 Jan. 1912. Local Agents (Indianapolis), Box 37A.

67. IRO Records, Edward A. Kahn to David M. Bressler, 15 April 1914. Local Agents (Indianapolis), Box 37A.

68. IRO Records, Harry T. Schloss to George David, 9 June 1902. Local Agents (Terre Haute), Box 39.

69. IRO Records, Harry T. Schloss to Jacob Furth, 10 Oct. 1904. Local Agents (Terre Haute), Box 39.

70. IRO Records, General Manager to Harry T. Schloss, 13 Oct. 1904. Local Agents (Terre Haute), Box 39. In New York, immigrant heads of households relying solely on their own labor frequently could not fully support their families. The labor of other members of the household, including children, often proved essential for family self-support at a minimal level. See Appendix, Table 11.

71. IRO Records, Ultra Skirt Company to Harry T. Schloss, 12 Jan. 1905. Local Agents (Terre Haute), Box 39.

72. IRO Records, Harry T. Schloss to David M. Bressler, 16 Jan. 1905. Local Agents (Terre Haute), Box 39.

73. Ibid.

74. IRO Records, David M. Bressler to Harry T. Schloss, 16 Jan. 1905. Local Agents (Terre Haute), Box 39.

75. Ibid.

76. IRO Records, Edward A. Kahn to David M. Bressler, 16 Oct. 1908. Local Agents (Indianapolis), Box 37A.

77. IRO Records, David M. Bressler to Edward A. Kahn, 23 Oct. 1908. Local Agents (Indianapolis), Box 37A.

78. David Bressler, "The Removal Work," in *Proceedings of the Third National Conference of Jewish Charities in the United States* (New York: Philip Cowen, 1904), 143.

79. IRO Records, Industrial Removal Office to Sol S. Kiser, 10 July 1905. Local Agents (Indianapolis), Sol S. Kiser File, Box 38.

80. IRO Records, General Manager to Sol S. Kiser, 10 July 1905. Local Agents (Indianapolis), Sol S. Kiser File, Box 38.

81. IRO Records, Sol S. Kiser to David M. Bressler, 18 July 1905. Local Agents (Indianapolis), Sol S. Kiser File, Box 38.

82. IRO Records, Sol S. Kiser to David M. Bressler, 9 Sept. 1905. Local Agents (Indianapolis), Sol S. Kiser File, Box 38.

83. *Fourth Annual Report of the Jewish Federation of Indianapolis, April 1, 1908–March 31, 1909*, 10.

84. *Fifth Annual Report of the Jewish Federation of Indianapolis, April 1, 1909–March 31, 1910*, 14.

85. IRO Records, Stanley Bero to David M. Bressler, 3 Dec. 1907. Traveling Agents, Box 18.

86. IRO Records, David M. Bressler to Stanley Bero, 4 Dec. 1907. Traveling Agents, Box 18.

87. IRO Records, David M. Bressler to Emil Leipziger, 7 Jan. 1904. Local Agents (Terre Haute), Box 39.

88. IRO Records, Emil Leipziger to David M. Bressler, 11 Jan. 1904. Local Agents (Terre Haute), Box 39.

89. Jack Glazier, "Stigma, Identity, and Sephardic-Ashkenazic Relations in Indianapolis," in *Persistence and Flexibility: Anthropological Perspectives on the American Jewish Experience,* ed. Walter P. Zenner (Albany: State University of New York Press, 1988), 47–48.

90. IRO Records, S. B. Kaufman to David M. Bressler, 5 Jan. 1910. Local Agents (Indianapolis) Box 37A.

91. Ande Manners, *Poor Cousins* (Greenwich, Conn.: Fawcett, 1972), 53.

92. IRO Records, S. B. Kaufman to David M. Bressler, 11 Aug. 1910. Local Agents, (Indianapolis), Box 37A.

93. Ibid.

94. Ibid.

95. IRO Records, David M. Bressler to S. B. Kaufman, 11 Aug. 1910. Local Agents (Indianapolis), Box 37A.

96. *Indianapolis Star,* 11 Aug. 1910, 3.

97. IRO Records, S. B. Kaufman to David M. Bressler, 8 Aug. 1910. Local Agents (Indianapolis), Box 37A.

98. IRO Records, David M. Bressler to S. B. Kaufman, 11 Aug. 1910. Local Agents (Indianapolis), Box 37A.

99. IRO Records, David M. Bressler to S. B. Kaufman, 15 Aug. 1910. Local Agents (Indianapolis), Box 37A.

100. IRO Records, S. B. Kaufman to David M. Bressler, 14 Aug. 1910. Local Agents (Indianapolis) Box 37A.

101. IRO Records, David M. Bressler to S. B. Kaufman, 16 Aug. 1910. Local Agents (Indianapolis), Box 37A.

102. Ibid.

103. IRO Records, S. B. Kaufman to David M. Bressler, 18 Aug. 1910. Local Agents (Indianapolis), Box 37A.

104. Ibid.

105. IRO Records, S. B. Kaufman to David M. Bressler, 31 Aug. 1910. Local Agents (Indianapolis), Box 37A.

106. Ibid.

107. IRO Records, David M. Bressler to S. B. Kaufman, 2 Sept. 1910. Local Agents (Indianapolis), Box 37A.

108. IRO Records, S. B. Kaufman to David M. Bressler, 4 Sept. 1910. Local Agents (Indianapolis), Box 37A.

109. IRO Records, David M. Bressler to S. B. Kaufman, 7 Sept. 1910. Local Agents (Indianapolis), Box 37A.

110. *Fourteenth Annual Report of the Industrial Removal Office for the Year 1914*, 3.

111. IRO Records, Chairman of the IRO to S. B. Kaufman, 9 Oct. 1914. Local Agents (Indianapolis), Box 37A.

112. *Thirteenth Annual Report of the Industrial Removal Office for the Year 1913*, 11, and insert, Table 1.

113. *Fourteenth Annual Report of the Industrial Removal Office for Year 1914*, 9; *Distribution* 2 (February–March 1916): 9; *Distribution* 3 (February 1917): 7; *Seventeenth Annual Report of the Industrial Removal Office for the Year 1917*, 3.

114. *Thirteenth Annual Report of the Industrial Removal Office for the Year 1913*, 11.

115. *Fourteenth Annual Report of the Industrial Removal Office for the Year 1914*, 9.

116. *Distribution* 2 (February–March 1916): 9; *Distribution* 3 (February 1917): 7; *Seventeenth Annual Report of the Industrial Removal Office for the Year 1917*, 3.

117. Owing to lacunae in the records, this figure represents an estimate. It is based on figures provided in IRO resettlement maps for the period 1904–1913; JAIAS annual reports, especially before 1904; and IRO annual reports. It cannot be determined how many people settled in Indianapolis as a result of a prior connection to an IRO settler already located in the city, but the number may have been substantial. Still, figures provided by the Jewish Federation seem exaggerated. By March 1911, the estimate of the number of families settling under IRO sponsorship or through a connection to a previously located IRO family put the number between 400 and 500 *(Sixth Annual Report of the Jewish Federation of Indianapolis, April 1, 1910–March 31, 1911)*.

## Chapter 5. Conclusion

1. Richard D. Lamm and Gary Imhoff, *The Immigration Time Bomb* (New York: E. P. Dutton, 1985).

2. Julian L. Simon, *The Economic Consequences of Immigration* (Oxford: Basil Blackwell, 1989).

3. Thomas Muller, "Economic Effects of Immigration," in *Clamor at the Gates*, ed. Nathan Glazer (San Francisco: ICS Press, 1985), 115.

4. Roger D. Waldinger, *Through the Eye of the Needle: Immigrants and Enterprise in New York's Garment Trades* (New York: New York University Press, 1986).

5. Peter Kwong, *The New Chinatown* (New York: Hill and Wang, 1987), 148.

6. Herbert Gans, "Symbolic Ethnicity: The Future of Ethnic Groups and Cultures in America," *Ethnic and Racial Studies* 2 (1979).

7. Ibid., 5.

8. Ibid., 8–9.

9. Joshua Fishman et al., *Language Loyalty in the United States* (London: Mouton and Co., 1966) 43.

10. Richard Alba, *Ethnic Identity: The Transformation of White America* (New Haven: Yale University Press, 1990), 12–15, 93; Stephen Steinberg, *The Ethnic Myth: Race, Ethnicity, and Class in America* (Boston: Beacon Press, 1989), 68–69.

11. Charles Silberman, *A Certain People* (New York: Summit Books, 1985). A number of critics do not share Silberman's confidence about Jewish life in the United States. See Arthur Hertzberg, "The Triumph of the Jews," *New York Review of Books* 32 (1985).

12. Irving Howe, *World of Our Fathers* (New York: Simon and Schuster, 1976), 253.

13. Steinberg, *The Ethnic Myth*, 53.

14. Michael Novak, *The Rise of the Unmeltable Ethnics* (New York: Macmillan, 1971).

15. Nathan Glazer and Daniel Patrick Moynihan, *Beyond the Melting Pot*, 2nd ed. (Cambridge: M.I.T. Press, 1970).

16. Gans, "Symbolic Ethnicity," 3; Steinberg, *The Ethnic Myth*, 72–73.

17. Curricular changes in higher education, particularly regarding the literary canon, have generated heated academic conflict during the past ten years. One of the opening salvos was fired by Allan Bloom in *The Closing of the American Mind: How Higher Education Has Failed Democracy and Impoverished the Soul of Today's Youth* (New York: Simon and Schuster, 1987). Of the rejoinders to Bloom's argument, Lawrence W. Levine's *The Opening of the American Mind: Canons, Culture, and History* (Boston: Beacon Press, 1996) is among the best. Curricular change in public schools under the impact of multiculturalism is the focus of Nathan Glazer's recent book, *We Are All Multiculturalists Now* (Cambridge: Harvard University Press, 1997). Glazer regards the innovations as salutary in promoting respect. However, he finds reason for regret because the source of multiculturalism in his view lies in a national failure to surmount the black–white racial divide.

18. Michael Gold, *Jews Without Money* (New York: Liveright, 1930), 37. Recently republished by Carroll and Graf, the new edition is introduced by Alfred Kazin, who points out Gold's ignorance about the Jewish underworld of Europe, portrayed in the stories of Isaac Babel.

19. Alejandro Portes and Richard Schauffler, "Language and the Second Generation: Bilingualism Yesterday and Today," *International Migration Review* 28 (Winter 1994): 658–659.

20. Of the many books written in reaction to the authoritarian, antidemocratic variety of multiculturalism, the following are frequently cited: Arthur M. Schlesinger, Jr., *The Disuniting of America* (New York: W. W. Norton, 1992); Robert Hughes, *Culture of Complaint: The Fraying of America* (New York: Oxford University Press, 1993); and Richard Bernstein, *Dictatorship of Virtue: Multiculturalism and the Battle for America's Future* (New York: Alfred A. Knopf, 1994). Hughes does not restrict himself to the extremes of the multicultural left, but with equal contempt skewers their authoritarian counterparts of the right. His criticisms are a useful reminder that the widely ramifying debate about multiculturalism is not reducible to a simple opposition between the political right and left. Levine, in *The Opening of the American Mind*, does not share any

of the concerns of the critics of higher education disturbed by intolerant multicultur-alism. He facilely dismisses the excesses of the latter as aberrations that have been in-vested with undue importance. See also " 'The University Is Not the U.S. Army': A Conversation with Lawrence W. Levine," *Humanities* 18 (January/February 1997): 7.

Several observers discuss the two strains of multiculturalism identified in this chap-ter. K. Anthony Appiah distinguishes between liberal and illiberal multiculturalism in "The Multiculturalist Misunderstanding," *The New York Review of Books* 44 (1997): 34. David Maybury-Lewis separates serious from extreme multiculturalism. He supports the former in fostering the accommodation between ethnic groups in plural states and in protecting the identities and interests of indigenous peoples. See "A New World Dilemma: The Indian Question in the Americas," *Symbols* (Fall 1993): 17–23.

21. Alejandro Portes and Min Zhou, "The New Second Generation: Segmented As-similation and Its Variants," *Annals of the American Academy of Political and Social Sci-ence* 530 (November 1993): 81–82.

22. Alejandro Portes and Alex Stepick, *City on the Edge* (Berkeley: University of California Press, 1993), 8.

23. Portes and Zhou, "The New Second Generation," 82.

24. For excellent discussions of contemporary problems of pluralism and assimila-tion, see John Higham, "Another American Dilemma," in *Send These to Me*, rev. ed. (Baltimore: Johns Hopkins University Press, 1984), 233–248; and David Hollinger, *Postethnic America* (New York: Basic Books, 1995).

See also Rudolfo O. de la Garza et al., *Latino Voices: Mexican, Puerto Rican and Cuban Perspectives on American Politics* (Boulder: Westview Press, 1992). This extensive survey undermines conventional outlooks of both the right and the left. De la Garza and his colleagues provide data that expose the fantasies of those who imagine a politi-cal and cultural fifth column within American borders. The survey's respondents be-lieve in the importance of learning English, claim few personal experiences of discrimination, maintain a high level of trust in government, and hold moderate to conservative political viewpoints. The data also suggest that Latinos do not constitute a single political community. In effect, the respondents express attitudes that are dra-matically at odds with those of ethnic leaders resistant to assimilation.

25. Horace Kallen, "Democracy Versus the Melting Pot: A Study of American Na-tionality," Part 2 *The Nation* (25 Feb. 1915): 218.

# Index